CHILDREN'S AND YA
BOOKS IN THE
COLLEGE CLASSROOM

Fantasy Media in the Classroom:
Essays on Teaching with Film, Television, Literature,
Graphic Novels and Video Games, edited by Emily Dial-Driver,
Sally Emmons and Jim Ford (McFarland, 2012)

The Truth of Buffy: Essays on Fiction Illuminating Reality,
edited by Emily Dial-Driver, Sally Emmons-Featherston,
Jim Ford and Carolyn Anne Taylor (McFarland, 2008)

CHILDREN'S AND YA BOOKS IN THE COLLEGE CLASSROOM

Essays on Instructional Methods

Edited by
Emily Dial-Driver,
Jim Ford *and* Sara N. Beam

McFarland & Company, Inc., Publishers
Jefferson, North Carolina

LIBRARY OF CONGRESS CATALOGUING-IN-PUBLICATION DATA

Children's and YA books in the college classroom : essays on
  instructional methods / edited by Emily Dial-Driver, Jim Ford
  and Sara N. Beam.
      p.   cm.
  Includes bibliographical references and index.

  ISBN 978-0-7864-9502-3 (softcover : acid free paper) ∞
  ISBN 978-1-4766-2115-9 (ebook)

  1. Children's literature—Study and teaching (Higher)
  2. Young adult literature—Study and teaching.   I. Dial-Driver,
  Emily, editor.   II. Ford, Jim, 1972– editor.   III. Beam, Sara
  N., 1980– editor.

  PN1009.A1C498 2015
  809'.892820711—dc23

                                                    2015003525

BRITISH LIBRARY CATALOGUING DATA ARE AVAILABLE

Front cover image: An illustration from the student project
Unmonsterly Matilda, a handmade book by Kristen Cleary,
Gretchen Eagle Chaffin, Hannah Hanley, Francyne Melberg
and Melody Davis

Printed in the United States of America

McFarland & Company, Inc., Publishers
  Box 611, Jefferson, North Carolina 28640
  www.mcfarlandpub.com

Table of Contents

Part III: Student Perspectives

Preface

EMILY DIAL-DRIVER

Happenstance and serendipity can lead us to many good outcomes.

Happenstance, an event that occurs, can cause tragedies, make connections possible, or cause, as Longfellow asserts, those two ships to pass in the night with no lights on board. Serendipity, which may be a happier event than happenstance, is accidental, but accidental in a way that leads to a good end.

Both of those words apply to the genesis of this book.

Happenstance. This occurred when I was left with a colleague, a silent colleague, awaiting a meeting. One might sit quietly and meditate in the company of a silent colleague. I, however, can chatter. So I did, and I happened to mention that I had read a children's book to one of my classes, a real children's book: *The Paper Bag Princess* (Munsch).

Dr. Silent raised an eyebrow and asked what class I had read to. I answered, "Composition I."

That answer resulted in what could be written as "Hummph" and a dismissal by Dr. Silent who simply walked off to the water fountain. I was chagrined. Then came serendipity. Saddened—and, to be honest, a bit worried about the way my methods might be viewed—I told what had happened to another colleague who said, "I use works for children in *my* class."

Our discussion centered on *her* use of "The Little Red Hen" in her nursing class and on *my* use in creative writing classes of lines from Thurber's *The Wonderful O* and *The White Deer* to illustrate word choice and use, as well as my use of what pretends to be a children's book, *The Pedant and the Shuffly: A Fable* (Billairs and Fitschen), in revealing how one cannot judge the worth of a book by its childish appearance.

Then there's *Wonder*, the story of a boy with facial deformities told by multiple narrators. It fulfills the definition of a work worth reading on its own

1

terms, with literary elements (remember those multiple narrators), careful use of words and rhetorical devices, and thematic material. In *Wonder* "everyone" is an Other *to* others and the overarching ethical model is that one should be kind. In addition, disabilities/differences studies have always been and are currently growing in importance. And, it's good. Really. Good. Knowing all that, that there is value in the pursuit, that we are not alone, the quest began.

I began to seek out those who were secretive about the methods they used in teaching concepts that included children's works. It turns out that many college educators use literature written for children or young adults in their classes. It's like a silent secret, however, and not a silent secret *society* because the whole thing is generally not publicized to other educators. I suppose the hiding is out of fear that, as Dr. Silent reacted, the pedagogical methods might be dissed by others.

And, as I discovered and continue to discover, the methods are innovative and interesting and, most important of all, *effective*.

So, in order to bring the practice into the light, we, the writers of these essays, decided that we would publically admit to our secret and tell others about what we do.

Along the way we enlisted several people to aid us in proofing and fact-checking and all those other important tasks: Jessica Limke, Aubrey Nagy, Bryce Briner, Mary Mackie, Jessica Robinette, Shanna Harrison, Briana Kelley, and Abby Wraight.

We, editors and contributors alike, hope that, by revealing our secret methods, we might invite others to join the society we hope will no longer be silent. We hope that others enjoy and celebrate the engaging, rewarding, useful, and beneficial pedagogical practice of teaching adult-level concepts and conventions and developing critical thinking, academic, and intellectual skills with the help of literature for young, sometimes very young, people.

It makes life interesting. I hope you find our discoveries so.

Works Cited

Bellairs, John, and Marilyn Fitschen. *The Pedant and the Shuffly*. New York: Macmillan, 1968. Print.

Longfellow, Henry Wadsworth. "The Theologian's Tale: Elizabeth." *Tales of a Wayside Inn*. 1863. Boston: Houghton Mifflin, 1880. *Google Books*. Web. 1 Oct. 2014.

Munsch, Robert (writer), and Michael Martchenko (illus.). *The Paper Bag Princess*. Toronto: Annick, 1992. Print.

Palacio, R. J. *Wonder*. New York: Knopf, 2012. Print.

Thurber, James. *The White Deer*. 1945 New York: Harcourt, 1973. Print.

_____. *The Wonderful O*. Ill. Marc Simont. New York: Simon & Schuster, 1957. Print.

Introduction

Jim Ford

It all starts with Harry Potter, so "they" say. The Boy Who Lived, the publishing phenomenon, the orphan wizard whose annual experiences at Hogwarts are so much better than any actual school year—Harry Potter is the paradigmatic case of the power of young adult literature.

It starts well before that, of course, as evidenced by the following pages, with fairy tales, Golden Books, myths and legends, stories of all kinds that charm and intrigue readers of all ages. But the Harry Potter series is crucial to so many students' experience with and expectations of books, and the realization that college literature can be as compelling, intriguing, and enjoyable as Harry Potter highlights the possibilities for using children's and young adult literature in the college classroom.

Young adult literature—the best of it, anyway—offers a number of advantages as educational material. First, such works often meet students where they are, resonating with a young adult's experiences and outlook. The reading level of young adult works can be much more manageable, particularly for college freshmen who may be working their way up to traditional college literature. These stories have their depth and significance, which can be revealed using traditional literary techniques of analysis and reflection. It is easier to teach students how to use those techniques when the object is something the students already understand at a basic level. Most importantly, these are works that students genuinely enjoy, a crucial reminder that reading should be a pleasurable activity. Great stories are worth reading, wherever one may find them.

This study develops a variety of ways to integrate children's and young adult literature into the college classroom. In addition to themes, topics, and suggested materials, it provides techniques, practical approaches, and actual assignments that demonstrate proven ways to use these works to improve teaching and learning. It begins "Inside the English Classroom," both because that is the typical setting for studying literature and because this book began with the teaching experiences of English professors. The nine essays in this part use a variety of works and approaches to enrich teaching in high school as well as college English classes. The second part moves "Beyond the English Classroom," with fourteen essays covering a wide range of disciplines and perspectives. Perhaps surprisingly, it is the largest section of the book, featuring classes from sociology to fine arts, from computer science to political science, and from biology to communications. The sheer range of these disciplines, and the wide variety of works, from traditional Native American stories to fairy tales from several different cultures, suggest the tremendous possibilities for featuring such literature in the college classroom. The third part, "Student Perspectives," concludes with student reflections on their encounters with young adult literature, and how such works can inform college teaching and learning. These five essays provide solid evidence—in students' own words—of the dramatic difference young adult works can make for a college student.

The first essay is Emily Dial-Driver's "Out of the Sandbox." Though it begins our section on the English classroom, its applications are much wider. It introduces ways in which a number of children's stories can be entries to lessons in composition, introduction to literature, and introduction to philosophy. Like a number of the essays that follow, Dial-Driver details specific assignments and classroom prompts that put into practice the theoretical benefits of "kiddie lit."

The pedagogical focus continues with Sara N. Beam's "In Appreciation of Mere 'Horseflesh,'" one of several essays that focus on freshman composition in particular. Beam describes how *Black Beauty* is a great resource for teaching composition students a deeper understanding of various textual features, particularly genre. Similarly, Scott Reed and Frances E. Morris use fairy tales to teach such students about the evaluation and construction of argument in their essay "Magical Persuasion." Nataliya Romenesko takes an international turn along the same lines in "Once Upon a Time," a study that highlights how Russian fairy tales yield insights into a nation's culture and history, as well as aid English composition. Robin M. Murphy and Macy McDonald bring the conversation back to young adult literature proper in "Making a Case," an examination of the creative uses that some contemporary young adult works make of classical myths and legends. Studying those allusions lends a new dimension to their college rhetoric courses. Each of these essays appreciates these works in their own right while demonstrating their value to college writing courses.

These works enrich the college classroom, but the applications for high school teaching are also significant, as the next two essays argue. Jesse Stallings describes his approach in a course on graphic texts in his essay "Graphic Language (Devices) in the High School Classroom." Stallings includes several techniques that teach students how to understand a graphic novel and shows how that can help them appreciate all sorts of novels (graphic and otherwise). Mike Turvey's "Steppin' Out with 'Jabberwocky'" focuses on creative writing in particular and on how a creative process that begins with Lewis Carroll's poem improves the high school classroom.

The composition process remains the focus in the eighth essay, "Composing a Work That No One Hero Could Compose Alone," by Sara N. Beam and Holly Clay-Buck. Through a close reading of a newer *Young Avengers* comics run, Beam and Clay-Buck describe collaboration as a model for composition in the twenty-first century. Their collaborative work illustrates a number of worthwhile approaches and ideas.

The final essay in the first part is "The Truth About Native Stories," in which Sally Emmons begins by describing unsuccessful attempts to include Native American literature in the college classroom. Emmons then demonstrates how to do it right and explains how Native American children's literature functions as an introduction to tribal life. Her essay takes seriously the challenges as well as the benefits of these approaches.

The second part begins on a related note with Hugh Foley's "Shifting Perspectives." It compares modern Native American children's literature with earlier uses of Native American characters and themes by non–Native authors. In so doing it shows how the mistakes and misunderstandings of the past can be educationally beneficial today. Continuing the theme, David Newcomb describes his encounter with a particular Native tale, "The Story, Myth, Legend of Jumping Mouse," and how adopting that tale in his classroom enabled a deeper understanding of key ideas and themes. Gioia Kerlin does something similar with a piece of Spanish literature in "Happy Hedgehogs, Happy Students," proving that the possibilities for children's tales extend beyond the English language.

The previous essays feature stories from the past with which students are largely unfamiliar, but more popular young adult works are also pedagogically rich opportunities. Jacqueline Bach, Melanie Hundley and Emily Tarver combine to show how in "*Unwind*ing Ethical Questions." They use a young adult series to approach ethical questions, an approach suitable for a number of general education courses. In this case they focus on Neal Schusterman's Unwind series, but the approach is applicable to a number of other works as well.

The next three essays consider the value of creating new works, either actual children's literature or texts composed using children's literature as a model. This begins with Laura Gray and Gary Moeller's "Children's Books from Serious, Adult Concepts." Based on their experiences with an interdisciplinary, team-taught women's studies course, it reviews a particularly intriguing assignment: the creation of a children's book in a course that tackles serious adult themes and works. Similarly, Michael McKeon's essay, "Image and Text in *The Tale of Peter Rabbit*," articulates the ways in which Beatrix Potter's classic is a model for senior capstone students, illustrating a strong relationship between image and text. Peter Macpherson uses fairy tales to help teach his game design students in "Trees, Not Poles." The assignment to create a story that branches in multiple directions as an exercise in game development is another example of the wide applicability of children's and young adult literature.

The collection moves from computer science to social science, as the next two essays demonstrate ways to use children's literature to understand politics and history. Carolyn Taylor's "Freedom" emphasizes key political ideas and values, while Paul B. Hatley's "Thinking About the Unthinkable" discusses how a particular text of children's literature can help history students understand the use of atomic bombs in World War II in a more than intellectual manner. Such works can be an opening into the most difficult of topics.

Seemingly simple tales often convey deep truths. D. Sue Katz Amburn provides some examples in "Biology Tales," explaining how fairy tale-like stories help students understand complex ideas in biology classrooms. Gregory Stevenson approaches "Biblical Studies through Yertle, Aslan and Little Red Riding Hood." Francis A. Grabowski III uses *The Giving Tree* to illuminate friendship in "Timber!!!" In a lively dialogue, Weldon Lee Williams and David Blakely discuss the value of such literature for teaching voice in communications and theatre. While the subjects and the specific works vary, the basic point does not: Children's literature can enhance the college classroom.

The final essay in the second part is Juliet Evusa's "Boys and Girls Stay in with Media." Evusa contextualizes various judgments (and stereotypes) in a mass media course. In doing so, she shows once again how adult topics and themes are sometimes more visible in children's and young adult literature. Along the way she includes a number of vivid reactions and comments from the students themselves, demonstrating the educational potential of such literature.

Those reactions are the primary focus of the third part, "Student Perspectives." It features five essays from successful students, beginning with Erika

Carter's "The Whole Picture." These essays prove just how effective the study of children's literature can be, in the students' own words. They include reflections on the nature of humanities as well as more specific ethical ("Sources of Morality" by Kimberly Qualls) and gender issues ("My Lady Hero" by H. J. Bates). Jessica Limke's "Tulsa's Coming-of-Age Stories" captures a particular time and place, through a close study of S. E. Hinton's classic young adult works. Finally, Davey Rumsey's "Into the Swamp" returns to graphic novels, focusing on Alan Moore's *Swamp Thing*. These essays articulate what teachers so often hope—the power of great literature to connect and move our students.

All in all, these twenty-eight essays feature a wealth of ideas, techniques, and assignments. In some classes children's literature is the sole focus. In others, young adult literature serves as a gateway to more traditional college classics. My personal favorite is to pair young adult novels with adult literature by the same author (good possibilities are Neil Gaiman's *Coraline* and *American Gods*, Nicholas Hornby's *Slam* and *About a Boy*, J.R.R. Tolkien's *Hobbit* and *The Lord of the Rings*), an approach that even works with J.K. Rowling's *Harry Potter*. (For more on the pedagogical uses of *Harry Potter* and other fantasy works, please see *Fantasy Media in the Classroom: Essays on Teaching with Film, Television, Literature, Graphic Novels and Video Games* published by McFarland in 2012 and edited by Emily Dial-Driver, Sally Emmons, and Jim Ford.) While this volume moves beyond Harry Potter to some less obvious choices, the classics of young adult literature are equally worthy.

Whatever the approach, and in any classroom, the thoughtful inclusion of children's and young adult literature expands and enriches the college classroom. We hope that the works, themes, and recommendations that follow inspire your own teaching and reveal new ways to inspire students with the love of great literature.

Out of the Sandbox
EMILY DIAL-DRIVER

College teaching is aimed at adult learners: late teens, returning adults, people who are mature. Courses of study are more demanding than high school and require higher orders of thought; courses generally require not only learning names, dates, and facts, but also utilizing analysis, evaluation, and synthesis.

However, the implication that one leaves "childish things," including children's literature, behind is not entirely true. Those things are part of the background and history of a person and can be recalled—and recalled usefully. In addition, those "childish" works of literature can have hidden depths, say, *Alice in Wonderland* or *The Wonderful Wizard of Oz*, fully worth studying in their own right.

I'm not going to do an apologia for studying children's literature on its own here but only talk about its use as an auxiliary aide to those supposedly-more-acceptable-in-college "adult" works.

Use of children's literature as an aide can be valuable in different kinds of classes, many of which are featured in this volume. I myself have referred to various works of children's and young adult literature in various classes. In composition classes, I've used both *Martina the Beautiful Cockroach* (Deedy) to introduce semantic levels and *Marvelous Mattie* (McCully) to introduce a unit on inventions. Martina, the cockroach, is ready for suitors, but her grandmother tells her she needs to find out how the suitor will react in anger; thus, Martina is instructed to spill coffee on each suitor. Each suitor reacts differently and, of course, all but the last act inappropriately, causing Martina to reject all but the last. She tells the arrogant rooster, "You are much too cocky for me," and the vicious lizard, "You are much too cold-blooded for me." Here we find that a child would not understand all the possible meanings and connotations of "cocky" and "cold-blooded," but an adult would be aware of the double and triple meanings of each expression, the levels of semantics.

Mattie (Margaret E. Knight), in McCully's *Marvelous Mattie*, is the inventor of several items, among them a shield to prevent mill loom shuttles from flying off and injuring workers. She also invented the modern paper bag and the paper bag-making machine (patents in 1870 and 1878), still in use today. This book has the advantage of showing students that simple things, like paper bags, can be interesting; that inventions can be made by people they've never heard of; and those inventions can be worth researching. This encourages them to think of items besides cars and iPhones that might be significant and fascinating.

In Literary Traditions, an upper division course, during a discussion on Shakespeare, I have referenced the Twilight series in relation to *Romeo and Juliet*. (I have to admit the reference to Twilight was completely derogatory.)

The Twilight series is very popular with high school girls especially, and its relation to *Romeo and Juliet* is obvious. The Twilight characters Bella and Edward and the Shakespeare characters Romeo and Juliet are separated, one set by a family feud and one set by a cultural clash (if one can say that the difference between vampire and non-vampire is a cultural clash). That is not why I was so derogatory. I see the basic bones of Twilight as Bella waiting to be rescued and whining, "Have sex with me. Have sex with me. You won't have sex with me; make me a vampire and have sex with me. Then I can join your family, forsake mine, and have a bloody baby." Ick. (That is not what the fans want to hear. But maybe it might make them think.)

Romeo and Juliet was written in another time; Twilight is contemporary. Have we learned nothing? Are women still just wimps?

Then we can go on to discuss the similarities and differences in philosophy to such works as Butler's *The Parable of the Sower* and Hurston's *Their Eyes Were Watching God*. In *Parable* the main character is female and the driving force behind the travel and "rescue" of a band of people escaping from a post-apocalyptical society and trying to build a better world; in *Their Eyes* the main character is female and finding her own identity, separate from her relationship to a man—and from much of the society in which she lives. Much about these novels is antithetical to the "wimpy female" character we have seen and still do see in literature.

So one is not limited in the uses of children's literature at any level. However, I would like to highlight two classes in which children's works have been especially helpful: Introduction to Literature and Introduction to Philosophy.

Introduction to Literature

By the time students reach college, they may have heard literary terms and their definitions for years. Some have heard them, but forgotten or ignored them. Others have heard them and are bored by reiteration. Some poor souls may not have even "heard" them.

This means, in order for everyone to begin on that "level playing field" (the one that doesn't actually exist) in an introductory class in literature, the terms have to be introduced and illustrated. We want the resistant ones to pay attention; we want the uninformed to be informed; we don't want to allow the already informed to experience boredom or to think the class will be no more than duplication of what they have already mastered (it's much, much more—but they don't know that until they've actually *had* the class).

So what's the solution?

We discuss literary terms in a way with which few (or maybe none) of the students are familiar: in terms of works written for young children.

I begin by talking about how people think of analysis of literature as "picking it to death" and how that makes it sound as if literary analysis and criticism is a negative thing and leads to less enjoyment. Hah.

Then I read Maurice Sendak's *Where the Wild Things Are*. Some students are already familiar with this work (or the film), but having it read in a college class at least gets their attention. Before I begin reading, I have them gather in the close semi-circle common in kindergarten and lower elementary so they can experience the pictures when I turn the book toward them. Again, this surprises them. It's unexpected. It's "weird."

So the story of the mischievous Max and his journey to the Wild Things unfolds and ends with his return to his room and warm supper.

I ask them, "Does Max actually get in a boat and go visit the Wild Things?" The discussion begins, leading to their realization that the story is a metaphor: the journey to the Wild Things is Max's anger and frustration at being sent to his room. The story is filled with symbols (for example, the Wild Things with their roars standing in for Max's rage and the boat for the imagination) and images (Max in his wolf suit, the chase of the dog with the fork, the boat, the Wild Things again, and others). It even includes an epiphany, whether or not the child consciously recognizes it: the mother will love Max even if she's angry at him because he's done mischief.

Because visual literacy is important also, we discuss that the text is not the whole story, that the pictures move the story along even without any textual clues. We talk about the pictures' effects and the tale they tell, opening the discussion for the rationale behind not having text accompanying the pictures.

And *Where the Wild Things Are* has levels of meaning. The way a child relates to the story is different from how an adult relates, the adult having a more sophisticated understanding. It doesn't mean that children cannot enjoy and appreciate the book (children obviously do), but it means that adults, who have more life experience and education, can appreciate the book on additional levels, intellectually and philosophically, to which children cannot yet aspire. Adult appreciation does not lessen enjoyment of *Wild Things*; it adds elements of additional appreciation. This is a concrete example of how understanding analysis, interpretation, and criticism of literary works (written, taped, filmed— for any and all ages) adds elements of additional appreciation for the student of literature.

Light bulbs do not actually flash, but the faces (and later assessment) reflect that new ideas are beginning to simmer.

That's where *Dear Mili* comes in. *Dear Mili* is a Grimm story about a little girl sent into the forest to escape the evils attacking her town. She stays for three days, is sent back home to her mother, and discovers thirty years have passed; she and her mother both die. A grim story. Lost and then discovered, *Dear Mili* first appeared in a letter Wilhelm Grimm wrote ("Illustrator"). What makes Mili interesting is, of course, the history of the work and the fact that Maurice Sendak of Wild Things fame did the illustrations. Even more interesting is what Sendak does with art. The illustrations are spooky enough, but he adds a layer. In one illustration, Mili is in the creepy forest, with some evidence of bones on the forest floor, in the foreground. Behind the mid-ground view of townspeople escaping across a bridge, are the towers of Auschwitz.

The point I make with this story is that one can appreciate the story if one takes it at face value. However, if one knows that those towers reference Auschwitz, it adds something to the story. In fact, that knowledge universalizes the work: bad things happen in all historic periods, and children are affected by these events.

Dear Mili is a great representation of how more knowledge can lead to a greater appreciation, a concept that is valuable later when discussing works, such as Eliot's "Journey of the Magi": a knowledge of history, culture, and the Bible add much to the appreciation of his engaging poem.

It's not enough to stop with the Wild Things or even Mili. The next story up is *The True Story of the Three Little Pigs by A. Wolf* (actually written by Jon Scieszka and illustrated by Lane Smith). This well-known story, told in this work from the point of view of the sneezing wolf instead of the poor huffed-at pigs, is a graphic (literally) representation of how stories differ when told by different narrators and/or to different audiences, which leads to a discussion of how students themselves change stories for different audiences and how their family members change stories, depending on who the narrator is—and what the purpose is for narrating. *Pigs* is also a good place to talk about characterization, especially of the wolf narrator, and personification (as is *The Brave Little Toaster*—so much fun!). It also serves to reveal the plot "arc," with points of conflict (each of the three pigs: pig against wolf and pig/wolf against nature in the characteristics of the building materials), climax (the capture of the wolf), resolution (the wolf is in jail), and denouement (the wolf still needs sugar!) in few words.

In addition, visual literacy is a topic of discussion, as we discuss how the illustrations complement the text as well as add elements to the text. For example, students notice that as the Wolf begins his story, the graphics include a pig nose in place of the "O" in "story." In his plaint that eating "bunnies and sheep and pigs" is just like our eating cheeseburgers, the illustration is of a gigantic, multi-layered cheeseburger-like sandwich, with noses, tails, ears, and hands just sticking out at the sides: this causes a few "Ewws." And, at the third little pig's house, the foreground in the illustration includes a pig foot (hand?) holding a microphone, leading to the next page in which the Wolf complains the "untrue" accusations of him are a result of media exaggeration. At this point we talk about how the images reinforce all elements of the selection, including tone and theme.

Both selections are excellent for discussions about tone and theme. They are good to compare. *Pigs* is, because we know the "real" story, ironic, humorous, and a little bit tongue in cheek. *Wild Things* is realistic in its portrayal of Max's initial actions and fantastic in its portrayal of Max's state of mind. It is both kind and revelatory.

Another concept that can be a bit difficult, and unfamiliar to students, is *deus ex machina*. Originating with the Greeks and their resolution of difficulties in some plays by the appearance from above and the corresponding actions of one of the pantheon of gods (thus, "the god in the machine"), the term is now more broadly applied to any unexpected and unusual resolution to some problem a character is having. Okay, so what does that mean? We turn to Tintin. Tintin is a boy of indeterminate age acting as an investigative reporter and detective. Each of the adventures is completely unrealistic: Tintin never seems to turn in any work; accompanied by his dog, Snowy, and one or more of the odd characters he meets—and collects—along the way, he has the opportunity to chase "bad guys" all over the world; despite being faced with gangs and even armies of the bad, he never is truly harmed; all his efforts are successful. (There are those who carp at the stories because they are so unrealistic. It's a comic!)

Thus, we come to the *deus ex machina* factor in many of Tintin's adventures. For example, in *The Shooting Star*, Tintin is threatened by a giant spider (the result of a meteorite [don't ask]) but a giant apple falls on the giant spider, crushing it and saving Tintin from a spidery fate (Herge 121–22). In *The Broken Ear*, Tintin, at the mercy of a gunman preparing to kill him, is saved by a lightning strike that releases his bonds and bounces him outside the house in which he is being held captive! He is completely free to continue his pursuit of those same bad guys (28–29). Less obvious is the sequence in *The Calculus Affair* in which Tintin, Calculus, and Captain Haddock are being pursued by agents of a foreign government. The car Tintin is driving is faced with a tank; as Tintin brakes, the car skids and is totally wrecked, but passenger and driver are thrown free, completely unhurt, and the damaged car convinces the pursuers that they have been killed, leaving them free to steal the tank (59–60)!

It's not just the main human characters affected by *deus ex machina*. Snowy, Tintin's faithful fox terrier, also benefits. In *The Red Sea Sharks* (96–97), Snowy sneaks a bone from a tethered wild cat. The large cat, leaping to retrieve the bone, breaks free from restraint by pulling loose a large chunk of the rock wall with the tether, which, just as the cat jumps Snowy, loops around and smacks the cat on the head, saving Snowy from disaster. And, later in the same story (124), an enemy tries to attach a limpet mine to the ship on which the adventurers are sailing, but Captain Haddock has ordered the anchor dropped, which bonks the bad guy on the head, causing him to drop the mine and a shark to swallow it.

Here again, in each of the works, the story and the pictures are symbiotic and make a point about how pictures not only illuminate the story, but move it forward. For example, the diver attempting the limpet attachment is shown losing the mine; a shark is swimming below him; and, subsequently, the shark explodes.

Not only visual elements and terms about prose works can be illustrated by children's works. Poetic terms can also be illuminated.

Students sometimes (often) have difficulty in learning rhyme schemes and meter. They are resistant; it's too *hard* (can you hear the whine?). But rhyme schemes can be easier to find in nursery rhymes. "Baa Baa Black Sheep" and "Wee Willie Winkie," for example, each have two stanzas of *abcb*—easy enough to discern. In fact, many nursery rhymes have the same pattern, and students can be interested to discover this similarity themselves.

Rhythm is a different problem. Students dance; they sing; they know song lyrics; they may even play instruments—and many still have problems with discerning meter in a poem. We start by talking about song, dance, and lyrics. And then we talk about the fact that all language has rhythm, with emphases and stresses. Even words have stresses, called accented syllables. This is still not enough.

So we turn to *The Jolly Jingle Book* by Leroy F. Jackson, which contains a number of poems that can be read with excessive emphasis, as in the lines from "Milky Moo": "We've *got* [all emphases are added here and following] a *cow* called *Mil*ky *Moo*. / She's *down* there *by* the *shed*," an example of iambic quatrameter followed by iambic trimeter. The "beats" can be clapped. Then there's also Dr. Seuss's *Green Eggs and Ham*, also clappable, illustrating the difference between "*I* am *Sam*. *Sam* I *am*" (5–7), with a caesura, and "I *do* not *like* them, / *Sam*-I-*Am*. / I *do* not *like* / green *eggs* and *ham*" (12). There are a plethora of others. The subsequent discussion then can turn to why children's poems are so very emphatic and why adult poetry is not, but that one can "hear" or "feel" the emphases nonetheless.

Turning to Tintin again, one can illustrate alliteration with many of Captain Haddock's curses: "Billions of blue blistering barnacles" (*Red Sea Sharks*, 121—and in multiple other places) and "blundering barbequed blister" (*Tintin and the Picaros*, 172), for instance.

The above are simply examples of what one may do with children's books. Other books, designed for various ages, can be used as illustrations of about every literary element possible. One might consider any favorite to introduce concepts. The only limit is your imagination—and the imaginations of your students.

Now for something a bit different.

Introduction to Philosophy

One of the best—and most rewarding, both for me and for the students—assignments in the Introduction to Philosophy course is based in a student's depth of understanding of one philosopher's particular philosophical tenet. The exercise begins with one sheet of paper which will become a small "book." In order to make the book, one follows the following instructions (you can skip the steps if you don't want to make a book!):

1. First lay the paper on the desk as if you were going to write on it. The page facing you is Side 1.

2. Fold the paper in half so that it's no longer 8½ by 11 inches but 8½ by 5½ inches, in essence making a square(ish) sandwich shape.

3. Fold the paper up in half once again from the sandwich shape, making a hot dog shape of 2¾ by 8½ inches.

4. Open the page completely.

5. With Side 1 up, fold the paper lengthways (the other direction from the previous folds), making a big "foot-long coney" shape of 4¼ by 11 inches.

6. Open the page completely, again keeping Side 1 up, and refold it to the sandwich (8½ by 5½ inches) shape.

7. Starting from the fold, tear or cut the vertical crease in the paper from the fold to the horizontal crease halfway down the folded page. [A person cutting the paper will want to have the fold at the bottom, cutting the vertical crease to the middle crease halfway up the page. Since most students do not come with scissors (except for the well-prepared and privileged few), those without scissors would probably need the fold at the top and would tear down the vertical crease from the fold to the middle horizontal crease halfway down the page.]

8. The book is almost assembled. The only thing left to do is, once again, to open the page flat, this time to Side 2, the folds poking up (so to speak), with the torn opening vertical.

9. Place the left hand on the left side of the tear and the right hand on the right side.

10. Pinching the crease with the fingers, pull the page gently apart, not tearing it more, by rotating the hands so the outside of each hand faces down and the thumb is up, until the torn/cut opening first becomes a diamond and further pulling to the side and pushing to the middle causes the entire structure to look something like a plus sign. Thus are formed the eight pages of the book.

11. At that point the creases need be smoothed into submission, making each section a playing card shape, and the "pages" manipulated (folded) until they all point the same direction, constructing the book of eight total pages of 2¾ by 4¼ inches.

If this is just too confusing, directions on making a book from a single page appear on numerous websites, complete with pictures. However, it is always good for students to practice following directions, and this is a perfect way for them to do so.

Whether or not students follow the directions or search a website, if they do the steps, they end up with an eight-page book. Students then choose a tenet of one philosopher. They write and illustrate an explanation of that tenet for an audience of second to fourth-grade children, each student choosing a particular audience in that grade range.

Why would you want to do this exercise? As most of us know, we have to know a topic really, really well to be able to teach it to someone, even of college age. But we have to even more fully understand the topic to be able to "translate" that topic so those unaccustomed to the vocabulary of the field and not already acquainted with the underlying premises of philosophical discussion can understand what we are trying to convey.

Another aspect is the length. There's not much space in eight 2¾ by 4¼ inch pages, especially when you factor in illustrations. So succinctness is vital. And to be succinct, one must be clever and understand what is to be conveyed. One of the precepts I remember from a public speaker giving tips is that almost anyone can give a thirty-minute speech about a topic because it's possible to ramble, but few can do a creditable job in three minutes since the speaker has to know exactly the points that are important and how to effectively make those points.

An added element of the project is presentation. This meets objectives of oral presentation and the ability to interact with questioners. Each student reads his or her book to the class, answering questions about the topic. Additional questions include information on the composition of the book: Why was one choice made over another? Would this other choice have served the purpose better? and so forth. This also serves as a review of important topics covered in the class.

Following are examples written for a second grade audience.

- One student made a book called *Philosophy Is....* In this book each page of text is followed by a page of illustration: "*Philein*—Greek for ... to love" is accompanied by an illustration of a heart with the word "Love" written on it; "and ... *sophia*—Greek for ... wisdom" is illustrated with a picture of a book from which golden rays emanate; "The love of wisdom" is followed by a picture of a stained glass window that includes a book and a heart. The final page simply says, "Philosophy." (Adam Bennett)

This little book elicited a conversation about what philosophy actually means, and the various systems of inquiry, including epistemology (the study of knowledge and what it is and what it means), ethics (the study of values, morality, and personal and social conduct), and metaphysics (the study of reality and existence) (Velasquez 11–17). In other words, it reviewed the entire class!

Another little book was based on the sayings of Confucius, including those on being helpful, obedient, and respectful, and, of course, "Treat others how you want to be treated."

Responding to this little book, the class discussed a number of things, among them ethics and Confucius's expression of ethics in *The Analects*, and, especially, the relationship between Confucian precepts and the Golden Rule (Velasquez 158–61).

Yet another little book featured Carol Gilligan's philosophy and included several of her precepts, among them care of self and others and a balance between.

Discussion centered on this book compared Gilligan's "ethics of care" (Velasquez 544–49), with its emphasis on how people respond to situations; to the ethics of utilitarianism, emphasizing the greatest good for the largest number of people (507–14); and to Kant's categorical imperative, emphasizing that each actor should act as if everyone should act in that way in the situation (523–30). The classes further discussed the current feeling that Gilligan herself is now taking, that males and females approach morality in similar ways (Velasquez 548).

- In the final example, *The Complete Guide to Nihilism*, the first three pages include the title page, a copyright page with author, and a table of contents: "Contents—Nihilist Beliefs: 18th Century/19th Century/20th Century/21st Century." The next five pages are blank. The final page says,

  The Complete Guide to Nihilism finally reveals the secrets of nihilistic beliefs. The Eighteenth and Nineteenth Century beliefs were translated from the undiscovered lost journals of Arthur Schopenhauer (1788–1860). The Twentieth Century beliefs were taken from the unwritten papers of Richard Taylor, contemporary American philosopher. The possible evolution of nihilism is discussed in the Twenty-first Century section [Patricia Sanders].

The difficulty with the last example is that it does not actually deal with nihilism. In fact, presenting this book to the intended audience would serve little purpose except confusion. However, the presentation of the book in class elicited laughter. When the class settled, a long discussion ensued about what decisions and information might have actually been necessary to make a book on nihilism for second graders. More importantly, the discussion focused on the philosophy of nihilism (all is meaningless) and on Schopenhauer and Taylor and their nihilistic beliefs (Velasquez 691–93).

This assignment is both amusing and effective and serves multiple purposes.

Conclusion

Children's literature does not necessarily mean simple. It is not for the simple-minded. Children's literature is another arm of the sophisticated and engaging world of literary and visual literacy. And it's fun.

Works Cited

Butler, Octavia E. *The Parable of the Sower.* New York: Grand Central, 2000. Print.

Deedy, Carmen Agra. Illus. Michael Austin. *Martina the Beautiful Cockroach: A Cuban Folktale.* New York: Scholastic, 2007. Print.

Grimm, Wilheim. Illus. Maurice Sendak. *Dear Mili.* Trans. Ralph Manheim. New York: Farrar, Straus and Giroux, 1988. Print.

Hervé. *The Broken Ear. The Adventures of Tintin,* Vol. 2. New York: Little, Brown, 1978. 1–64. Print.

_____. *The Calculus Affair. The Adventures of Tintin,* Vol. 6. New York: Little, Brown, 1978. 1–64. Print.

_____. *Red Sea Sharks. The Adventures of Tintin,* Vol. 6. New York: Little, Brown, 1978. 65–127. Print.

_____. *The Shooting Star. The Adventures of Tintin,* Vol. 3. New York: Little, Brown, 1978. 65–127. Print.

_____. *Tintin and the Picaros. The Adventures of Tintin,* Vol. 7. New York: Little, Brown, 1978. 128–92. Print.

Hurston, Zora Neale. *Their Eyes Were Watching God.* New York: Harper, 2006. Print.

"Illustrator Maurice Sendak Works His Melancholy Magic on a Long-Forgotten Grimm Fairy Tale." *People* 30.23 (5 Dec. 1988): n.p. Print.

Jackson, Leroy F. *The Jolly Jingle Book.* Ill. Clare McKinley. New York: Rand McNally, 1961. Print.

McCully, Emily Arnold. *Marvelous Mattie: How Margaret E. Knight Became an Inventor.* New York: Farrar, Straus and Giroux, 2006. Print.

Scieszka, Jon. Ill. Lane Smith. *The True Story of the Three Little Pigs by A. Wolf.* New York: Puffin, 1996. Print.

Sendak, Maurice. *Where the Wild Things Are,* 50th anniv. ed. New York: HarperCollins, 2014. Print.

Seuss, Dr. *Green Eggs and Ham.* New York: Random, 2013. Print.

Shakespeare, William. *Romeo and Juliet.* MIT. Web. 10 Feb. 2013.

Velasquez, Manuel. *Philosophy: A Text with Readings,* 7th ed. New York: Wadsworth, 1999. Print.

In Appreciation
of Mere "Horseflesh"
Sara N. Beam

With debate in the air about Oklahoma horseflesh, Spring 2013 seemed an appropriate time to bring a horse into a classroom. Not a real horse, but a text authored by one, "translated from the original equine," as the novel subtitle notes. Proponents of OK House Bill 1999, which would legalize horse slaughter for human consumption (export only), said that it would keep jobs in Oklahoma rather than send them to Mexico and would stem horse abuse, evidently a large problem in Oklahoma. Opponents said that inspecting meat for other countries is not the U.S.'s job and that raising horses for meat would not be as profitable as raising cattle; other opponents simply opposed the consumption of horsemeat and the practice of raising animals for human consumption. By late March, Oklahoma Governor Mary Fallin signed HB 1999 into law (Eckhoff). So, bringing *Black Beauty*, a text about perspective—specifically, animal perspective—to a college composition classroom was a way of inspiring discussion about rhetoric and writing regarding (human and non-human) animal rights in a grounded way.

The quoted word "horseflesh" in the title is in reference to a line from the horse character Ginger, who, unlike the horse protagonist Black Beauty, was not raised by kind people. She underscores Beauty's privileged position as one who was lucky enough to be born to a mother who belonged to a kind master and to have, so far, encountered few cruel people. The master she was reared by had "no gentleness ... but only hardness," and Ginger "felt from the first that what he wanted was to wear all the spirit out of me, and just make me into a quiet, humble, obedient piece of horseflesh. 'Horseflesh!'" (Sewell 25). She was treated like an object rather than a subject, a resource to be consumed. Beauty's and the reader's final glimpse of Ginger is her corpse being hauled off to the knacker's (165–66).

The full title of the novel is *Black Beauty: The Autobiography of a Horse, Translated from the Original Equine*. The text was published in England in 1877 for an audience of working-class people whose livelihoods depended on horses. The novel's purpose was to help train an audience with lower literacy rates about the care, training, and keeping of horses. Appearing just eighteen years after Darwin's *On the Origin of Species*, the text was produced in and entered a culture debating and exploring the connections between animals and humans; "animal-related discourse," or discussion, at this time was "both enormous and diverse" (Morse and Danahay 3). As Morse and Danahay explain, "The effect of Darwin's ideas was both to make the human more animal and the animal more human, destabilizing boundaries in both directions" (2). The timeframe the text appears in is crucial: in the recent past was not only Darwin's text but also American Harriet Beecher Stowe's 1852 anti-slavery novel *Uncle Tom's Cabin; or, Life Among the Lowly*; the Crimean War, in which horses served as weapons, transportation, and beasts of burden; the 1870 Married Women's Property Act, which allowed women to continue to legally own property or wages while married; and the 1870 Education Act, which made elementary education mandatory. Sewell's text, an *autobiography* of a *horse*, was an exploration of the human/animal divide, a literary experiment in form and style that consciously engaged its audience in the discourse about animal and human rights, giving readers a way into the many facets of the debates in simple language. Notably, when *Black Beauty* was marketed in the U.S. in 1890 by the Massachusetts Society for the Prevention of Cruelty to Animals, founder George Angell re-named the work *Black Beauty. His Grooms and Companions. The "Uncle Tom's Cabin" of the Horse* (Gavin 187–88).

Black Beauty is a training text. It is a pet book of mine, but Spring 2013 was the first time I'd brought it to a freshman writing class. The students were still shy, and I was hoping interaction with an animal would calm and soothe them. "We use nonhuman animals to understand, validate, and further ourselves" (Dorré 5), and *Black Beauty* can be used, I believe, to further students' understandings of rhetoric, fiction writing, critical thinking, and empathetic imagination. Though this story depends on magical realism, as it asks readers to go along with the idea of talking horses, and though it has long been marketed to children as a work for children, it was not written for an audience of children—however, its accessible language and imaginative style are qualities that apparently mean, to some, it is most suited for children. For example, Black and Warren's 1911 "A Brief Suggestive List of Reading for Children in the Elementary School" from *The Elementary School Teacher* recommends *Black Beauty* for fourth graders (147). Sewell herself was an educator, teaching adult education, for example, in Wick (Gavin 142). She was an innovative teacher, engaging her students by bringing to class "a bullock's or a sheep's eye which she would then dissect for her 'astonished' students in order to reveal the amazing mechanism of sight" (144). Written by a teacher, meant for learning purposes, *Black Beauty* is, like most literature now marketed to children, more complex than most people assume it to be. Its literary features and interesting textual history make it a great text to explore and investigate in a college composition classroom.

Kylene Beers and Robert E. Probst's work on the value of literature in the classroom was a vital supplement to my classroom activity; their text offers discrete tools for students who are under-equipped to discuss literature. Beers and Probst argue for the efficacy of studying fiction, pushing back against dual efforts to increase standardized testing and to decrease the value of studying literary texts. Their argument is also in response to the changes to reading practices that have come with the digital age. What does reading mean today, and how has reading online enhanced and/or hindered students' reading skills? Whatever the various answers may be, and there are lots of suggestions out there, students need specific tools to help them focus and find a way into a literary text. Beers maintains that "Nonfiction lets us *learn* more; fiction lets us *be* more" (qtd. in Beers and Probst 17). Moreover, a group or community of people collaboratively analyzing the same text can open up the work to multiple interpretations; however, Beers and Probst don't want those communities to settle for just any discussion. Rigorous discussion is the goal, discussion wherein groups avoid "inauthentic" or "monologic" classroom discourse and instead engage in "authentic"/"dialogic" conversation, one that is fueled by effective, direct open-ended questions (29). Thus, Beers and Probst offer six "Signposts to Notice and Note": "Contrasts and Contradictions," "Aha Moments," "Tough Questions," "Words of the Wiser," "Again and Again," and "Memory Moment" (71–73). The definition of each is fairly self-explanatory because the language Beers and Probst have chosen for these terms is simple (which is not to say the ideas are one dimensional!). Each Signpost comes with a specific "anchor question" to consider in conversation or in writing. The questions as matched with their Signposts are as follows:

> Contrasts and Contradictions: Why would the character act (feel) this way?
> Aha Moments: How might this change things?
> Tough Questions: What does this question make me wonder about?

Words of the Wiser: What's the life lesson and how might it affect the character?

Again and Again: Why might the author bring this up again and again?

Memory Moment: Why might this memory be important? [79].

The Signposts are useful to students of all ages at all levels of schooling, from primary to secondary to higher education to adult education. When students search for Signposts, note the pages they occur on, and use specific references to the text as they ponder the questions, they are engaging in critical and creative thinking about literature, as well as about themselves (reflection) and about humanity at large (when they expand ideas to the world and people they know). I'll explain why and how the Signposts and questions worked in a Composition I course in conjunction with *Black Beauty*.

Today, educators face increasing pressure to justify every piece of literature we want to teach in English classrooms. *Black Beauty* is a book that can work well not only in a Victorian literature, children's literature, or literature survey class, but also in a Composition I/II course. The novel did its job effectively, walking the students through the doorway from nonfiction to fiction, allowing them to feel out how an obvious work of imagination could perform the duties of more "realistic" essay writing—duties like employing details to create a realistic setting, speaking at an audience-appropriate level, transitioning between events in a narrative, providing a new perspective on controversial yet debate-worn topics, and effectively convincing a range of readers to re-imagine and revise their treatment of animal and human Others.

What I'd particularly like to focus on here in this essay, and what I'd recommend discussing about *Black Beauty* in a composition classroom, are genre and textual features. Regarding genre, this book could be classified as animal autobiography, children's literature, fable, fictional autobiography, and more: "As the 'autobiography' of a working-class creature," offer Morse and Danahay, "Sewell also places BB's narrative in the genre of working-class autobiographies" (187). Furthermore, the novel could also be classified as social problem or social protest fiction. The novel is topical in its protests against the use of the bearing-rein; Gavin notes that "Anna with typical intrepidity had sent a copy to Edward Fordham Flower, a leading campaigner against 'the barbarous and senseless use of spurs, whips, curbs, gag bits, and bearing-reins'" (193). Along with highlighting the bodily cruelty caused by the bearing-rein, the novel also highlights inhumane tail- and ear-cropping practices. How funny it is that this Victorian-era social problem/protest book is marketed to kids—when you pause and think about it, it's a bit like marketing *Mary Barton* to children! (Only in *Mary Barton*, it's the working class and poor who are miraculously able to speak.) Two other elements to examine in the text are its use of illustration and the fact that there are a wide variety of versions of the text available for purchase. For example, the 1977 Illustrated Classics Edition by Playmore, Inc., is an abridged version of the text with illustrations that are not original to the work. This text and others like it take liberties with the original content and adjust it as they see fit in the name of appealing to an audience of children—or to an audience of parents with differing ideas about what is appropriate reading material for children.

In my Composition I course at RSU, paddocked between a series of readings about post-conviction DNA testing and Richard Wright's "The Library Card," *Black Beauty* stared at students innocuously, waiting for interaction. There would be no test over the material, only a 40-minute discussion, where the class would apply Kylene Beers and Robert E. Probst's critical reading strategies. The text fit well as a link between non-fiction and fiction writing because it was designed to enunciate clearly and concisely arguments about how we should treat others. The selected chapters, one and ten, respectively included descriptive narrative of Black Beauty's colthood and a debate among full-grown Black Beauty and his peers about their status. First-year college writers were able to read between the lines and to separate form from content and later to recognize horses as "a decoding machinery" (Dorré 47), with Beauty's "autobiography" carrying reverberations of a slave narrative and the plights of the working class (37, 44).

The students were curious about Sewell as a writer; they were interested in Sewell's biographical information, the story of her life. Too often, the text of focus is detached from humanity, in students' eyes. Without a mental picture of the author's life and times, they lack incentive to invest time in the text. As someone who had studied nature since she was a young child, as a beekeeper, and as a person with mobility issues (due to a foot or ankle injury that occurred when she was a teenager) and a chronic unclear medical problem ("probably Lupus," but scholars are unsure) that left her dependent on horses for transport (Gavin 34–35, 208), Sewell was aware of the lives of animals. Gavin notes that "Even in childhood Anna was not afraid to speak out against cruelty. She was especially indignant over the people she dubbed 'bobies' who shot birds for pleasure" (23). Furthermore, "prevention and alleviation of all forms of cruelty was a strong Quaker principle" (23). We noted that Sewell's family relocated and started over many times; she had to find a way to revise her life, deal with fate controlled by outside forces, and find stability in family, reading/writing, teaching, charity work, and her work with animals. This biographical information, plus the concrete tools offered by Beers and

Probst, seemed to help the students avoid feeling lost, overwhelmed, unmotivated.

After the brief lecture on Sewell's injury, disability, Quaker background, and reliance on horses as aid, I encouraged the class to refer to the excerpt from the text and look for one of the Six Signposts of their choosing. I referred to a student's comment from the last class meeting, when I'd told them about why and how children's literature was used in college classrooms: when asked why children's literature might be valuable, one of the more vocal students, Bailey Thompson, had cleverly noted, "A little simplicity never hurt nobody." The conversation about *Black Beauty* actually began after I asked the students, who were mostly from areas of Oklahoma considered rural, if they'd ever ridden a horse or been around one before. About one-third of the class of 22 said they had. Following that, I asked if any of them had ever read the text before—none had. Queries about how the text read revealed that, to them, the text seemed dated but gave them an idea of different forms of English and about how language evolves over time—they said the narration seemed unnaturally formal. When asked what this means, they pointed to stilted-sounding lines that use older forms of words and did not use contractions, like "*Whilst* I was young I lived *upon* my mother's milk, as I *could not* eat grass" (3; emphasis added).

The first Signpost they picked up on was Beauty's mother's advice to him about his breeding and morals. She states, "The colts who live here are very good colts, but they are cart-horse colts, and, of course, they have not learned manners. You have been well bred and well born.... I hope you will grow up gentle and good, and never learn bad ways; do your work with a good will, lift your feet up when you trot, and never bite or kick even in play" (3–4). Students spent a few minutes discussing this moment they identified as Word of the Wiser moment in the text. We talked about Mother as a character; students noticed that her name is Duchess and that she models manners and breeding. To students, the life lessons here are about identity, stereotypes of mothers and motherhood, and how to treat others, and the takeaway for Beauty's character is his motivation to behave in an orderly manner, unlike the misbehaving boys (3–4).

The next issue students touched on was that of cropping ears and tails, something that comes up in Chapter 10. Chapter 10 features arguments by animal characters, from their own perspectives, about animal abuse and animal rights. The group of horses consists of Black Beauty, Ginger, Merrylegs the Shetland pony, Justice the carting and luggage horse, and Sir Oliver the retired hunting horse. Beauty opens the chapter by remarking on Ginger's and his build and stature and how much they look forward to "being saddled for a riding party" (36). He then reflects on how his riders' treatment affects him, particularly the way they handle the reins: "Oh! If people knew what a comfort to horses a light hand is, and how it keeps a good mouth and a good temper, they surely would not chuck, and drag, and pull at the rein as they often do" (36). This leads to a discussion of fashion and how humans sometimes mistreat animals for the sake of looking fashionable. Ginger notes that fashion must be the inspiration for the painful bearing rein she was made to wear in London (38). Sir Oliver agrees and then rails against mistreatment of animals for the sake of fashion. Regarding ear and tail cropping on dogs, he says, "To my mind, fashion is one of the wickedest things in the world.... Why don't they cut their own children's ears into points to make them look sharp? Why don't they cut the end off their noses to make them look plucky? One would be just as sensible as the other. What right have they to torment and disfigure God's creatures?" (38–39). Sir Oliver and Ginger express anger and resentment as they describe cruel behavior of humans. Justice and Merrylegs step in and defend good people, arguing that the master, John, and James represent human capacity to carefully consider animals' perspective.

Students noticed this moment as one of Contrast and Contradiction. We discussed argumentation and making a case and debated how effective Sewell's use of animal characters in dialogue was: was the text overly sentimental propaganda, or was it rhetorically effective? Students mentioned recent horse abuse cases in Oklahoma, and we referenced points of debate about the issue of the recent horse slaughter bill. Students also discussed the repeated use of the term "fashion," and we noted that it does not necessarily refer to runway fashion, but just what's considered cool or acceptable.

Students also used this moment in the text to recognize how the attitudes and mannerisms of characters toward a certain topic moved character development along. One student pointed to the line, "I always carried the mistress," by Beauty (36), which means he is well-behaved, dependable, and handsome. They contrasted Beauty with Ginger, whose life experience has up until this point been so different from Black Beauty's and whose name denotes spiciness. The contrast in attitudes between the ill-treated horses Ginger and Sir Oliver and the well-treated horses Black Beauty and Justice stood out to the students. The distinction highlights the notion that a creature's behavior is molded by its experience. I asked students what else they'd noticed, and they discussed the setting of the work, specifically, the setting of Beauty's first home as depicted in Chapter One. The description starts, "The first place that I can well remember was a large pleasant meadow with a pond of clear water in it"

(3). This was an idyllic place with "shady trees," "plowed field," "master's house," and "running brook" (3). This is a Memory Moment, and the question that pairs with it asks readers to consider the memory's importance. In this case, the memory links to Beauty's upbringing and the formation of his personality and temperament.

Since we were investigating and unpacking this text in a low-stakes setting, one of the most important lessons I hoped students would get out of it was a conscious mindset about and a framework for discussing literary genres. I mentioned *Black Beauty* was connected to animal fables, and no one knew what those were. So, after I gave the class a brief example (Aesop's "The Tortoise and the Hare"), we made a plan that after class I'd send them an email with more information. In the meantime, we considered animal rights and ethics: as Jeremy Bentham argues of "agents ... susceptible of feeling happiness" in 1823 in a passage often quoted in histories of animal rights debates, "the question is not, Can they *reason*? nor, Can they *talk*? but, Can they *suffer*?" In the middle of the burgeoning animal rights movement, and situated in the same timeframe as push back against the British Imperial project, the women's suffrage movement, the labor rights movement, etc., is Sewell's animal autobiography arguing that "we have no right to distress any of God's creatures without a very good reason; we call them dumb animals, and so they are, for they cannot tell us how they feel, but they do not suffer less because they have no words" (192). Her text makes much the same argument as the 1876 Act to Amend the Law Relating to Cruelty to Animals, which controlled animal experimentation practices, attempting to further limit animal suffering (*The Public General Statutes* 459). It makes sense then that Sewell's most recent autobiographer gives such emphasis to this detail from Sewell's life: "'If I ask [Anna] to arrange the fruit she will always turn the worst side out,' complained her mother, who from aesthetic reasons quite disapproved of this procedure" (Gavin 160). *Black Beauty* is a social problem novel exposing the maltreatment of animals and the reasons behind cruelty, attempting simultaneously to prevent further cruelty by teaching perspective.

The goals for the discussion included helping students recognize narration, literary genres, audience, and characterization; helping students transfer knowledge about modes of writing from analysis of nonfiction to analysis of fiction; and opening the door for them to learn how to discuss and write about fiction. These goals were accomplished because, first, the close reading strategies offered by Beers and Probst actually did give the students concrete tools to use. Second, the training ground text of *Black Beauty* gave them some safe content to try out. Third, the low-stakes nature of the discussion exercise gave students confidence and space to grow. When we later held formal discussions of *Fahrenheit 451*, students participated in ways grounded in class vocabulary and textual evidence. Showing students how to carefully and respectfully employ this "simple" text modeled for them how to care for and respect all literature. Sewell's "little book, its special aim being to induce kindness, sympathy, and an understanding treatment of horses" (her own words) (Gavin 178), is a training text, a working text, something well-crafted and lasting. Its larger lessons are ones of compassion, especially for those considered less-than. The nuanced book gives a voice and subjectivity to human and non-human animals who were/are disenfranchised, and the text is worthy of and useful to the college composition classroom.

Works Cited

Beam, Sara. Email to students. 5 March 2013.

Beers, Kylene, and Robert E. Probst. *Notice and Note: Strategies for Close Reading*. Portsmouth, NH: Heinemann, 2013. Print.

Bentham, Jeremy. "Of the Limits of the Penal Branch of Jurisprudence." *An Introduction to the Principles of Morals and Legislation*, 2d ed. 1823. *Library of Economics and Liberty*. Liberty Fund, 2002. Web. 4 June 2014.

Black, Jesse, and Irene Warren. "A Brief Suggestive List of Reading for Children in Elementary School." *The Elementary School Teacher* 12.4 (Dec. 1911): 145–50. *JSTOR*. Web. 15 May 2013.

Dorré, Gina. "Horses and Corsets: Black Beauty, Dress Reform, and the Fashioning of the Victorian Woman." *Victorian Fiction and the Cult of the Horse*. Cornwall: Ashgate, 2006. 95–120. Print.

Eckhoff, Vickery. "Over Public Outcry, Governor Signs Horse Slaughter Bill." *Forbes*. N.p., 2 Apr. 2013. Web. 29 May 2014.

Ferguson, Moira. "Breaking in Englishness: Black Beauty and the Politics of Gender, Race, and Class." *Women: A Cultural Review* 5 (1994): 34–52. Print.

Gaskell, Elizabeth. *Mary Barton. A Tale of Manchester Life*. 1848. Ed. Macdonald Daly. London: Penguin Classics, 1996. Print.

Gavin, Adrienne E. *Dark Horse: A Life of Anna Sewell*. Gloucestershire: Sutton, 2004. Print.

Morse, Deborah D., and Martin A. Danahay, eds. *Victorian Animal Dreams: Representations of Animals in Victorian Literature*. Hampshire: Ashgate, 2007. Print.

The Public General Statutes Passed in the Thirty-Ninth and Fortieth Years of the Reign of Her Majesty Queen Victoria. London: Eyre and Spottiswoode, Queen's Printing Office, 1876. Web. 3 June 2014.

Sewell, Anna. *Black Beauty*. Illustrated Classics Editions. Ed. Deidre S. Laiken. New York: Playmore, 1977. Print.

_____. *Black Beauty*. New York: Aladdin Classics, 2001. Print.

Wright, Richard. "The Library Card." *The Prose Reader: Essays for Thinking, Reading, and Writing*, 9th ed. Ed. Kim Flachmann and Michael Flachmann. Boston: Prentice Hall, 2011. 546–553.

Magical Persuasion

SCOTT REED *and* FRANCES E. MORRIS

"Little Pigs! Little Pigs! Let me come in! Not by the hair of your chinny chin, chin? Then I'll huff, and I'll puff, and I'll blooow your house down!"

Children enjoy the story of three chubby little pigs menaced by a wolf, the quintessential creepy stranger. They worry for the pig's safety, gain a sense of our own fragility, and root against the snarling villain. When they hear about a little girl with striking attire who journeyed through a dark forest, making her way to her grandmother's house, they worry, stalked by a shadowy predator. When Red Riding Hood stood warily at her grandmother's bed, exclaiming, "My, Grandma, what big teeth you have!" and the wolf replied, "The better to eat you with!" there is fear for her.

Children probably do not consider there might be a point to these exciting tales. Have you, reader, sitting comfortably in your nook, ever considered what special hold fairy tales have on the children who hear them and the adults who pass them on? Don't fairy tales have it all—a gripping plot, relatable characters, larger-than-life villains, a moral?

Why is the queen obsessed with her mirror? Why does Rapunzel let down her hair? A fairy tale is arguably a moral lesson related through story. Understanding a fairy tale as a form of argument can provide insight into how appeals are made and how arguments are built to get people to think and act as intended. Like a fairy tale, a successful argument makes a magical connection to its audience—sometimes through pure enchantment, sometimes through evil sorcery. As composition teachers, we may have overwhelmed our students with too much terminology and theory: claim, evidence, warrant, assumption, syllogism, enthymeme, rhetorical appeals, logical fallacies, *ad nauseam*. Just as Hansel and Grethel find their way through the forest with bread crumbs, so too do our students need a path through the academic maze, to connect with the wonder of why an argument works. To facilitate our students' understanding, we journey back to the familiar and fanciful fairy tale. We find the rhetorical appeals, syllogisms, and logical fallacies in "Rapunzel," "Hansel and Grethel," "The Emperor's New Clothes," and more. Please, sit with us and remember once upon a time when learning was fun.

Learning is often not engaging for the student. Everything seems to have been said that can be said about any topic. Students no longer need to make the leaps in logic or discover the truth from the material because some source has apparently already done that for them. Reading for comprehension is lost to skimming. Writing is reduced to summarizing. Research is now just browsing through search engine results. What is lost (or never sought because there are so many breadcrumbs in the way) in this newer, supposedly-more-efficient method is the search for and discovery of a student's own point of view—the ability to analyze. This loss in perspective is frightening.

Composition courses still teach argument and all of the parts that Socrates, Toulmin, and other advocates of rhetoric have handed down, but the missing link is that vital exploration of the text that students need to discover how and why an author has constructed an argument. When we ask them to identify the types of rhetorical appeal, for example, in Martin Luther King's "Letter from a Birmingham Jail," they can all too easily find the examples they need from Google. When we ask them to identify the premises and conclusions behind "The Declaration of Independence," they can download the answers on their phones. When we ask them to point out the flaws in logic expounded by Rush Limbaugh in "The Latest from the Feminist Front," they can find them neatly outlined by multiple sources in any given database.

As composition teachers on the front lines who have been losing this battle with the Internet, we turned to sources that have been overlooked in the Information Age, sources that, nevertheless, were the first arguments most of us were exposed to—fairy tales. Fairy tales, some of Western culture's earliest and most basic arguments of cultural mores, contain a rich yet straightforward argument. At Rogers State University, we built our Composition II courses, especially the online ones, around developing a deeper understanding of how argument works, and we use fairy tales to help students reach that understanding. Following a brief overview of the three types of rhetorical appeal—pathos, logos, and ethos—we introduce students to the concept we just discussed and provide an example in the lecture excerpt below:

Rhetorical Appeals in Fairy Tales

The Brothers Grimm's "Rapunzel" can be interpreted as a tale filled with moral lessons that are instilled into readers by appealing to their fear of loneliness and their desire to find love—to be connected to others. The enchantress in the story, Dame Gothel, is so afraid of being alone that she imprisons the maturing Rapunzel in order to ensure that she will always have a companion. Rapunzel, trapped and unhappy, lets down her hair to connect with someone on a deeper level than she can find with the enchantress. She seeks and finds love with the prince. They build this love through trust, sacrifice, and perseverance. Although initially afraid of the prince, Rapunzel dares to hope that "'[h]e will love me more than old Dame Gothel does," and she agrees to "willingly go away" with him (Grimm). Both the prince and Rapunzel sacrifice their personal safety to defy the enchantress and be together. The determined couple hatches a plan to build a ladder piece by piece to help Rapunzel to escape. Dame Gothel, of course, catches them in the midst of their plot. The prince falls from the tower and is blinded, and the enchantress exiles Rapunzel to the desert. Still, after two years, the two are eventually reunited in love. Ironically, the enchantress and audience both learn that true emotional connections cannot be forced; they must be earned through trust and sacrifice. You should now see that "Rapunzel," as do many fairy tales, successfully delivers its message through pathos. However, emotion is not the only appeal in "Rapunzel"; an analysis of logos could easily be built by examining the cause and effect (logical appeal) elements in the tale.

1. Rhetorical appeal is but one facet of how the message of Grimm's "Rapunzel" is delivered. The argument, its logic, is built on the basic structure all arguments are built on—the syllogism. A syllogism is a three part structure that leads an audience through clear evidence and reason to a sound conclusion.

2. The first part of the syllogism is the **claim** (conclusion). A claim, as we have discussed, is the opinion, attitude, or stance you have on a given subject. For example, you could argue that as powerful as the enchantress is, she cannot force Rapunzel to love her. The claim is that love is earned and cannot be forced. This claim then must be supported with the evidence found in the fairy tale.

3. The **minor premise** (support) of the syllogism is the specific evidence on which the conclusion is based. For example, despite the enchantress's overwhelming control of Rapunzel physically, she still does not control the maiden's heart.

4. The **major premise** (assumption) is the link between the minor premise (support) and the claim. Not everyone would make the same claim based on this evidence, but you can assert that the claim is logically linked to the evidence. For example, the assumption Grimm is making in "Rapunzel" is that a healthy society is built upon cooperation and respect. A society built upon tactics of force and domination will ultimately fail.

Understanding the implied assumption of an argument can be difficult and definitely takes practice, but once you are able to break an argument into its three basic parts, you can then understand how well you are presenting your own case and can recognize the strengths and flaws in the arguments of your opponents.

Through the assignment below, we followed up on the lecture by asking students to identify and analyze one or more rhetorical appeals and the structure of an argument they found in Grimm's "Hansel and Grethel":

Identifying Appeals and Argument Structure

Paragraph 1:

In a well-developed paragraph of at least ten sentences, analyze the fairy tale's use of one of the rhetorical appeals: logos, pathos, or ethos. Evaluate the fairy tale's worth/effectiveness in persuading its readers to adopt its message based on its use of one of these appeals. You must support your claims with specific evidence from the tale, and you must explain why the use of this appeal was or was not successful. Begin the paragraph with a topic sentence that identifies the author(s), the title, and makes a specific claim that addresses the use of this appeal.

Paragraph 2:

In a well-developed paragraph of at least ten sentences, identify the three basic parts of the fairy tale's syllogism: major premise, minor premise, and conclusion (or if you prefer, claim, support, and assumption). Once you have identified the parts of the argument, explain whether or not the argument is sound. Use specific evidence from the tale to support your analysis. Begin the paragraph with a topic sentence that identifies the author(s), the title, and makes a specific claim that indicates the soundness of the argument.

A good response from one of our students, Allyson Walls, typical of the many we received, reveals an appreciation of pathos and syllogism:

The story "Hansel and Grethel" by Jacob and Wilhelm Grimm successfully uses the pathos appeal to persuade the readers to accept the message or messages of the story. Throughout the whole story, basic fears and wants of humans are provided through the characters. Child abuse, murder, abandonment, human evil, betrayal of trust, and unconditional love are a few examples in the story that evoke emotions and question morals. The story seems to start out as a tragedy when the step-mother plans to abandon her children in the forest to save herself from starvation (Grimm). The story conjures hatred for the step-mother because she abandons her children, which is considered by many to be morally wrong in society. The story evokes pity when the children wander the forest and may "die of hunger and weariness" (Grimm). Hope for the children arises when they stumble upon a house made of candy (Grimm). Then comes fear for the children when they are captured by a witch, and hatred for the witch is evoked because she goes against societies' morals by being cannibalistic and wanting to cause harm to children. Hope arises once more when Grethel murders the witch, and the children make their way home once again (Grimm). The story eventually turns into one of victory when the children make it back to their father and live happily ever after (Grimm), which could perhaps evoke envy in the reader. The story is successful in the use of the pathos appeal because of the emotions it evokes continuously throughout the whole story.

Jacob and Wilhem Grimm's story "Hansel and Grethel" has a sound argument for perseverance. The syllogism for this story begins with the claim that determination and refusal to give up triumphs over bad situations. The minor premise is that no matter how lost the children of the story were or how bad their situation became, they were not discouraged and still tried to get back home. Finally the major premise is that if an individual does good things and continues to try to achieve their goal, they [*sic*] will succeed, and if individuals are bad and do wicked things, they will meet their demise. This story about perseverance is sound due to the many trials the children overcame. Hansel and Grethel face a situation where their step-mother wants to abandon them in the forest, yet the children keep trying to find their way home. When the children overhear their step-mother's plan, Hansel does not give up for he says to Grethel, "[D]o not distress thyself, I will soon find a way to help us" (Grimm). Twice, Hansel tries to make a trail leading back home (Grimm), which signifies his refusal to give up, and, even when they do not have a trail to follow, the children continue to walk, fighting starvation and exhaustion (Grimm). When the children come upon the wicked witch who wants to eat them, they do not give up, and they eventually cause the witch's demise and escape with her jewels. After the events with the wicked witch, the children continue on their journey home, and even when they come upon a body of water that they have no way to cross, they get help from a duck and continue on their journey. They walk until they finally make it home to their father and find perfect happiness. The step-mother and the witch also both meet their demise after they do terrible things. The witch murdered and ate children, and the step-mother abandoned two innocent children due to her own selfishness.

Once students felt comfortable identifying appeals and dissecting an argument's structure, we then asked them to look for any potential weaknesses in its logic. We gave them another breakdown of what we wanted from them though our own example below:

Identifying Logical Fallacies

Last week we discussed the three main parts of an argument. Breaking an argument apart should give you some insight into any potential weaknesses in logic. The flaws in logic are known as logical fallacies. Almost as many lists and terms for these fallacies exist as there are professors to create them. Being able to label a flaw as *ad hominem, non sequitur,* or a hasty generalization is not as important as being able to explain the weakness in the reasoning. Keep this in mind when you review the logical fallacies list and complete your assignment this week.

Let's continue working with arguments, using fairy tales as an example of argument structure and flaws—logical fallacies. The argument of Grimm's "The Six Swans," now centuries old and ingrained into Western culture, has stood the test of time, but it is not necessarily based on sound reasoning. For an argument to be sound, it needs three ingredients:

- First, its premises must be true; they must correspond to reality.
- Second, the conclusion based on those premises must be valid, meaning anyone could logically come to the same conclusion when reviewing the premises.
- Finally, if the premises are true and the conclusion is valid, then the argument is sound.

Often this is not the case, however. An argument may have a valid conclusion based on untrue premises, or it may have an invalid conclusion based on true premises. If an argument has either untrue premises or an invalid conclusion—or both—it contains a logical fallacy. This abstract description of logical fallacies becomes clearer when applied to a concrete example such as the argument in Grimm's "The Six Swans." Let's review the argument:

Claim: By assuming the perceived "traditional" virtues of womanhood, the maiden achieves her desired ends.

Support: Despite obstacles and dangers, the maiden keeps silent and labors on magical shirts for six years to restore her brothers to human form.

Assumption: Women who do what society expects of them will reap their just rewards.

Logical Fallacies: Hopefully, you see a stereotype here. What is inherently flawed with this type of logic? What if this logic were applied to you? What other fallacies can you find in Grimm's "The Six Swans"?

We suspend our beliefs when we read literature and watch films to be entertained, inspired, and instructed, but as educated people we must keep our wits about us and look for the message in the story and understand how it is delivered. Once you recognize the message, do you agree with it? Why or why not? Grimm's "The Six Swans" is a well-worn cautionary tale that reveals the power of emotional appeals and the subtlety by which arguments can be distorted to fulfill a goal. As a critical thinker you should be able to distinguish between truth and fiction and between reason and reaction.

Without connecting every link in the chain of logic, or perhaps we should say lack of logic, we have hopefully illustrated that seemingly strong arguments can be based on faulty premises. We then gave the following assignment for students to find the breaks in argument themselves:

Logical Fallacies Assignment

In a well-developed paragraph of at least ten sentences, identify at least one example of a logical fallacy in one of the following Brothers Grimm fairy tales: "Little Red-Cap," Little Snow White," or "The Golden Goose." Explain why you believe people have accepted this fallacy in the tale and provide evidence that supports your assertion that it is, in fact, a logical fallacy in the argument. Begin the paragraph with a topic sentence that identifies the author(s), the title, and makes a specific claim that identifies a logical fallacy in the fairy tale.

Holly DeGidts came up with a unique perspective on the logic of Grimm's "Little Red Cap":

In the fairytale "Little Red-Cap" the authors Jacob and Wilhelm Grimm rely on an appeal to authority to show why children should obey their mothers. In the story, Little Red-Cap is asked to travel through the woods to bring her grandmother a bottle of wine and a piece of cake. Before Little Red-Cap's trip, her mother directly tells the young girl not to stray from the path. Shortly after her departure, Little Red meets a wolf who tricks the girl off her path, giving him time to eat Little

Red-Cap's grandmother and wait to eat Little Red-Cap herself. After the wolf consumes both Little Red-Cap and her grandmother, a hunter saves them by cutting them out of the wolf's stomach. Weeks later, Little Red-Cap's mother asks her to make the same trip. Now heeding her mother's orders, Little Red-Cap ignores the wolf and arrives at her grandmother's house safely. The Brothers Grimm use the story of Little Red-Cap to urge their readers that following their parents' wishes will keep them safe. This logical fallacy operates on the requirement that parents always know what is best.

We concluded the lectures and assignments by asking the students to reflect in writing on how the whole process worked for them. Before this final writing assignment, however, we initiated an informal discussion that allowed students to share their perspectives on the arguments they found in the fairy tales. As the following response to the reflection assignment demonstrates, many of our students reported they found the informal discussion helpful, for it gave them insight into different approaches and allowed them to see that their own analyses were also valid. They realized that they could, in fact, analyze arguments on their own. The reflection assignment is included here:

Fairy Tales as Arguments Reflection

Write a well-developed paragraph of at least ten sentences. As always, begin your paragraph with a strong topic sentence which makes a claim that addresses your experience with analyzing fairy tales as an argument. Did this assignment help you learn to look for the parts of an argument? What did you like? What did you find difficult?

Composition student Haley Nye offered the following typical response on how analysis of fairy tales led to understanding of the structure of argument:

Analyzing fairy tales was a great help in learning how to decipher parts of an argument. I never would have thought that you could have created an argument from a fairy tale, and I found this very interesting. I knew all of the stories from past readings, but I really enjoyed rereading them for the assignments. Since the stories were so short in length, it really made them more enjoyable to read, absorb, and review when completing the assignments. I found the process of picking out the different elements rather amusing simply because they are tales made for children, but they contain very adult concepts. I do not think I found any part of these assignments difficult. It was essential to read the lecture for that week to understand what I would be doing in the assignments. After reading the lecture and Grimm's "Rapunzel," I found it very easy to grasp parts of an argument, but I could easily see how it would be very difficult for someone who had not done that reading prior to starting the assignment. I found the class discussions very enlightening, and wished we had included more of those types of assignments in those units. Hearing other people's ideas about what the claim, support, and assumption was helped to reinforce what each part could potentially consist of, and how to analyze the tales from different angles. Overall, the fairytale assignments were my favorite of all of the assignments we have done this semester.

In the age of Google, Ask.com, and Twitter, getting students to slow down and concentrate on the written word and its true power is challenging. Working with fairy tales has its drawbacks, but it does allow us to detour from the information highway to a quiet oasis that allows and encourages students to employ their minds. The discovery that they are capable of contributing valuable ideas and insight is worth the journey we take to get them there. For many of them, the trip is magical, startling, and empowering.

Works Cited

Degidts, Holly. "Unit 12. "*Composition II Online*. RSU Claremore, OK, 10 Nov. 2013.
Grimm, Brothers. *Children's and Household Tales*. Trans. Margaret Hunt. *World of Tales: Stories for Children, Folktales, Fairy Tales, and Fables from Around the World*. Web. 10 Aug. 2013.
Limbaugh, Rush. "The Latest from the Feminist 'Front.'" *See, I Told You So*. New York: Pocket Books, 1993. Print.
Nye, Haley. "Unit 15." *Composition II Online*. RSU Claremore, OK, 30 Apr. 2014
Walls, Allyson. "Unit 11." *Composition II Online*. RSU Claremore, OK, 6 Apr. 2014.

Once Upon a Time
Nataliya Romenesko

In a certain kingdom, beyond the thrice ninth land, there lived tsars who had three sons; widowed peasants who had beautiful daughters abused by their evil stepmothers; valiant talking horses and hungry-but-polite grey wolves; mighty knights known as bogatyrs; naïve simpletons destined to transform into good-looking princes; and gruesome villains with a knack for cannibalism and kidnapping. This magic-filled kingdom, populated by a host of charismatic characters and human-like animals, has existed in the popular imagination for centuries; its history, having originated within a primarily oral culture, evolved continuously to include an abundance of written records, also documented on stage and in film. Thousands of young but enthusiastic visitors wander within the kingdom's realm in the pursuit of its magical balance between right and wrong achieved as a result of the hero's misfortunes and exciting adventures. Although traditionally children-oriented in modern terms, the world of fairy tales has much to offer readers of all ages. Deeply rooted in an oral tradition, fairy tales, like no other genre, capture the most fundamental narratives of the nation's character and worldview and can thus yield invaluable cultural insights into its historical past.

Being both international and local, fairy tales incorporate global motifs of the universal human condition along with culturally specific themes closely tied to the region of their origin. While some of the fairy tale elements mentioned in the opening lines of this article are not geographically-bound, others are traditionally Slavic. Bogatyrs, for instance, are glorified warriors from the Russian *bylina*, a heroic oral epic; they are also often featured in the Russian fairy tale. According to Faith Wigzell, bogatyrs embody such "quintessentially Russian" qualities as "patriotism, strength, endurance and great capacity for drink" (41). In her introduction to *The Firebird and Other Russian Fairy Tales*,

Jacqueline Onassis approaches the same subject of "quintessential" Russianness from a more poetic perspective by pointing towards such elements of setting as "the damp black earth, the dense forest, the snow in deep winter, the wooden huts ... of the peasants and their lively village dances" as identifiably Russian (7). This poeticism, shrewdly noted by Onassis, permeates Russian fairy tales, imaginative folk narratives that recreate the rhythms of the peasant life. Deeply superstitious and often illiterate, the Russian peasant was "isolated culturally and, in many instances, geographically, from the mainstream of his [or her] nation's development" (Ivanits 4); even the rise and subsequent spread of Christianity did not eliminate more traditional pagan practices as Linda J. Ivanits convincingly demonstrates in her *Russian Folk Belief*. This unique blend of archaic and newly emerging belief systems resulted in a rather sophisticated fabric of agrarian rituals and religious festivities, both practical and mystical, directly reflected in the nation's most traditional narratives—its fairy tales.

Although teaching Russian language, culture, and literature has been relegated primarily to the Departments of Slavic Languages and Literatures across the U.S., studying elements of the Russian folklore can enrich introductory composition classes with cross-cultural perspectives. Separated by both geographical and ideological distances but invariably brought together by a relentless process of globalization, our nations have never stopped sharing and appreciating each other's cultural and literary heritage. While literary works of such canonical writers as Tolstoy, Dostoevsky, Pushkin, and Gogol (among others) reveal significant social, cultural, and historical truths about the Russian character, so does the Russian folklore that also serves as a source of inspiration for the Russian opera and ballet.

Realistically, a comprehensive examination of the Russian folklore, its origin, and subsequent dissemination will require time and resources beyond what an introductory writing class can potentially offer. However, a more focused investigation directed towards examining a limited number of Russian fairy tales and their most prominent characteristics will allow students to practice their critical thinking skills and develop a range of intercultural perspectives so essential in the world where "[l]ocal diversity and global connectedness confront us on a daily basis" (Connor 15). By immersing themselves into the magical world of the Russian fairy tale, students will have an opportunity to glimpse into a historically and socially remote Russian past, of which there is not much written record, and decide for themselves as to what constitutes a "quintessentially Russian" identity. After an introductory lecture, students will work in groups with their assigned fairy tales under their instructor's guidance and supervision. Their analysis will result in a presentation and a short reflective essay documenting their findings. If time allows, students will be encouraged to create a fairy tale of their own, incorporating various linguistic and structural formulae representative of the Russian fairy tale.

This tendency of the Russian fairy tale towards following an almost predetermined composition pattern with a typical set of characters was first noticed and explored by Vladimir Propp, who, in his *The Morphology of the Folk Tale*, attempted to analyze Russian fairy tales, aiming at an almost scientific precision in his literary investigation. Even though Propp's influential study, being formalist in nature and disregarding such important aspects of character analysis as motivation, psychological state, social class, and gender, his theory, when complemented by a more inclusive literary analysis, provides a solid foundation for examining the fairy tale's most basic narrative structure. According to Vladimir Propp, the fairy tale's plot is driven "by the functions of the dramatis personae in the order dictated by the tale itself" (25). Propp identifies thirty-one of such functions that follow the initial situation. A tale typically starts with an absentation, a departure of a family member, and an interdiction that is often violated by a hero. As a result, a villain enters the scene and, upon receiving valuable information about his victim, deceives the hero to cause him or her injury or harm. Next, a problem is made known, and the hero is dispatched. After an array of tests or interrogations, the hero obtains a magical object that provides guidance and delivers the hero to a goal of the journey. Soon after, the villain is defeated and pursues the hero unsuccessfully. Upon return, the hero encounters a false hero and has to assert his/her identity by fulfilling another task. In the end, the false hero is exposed, the villain is punished, and the hero, often transformed in appearance, is married and ascends the throne. It goes without saying that this logical sequence of events lying at the heart of the tale's structure permits a few variations; it, nonetheless, equips us with necessary terminology and focus in approaching the Russian fairy tale.

Another one of Propp's prominent contributions to the analysis of the Russian fairy tale is his classification of the tale's characters. He distinguishes between such character types as the hero (victim or seeker), the false hero, the villain, the benefactor who prepares the hero "for the transmission of a magical agent," the magical helper, the dispatcher, and the princess and her father, with the possibility of some characters taking on multiple roles (Propp 79). Of interest is that most functions, as well as character types, exhibit a certain duality: an interrogation is introduced and violated; a lack is made known and supplied; a hero is challenged by a false hero. This dual structure also coincides with the tale's overriding moral of the good conquering the evil and thus sustains a necessary balance of the fairy tale world. While the author of *Intercultural Rhetoric in the Writing Classroom*, Ulla Connor, describes a new intercultural approach as taking us "away from binary distinctions such as ... individualist and collectivist cultures" (8), these binaries are unavoidable when dealing with Russian fairy tales since "this ... system of binary opposites ... seems to be part of the linguistic and psychological makeup of the Slavs from pre-historic times" (Haney 2).

Besides its characteristic binaries, the rich language of the Russian fairy tale is "particularly rife with triplicity," ranging from a three-son family structure to a three-fold task or action sequence of the tale's characters (Croft 29). Even the setting often incorporates trebling (ex. "in the thrice-ninth kingdom") while the immediacy of magic transformations is emphasized by happening "in a trice." In his "People in Threes Going Up in Smoke and Other Triplicities in Russian Literature and Culture," Lee B. Croft notes that "[t]elling things three times in a triplistic way is a veritable hallmark of Russian literature" (42). Although convincing in demonstrating how this cultural tendency towards triplification is manifested in Russian naming practices (first name/patronymic/last name) and various grammatical categories of the Russian language, the author falls short of identifying its historical roots and leaves the issue open for further investigation. Jack Haney, in his turn, explains this phenomenon as a practical need of "the teller of the tales to gather his thoughts" and achieve higher impact on the audience by repeating things multiple times (3). Due to the lack of consistent and reliable written records, reconstructing the Slavic cultural past in its entirety is a challenge. Nonetheless, there is no doubt that triplicity, reflected in the Russian proverb "Third time is a charm," or, more literally, "God likes trinity" (Бог троицу любит), has deep cultural and religious roots. While triple structures are not exclusively confined to the world of the Russian fairy tale, their intense pervasiveness within the tale's language and plot is hard to overlook.

Among other language formulae typical of the Russian fairy tale are expressions of ambiguity such as "a long time, a short time" or "a short distance or a long one" used to describe a hero's journey. Dual in structure, they, along with such theatrical remarks as "lo and behold," attest to the oral tradition of the Russian fairy tale, whose narrator would use them as rhetorical means of maximizing his effect on the audience. Similarly, the tale's opening lines (*priskazka*) often do not clarify where the action is taking place; the setting is instead only cursorily delineated as "in a certain land there lived a certain character." This literary abstraction helps to focus the reader's attention on the character's journey and various magical occurrences, since achieving an exact

temporal and local precision is inconsequential to plot development. The clos-
ing lines (*kontsovka*) either proclaim the hero's marital bliss and prosperity or
bring a narrative closure in the form of a wedding-toast-like humorous statement. The tale's propensity towards such comic literary maneuvers helps to
strike a magical balance between its imaginary content, filled with exaggeration, and true-to-life motifs of pre-established social hierarchies and various
challenges associated with a peasant's daily life. The tale's fusion of realistic
and fantastical elements is also acknowledged in a popular Russian proverb:
"There is a grain of truth in every fairy tale" ("В каждой сказке есть доля
правды").

Before turning towards our discussion of a few selected fairy tales, we
should note that disputing what truly constitutes a fairy tale (or a wonder tale,
or a folk tale, the list to be continued) is outside the scope of this investigation.
The tales chosen for consideration come from Afanas'ev's collection entitled
Russian Fairy Tales and will be treated as such, difficulties of translation
notwithstanding. They will serve to introduce students to some of the most
iconic Russian fairy tale characters, along with more traditional aspects of the
tale's structure and language. In their semi-independent investigation, students
will meet simpleton-heroes, villain-heroes (including Baba Yaga and Koshchey
the Deathless), and female characters (who are rare). Although the above-
mentioned characters are archetypal and thus surface in numerous fairy tales,
here are a few tales I would recommend for closer analysis: "Ivanushko the
Fool" and "Emelya the Simplton"; "Baba Yaga" and "Koshchey the Deathless";
and "Vasilisa the Beautiful" and "Go I Know Not Whither, Bring Back I Know
Not What." Figure 1 is a sample of a guided-reading worksheet that students
can use for note-taking purposes. First, they read and analyze the two tales
(within one category) they have been assigned. After they record and later
present their findings, they fill out the rest while listening to their peers' presentations.

Among a gallery of vivid Russian folk characters, fools and simpletons
occupy a special place. Ingenious in their blissful ignorance, they often become
the object of ridicule because of their impracticality and almost childlike
naiveté. The grotesque extremities of the hero's behavior, however, serve well
to provide comic relief to the perplexed audience who stands to witness that
the fool's lack of hero-like characteristics as courage, wit, and determination
will not interrupt his inevitable ascent to wealth and power. Despite their
anti-heroic constitution, fools and simpletons manage to outsmart everyone
and climb the social ladder against all odds and in no time, typically assisted
by a magical helper of some kind. Why they, not only lazy but also short-

Fairy Tales	Literary Aspects	Plot/Structure	Characters (types; character; motivation)	Language Formulae	Tale's Moral (and/or beliefs it reflects)
Russian Fool Characters: • "Emelya the Simpleton" • "Ivanushko the Fool"		• • • • • • • •			
Russian Villain Characters: • "Baba Yaga" • "Koshchey the Deathless"		• • • • • • • •			
Russian Female Characters: • "Vasilisa the Beautiful" • "Go I Know" • "Koshchey the Not Whither"		• • • • • • • •			

Figure 1

tempered and even vengeful at times, are deserving of the magic help in the first place is another ethical dilemma presented by these types of characters.

Emelya the Simpleton, who appears in the fairy tale of the same name, is one of those lucky fools whose simplicity does not preclude his eventual rise to power. Emelya is the youngest of the three brothers and is a lazybones, who spends most of his days "lying on the stove and doing no work at all" (Afanas'ev 47). The tale starts with an absentation of the brothers, who, leaving for town, instruct Emelya to obey his sisters-in-law. Even though Emelya does not directly violate the brothers' interdiction (which takes the form of a request in this case), he is not incredibly enthusiastic when his sisters-in-law ask him (and thus dispatch the hero) to assist with their daily chores and send him to fetch some water. As luck has it, however, while getting water, Emelya catches a magical agent, a pike, that fulfills all his wishes and does all his work for him if only he says, "By the pike's command, by my own request" (47). Sadly enough, the pike's magic help does not keep Emelya out of trouble when he orders a stick to thrash some town people who happen to be in his way. Once this information reaches the tsar, who acts as a villain in the story, he proceeds to punish Emelya by throwing him into a barrel and then into the sea. Accompanying the main character aboard the barrel is the tsar's daughter, who is unfortunate enough to fall in love with the hero. Despite these temporary troubles, Emelya yet again resorts to magic and escapes the barrel to return triumphantly to the tsar's favor. The tale ends with "they began to live happily together and to prosper" (48).

In the end, the reader comes to sympathize with an ingenious but humorous main character whose swift advance within the social hierarchy, so improbable in more realistic terms, becomes possible in the fairy tale, which asserts its imaginative power to transcend any artificially established boundaries of peasant life. Despite his pronounced simplicity, Emelya is not fully void of ambition since his dream is to have "red boots, red caftan, and a red shirt" (Afanas'ev 46), all of which would be indicative of a higher social status. In her "Functions of Textile and Sartorial Artifacts in Russian Folktales," Victoria Ivleva points out that there is a "direct correspondence between appearance and social position" (272); this fact also explains why the hero's physical transformation often accompanies the change in his social status. While "Emelya the Simpleton" from Afanas'ev's collection omits this element of transformation, other renderings of this same tale mention Emelya's makeover to explain why the tsar's daughter falls in love with the main character. Among other elements characteristic of the Russian fairy tale, "Emelya the Simpleton" exhibits a traditional tendency towards triplicity: there are three brothers in the tale and three tasks Emelya performs before getting in trouble with the tsar. Although Emelya's ascent to power may seem questionable in moral terms, another character's random luck is even more puzzling, considering his rather staggering lack of common sense.

This disparity between the amount of effort and the end result is even more astonishing in case of "Ivanushko the Little Fool." In this tale, which in structure resembles the one discussed above, Ivanushko is the youngest son and his mother and two brothers repeatedly request his help with daily domestic chores. Although enthusiastic in his desire to help, Ivanushko accomplishes his tasks in such a nonsensical way, the readers wish he never undertook them. When asked to bring dumplings to his brothers working in the field, Ivanushko throws the food at his shadow, thinking it is a person who needs to be fed (63). When asked to buy a table and bring it back home, he leaves his purchase on the road, assuming the table has four legs and can thus make it home on its own (64). When asked to step in as a herdsman for his brothers, he plucks the sheep's eyes to prevent them from wandering off (63). Having lost their patience, the brothers plot to get rid of Ivanushko; the hero, however, manages to outsmart them and a certain nobleman, a random passer-by acting as an unsuspecting benefactor whose place (riches and all) Ivanushko takes in the end. Thus, yet again simplicity wins over treachery and impatience. Nonetheless, the reader must decide if the moral validity of Ivanushko's choices and downright absurdity of his behavior make him superior to his brothers and therefore deserving of a better end.

Despite such ethical complexity, the tale is concluded, "Ivanushko had a well; in this well was a bell; and that's all I have to tell" (Afanas'ev 65). Thus the audience knows that Ivanushko's grotesque behavior, albeit questionable in moral terms and far removed from practicality valued by the Russian peasant, is only meant to entertain and amuse. This, however, does not fully explain why fools and simpletons manage to capture the popular imagination, but both tales assign a certain ethical value to simplicity as a much appreciated quality of the human body and mind. In her *Russian Folk Belief*, Linda Ivanits points towards the peasant belief in "incapacities as masking extraordinary spiritual power" (111). Since "simpler...[people] saw more wonders" (Ivanits 65), it stands to reason that fools and simpletons featured in traditional fairy tales are deeply connected with the nature's magical powers. This phenomenon of "divine idiocy" (156) is further investigated by Dana Heller and Elena Volkova in their intriguing dialogue entitled "The Holy Fool in Russian and American Culture: A Dialogue."

While the tsar and the brothers appearing in the above-mentioned fairy tales exhibit a certain degree of maliciousness and cunning, on a "scary" scale, they are far below such super villains of the Russian folklore as Baba Yaga, the protectress of the forest, and Koshchey the Deathless, the embodiment of death. Part of the so-called "unclean force," in fairy tales, they coexist with such lesser supernatural spirits as rusalkas, leshys, and domovoys (among other beings occupying various domestic and natural environments) but enjoy a far more substantial area of influence. (Rusalkas are female spirits inhabiting rivers; they are notorious for using their charm to attract and drown men. Leshys are forest spirits guarding the forest and its animals; they can lead people astray. Domovoys are mischievous house spirits, often harmless, that watch out for the family whose house they co-inhabit, but, if made angry, they can cause harm.)

Baba Yaga, for instance, whose "classic Slavic origin" is highlighted by the majority of researchers (Grădinaru 316), inhabits the Russian forest but is not always confined to it due to the mobility granted by her mortar-and-pestle ride. She is the protector of the forest and the goddess of death who also "serves as initiator of the main character" (317). In "Baba Yaga," for instance, a heroine is expected to take care of the old witch (cleaning her hut and bathing her); she is also responsible for spinning yarn and cooking. By assigning three different tasks to the character, Baba Yaga allows her to reveal sincerity, kindness, and thoughtfulness, for which she is rewarded with beautiful dresses. On the other hand, two other female characters who display such negative characteristics as envy and spite are punished by Baba Yaga. All in all, when it comes to female characters, the moral of the story is far from dubious: being polite and hardworking is identified as an ethically appropriate behavior for a maiden, and Baba Yaga is the one who either condones or disapproves of the characters' behavior.

Therefore, despite her repulsive looks and occasional threats of cannibalism, Baba Yaga is a complex evil character: on the one hand, she is a villain who often pursues the hero; on the other hand, she is also a benefactor who assists the hero in his or her search. In "Baba Yaga," we observe a standard scenario of a victimized heroine, whose father, "a certain peasant" (Afanas'ev 194), succumbs to his evil new wife and abandons his own daughter in the service of Baba Yaga. Through the heroine's eyes, the reader sees "a little hut standing on chicken legs" (194) that can only be entered after saying the following magical words: "Little hut, little hut, stand with your back to the woods, and your front to me" (194). Baba Yaga, the Bony-Legged One, also gets a vivid, if somewhat fractured, description: "her head was in front, her right leg was in one corner, and her left leg in the other corner" (194). Both Baba Yaga's habitat and her fragmented body are meant to induce fear of an old hag, who, despite her reportedly Slavic origin, has a strong aversion to the Russian spirit. "I smell a Russian smell," she says menacingly when welcoming the peasant's daughter into her abode (194).

Left alone in Baba Yaga's hut, the girl meets her magical helper—a mouse that, in exchange for some food, assists the heroine in her plight. Every day Baba Yaga tests the heroine, and every day she exceeds her expectations. Positioned as a villain in the beginning of the tale, Baba Yaga then functions as a benefactor who bestows prosperity upon the maiden and thus ensures her successful future. Struck by his daughter's success, the peasant takes her back home. Thus, the heroine returns home where she has been substituted by the stepmother's daughter, a false hero, envious of the heroine's fortune. The tale's balance is restored when the stepmother's daughter, being rude with the mouse, fails to fulfill her daily tasks and is broken into pieces (reduced to bones) by Baba Yaga. Yet again, however, the tale's violent end is overshadowed by its humorous ending: "There's a tale for you, and a crock of butter for me" (Afanas'ev 195). The only part that's missing is "Cheers!"

As opposed to Baba Yaga, Koshchey the Deathless, "the Slavic prince of darkness" (Haney 3) and "a personification of the dreaded Tatar" (Onassis 8), typically acts as a kidnapper of female characters who are then rescued by their significant others. Despite his explicitly emphasized deathless-ness, skeleton-like Koshchey is not truly invincible. His death is hidden, matreshka style: it is protected by an egg that is located within a duck that is located within a hare on a remote island's tall oak tree (Afanas'ev 489). In other words, it is not easy to get to. In the tale "Koschey the Deathless," the characters manage to find out Koshchey's secret and kill the villain by striking him on the forehead with an egg containing his death. While this important moment of the heroes' triumph over evil creates one of the tale's focal points, the all-mighty–Koshchey's egg-inflicted death comes across as somewhat ironic.

Compared to the fairy tales previously discussed here, "Koshchey the Deathless" has a sophisticated structure that, in Propp's terms, incorporates more than one "move" or sequence of plot development. The character types involved, however, are no different from what we have seen before; there are simply more of them, propelling the tale's plot forward. The tale starts with a young Prince Ivan realizing his lack of a bride and being dispatched by his father, even though unwillingly, since in this tale Ivan is the only son. Early into his journey, Ivan saves a man, Bulat the Brave, from a beating and thus acquires a faithful servant or helper. Bulat the Brave assists Ivan in winning the affections of Vasilisa Kirbitievna, who, however unfortunately, gets snatched by Koshchey the Deathless, also occasionally referred to as the "old rattlebones" (Afanas'ev 487) by one of the characters. Thus, a new search ensues; it results in the villain's death with the help of disguise and what seems like an entire animal kingdom: a dog, an eagle, and a lobster. The villain's death does not eliminate the pursuit that is carried out by Koshchey's twelve sister-doves. They predict a series of three trials that await Prince Ivan upon his return home, but Bulat the Brave is the only one aware of the upcoming misfortunes. When he speaks up, he turns into a stone (493). Years later, Prince Ivan and Vasilisa Kirbitievna reverse the bad magic by slaying their own children and pouring their blood over Bulat's statue that, miraculously, comes to life, and so do the couple's children. The tale ends with a characteristic "I was at that feast too, I drank mead and wine there; it ran down my moustache but did not go into my mouth, yet my soul was drunk and sated" (494) as if the bloody incident has never occurred.

Being a longer narrative, "Koshchey the Deathless" contains a variety of language formulae typical of the Russian fairy tale: most actions and counter-actions happen in threes. Vasilisa Kirbitievna lives "[b]eyond thrice nine lands, in the thrice tenth kingdom" (Afanas'ev 485), and she spends three nights sweet-talking Koshchey into revealing the location of his death. Also, the vastness of Ivan's journey is emphasized through "for a long time or a short time," repeated on multiple occasions (487), while immediate results or miraculous transformations are typically predicated by "lo and behold" (490). What this tale also has in common with numerous others is that Prince Ivan does not truly achieve anything on his own. Confronted by repeated sequences of threefold misfortunes, he cries and is often incapacitated. Only a collective effort makes his achievements possible; among his helpers is Vasilisa Kirbitievna who directly contributes to Ivan's success. As opposed to other heroines we have encountered so far, she, whose destiny is shaped by multiple male characters in the tale, is proactive in finding out about Koshchey's death even when the latter meets each one of her three attempts with "You foolish woman! Your hair is long, but your wit is short" (488). Ironically, Koshchey, unable to spot her pretense, finds out for himself that the Russian proverb "У бабы волос долог, да ум короток," ("Woman's hair is long, but mind is short") might not necessarily ring true.

Vasilisa Kirbitievna, acting with a sense of agency, is not the only female character of her type. Though most are conditioned to follow a more traditional route of being praised for obedience, kindness, and outstanding needle work and then happily wedding a certain tsar, prince, or soldier, some female characters are more proactive in shaping their own destiny and determining their significant other's success. Beautiful in appearance, they also come across as strong-willed and intelligent maidens, whose practicality and power of foresight go well beyond what their husbands are capable of. Therefore, even though it might appear that "the heroines really do very little in the tales to direct their destiny" (Haney 3) and do not challenge established gender roles, their characters vary from tale to tale and do not always comply with convention. Despite the obvious fact that their behavior is far from modern manifestations of feminine free will, within a limited range of choices available to them, they choose and often choose wisely.

In "Vasilisa the Beautiful," a young heroine shares the same fate as the central female character of "Baba Yaga." Her journey, however, does not end with the girl's return home; instead, the tale introduces another move, a complication in the plot development. Initially, much like in "Baba Yaga," a victimized heroine, upon her evil stepmother's request, is sent to the old witch. Protected by her deceased mother's blessing, Vasilisa comes into possession of a magical doll that acts as her helper and advisor. After successfully completing a three-task sequence of domestic chores at Baba Yaga's hut, Vasilisa receives a glowing skull that she carries home as a source of light and that burns Vasilisa'a wrong-doers, her stepmother and two stepsisters, to ashes. Another move starts when Vasilisa comes to live with a certain childless old woman, weaves linen of superb quality, and is noticed by a tsar. Consequently, he falls in love with Vasilisa and marries her. Just like in previously discussed tales, the heroine is continuously assisted by magical power and female benefactors, Baba Yaga being one of them.

"Vasilisa the Beautiful" adds a few more pieces to the description of Baba Yaga's habitat, her means of transportation, and her servants. Baba Yaga's hut is surrounded by the fence made of human skulls; her doorposts are made of human legs; and she has human hands for bolts and sharp teeth for a lock. The witch rides in "a mortar, prodding it on with a pestle, and sweeping her traces with a broom" (Afanas'ev 442). Among her faithful servants are the three horsemen—daybreak in white, sunrise in red, and nightfall in black; she is also served by the three pairs of hands. Baba Yaga's intolerance of the Russian spirit is yet again emphasized: "Fie, fie! I smell a Russian smell!" she proclaims (442). However horrifying in her appearance and ways of life, the female character of Baba Yaga, charging Vasilisa with difficult daily tasks, acts as Vasilisa's pseudo-advisor by sharing her worldly wisdom, if in a rather intimidating teaching style.

On one hand, there is no doubt that such domestic chores as cleaning, cooking, and sorting out wheat serve as symbolic initiation rites of a young female. The tale is also rather explicit in praising female's lack of curiosity and the value of silence—"one who knows too much will grow old soon" (Afanas'ev 444)—and includes a seemingly inconspicuous mention of lady-like manners—"they always sat with folded hands, like ladies" (439). On the other hand, in the second part of the tale, Vasilisa takes a more active stance towards weaving her own destiny. When her linen is praised by the tsar and she is then commissioned to sew shirts, she remarks, "I knew all the time ... that I would have to do this work" (447). Polite, kind, hardworking, and, of course, exceptionally beautiful, she consciously uses the means available to her—her exceptional weaving skills—to advance within the social hierarchy and thus reach her own, however limited and marginalized, fairy tale happiness.

Similarly, in "Go I Know Not Whither, Bring Back I Know Not What," a bird-maiden, despite having no other name than "Fedot's wife," not only helps the hero succeed in his perilous adventures but also saves him from imminent death. Fedot, a tsar's favorite archer, meets his young wife during one of his hunting trips. Far from romantic, their first encounter results in Fedot shooting one of her wings. To his and the reader's surprise, the dove he was aiming at falls to the "damp earth" (Afanas'ev 504) and turns into a beautiful maiden whom he then weds. Their marital bliss, however, does not last long since when Fedot's boss, an unmarried tsar, finds out about Fedot's wife's unprecedented beauty, he plots to get rid of Fedot to take his place. The tsar is aided in his plot by his steward, who, in his turn, seeks Baba Yaga's advice on how to destroy Fedot and outsmart his wife. Even though their first two attempts are unsuccessful, the third task they assign to Fedot—"go I know not wither, bring me back I know not what" (511)—leaves even his wife puzzled. She then acts as a benefactor supplying the hero with a magic ball of yarn that leads the character directly to her mother and three beautiful sisters.

Fedot's in-laws, imbued with magical capacities, direct the hero in his search of "I know not what," which turns out to be another mystical being called Shmat Razum (literally, "a piece of wisdom"), an invisible genie capable of making any wishes come true. Fedot frees Shmat Razum from his previous, somewhat oppressive owners and wins his loyalty with a kind and cheerful attitude. In gratitude, Shmat Razum helps Fedot obtain three more magical objects on his way home, defeat the king, and ascend to power, with Fedot's wife becoming queen. Abundant in magic occurrences, this tale is also full of triplicities ("in a trice"; "thrice nine lands"; thirty years; three jars of milk) and incorporates a popular proverb: "[T]he morning is wiser than the evening" (Afanas'ev 505) that also repeatedly surfaces in "Vasilisa the Beautiful." Fedot's journey, vast in time and in geography, is described through such characteristic expressions as "a short distance or a long distance, after a long time or a short time" (514), whose ambiguity is only paralleled by the tale's title and I-know-not-what object of the hero's search.

Even though Fedot's success is ensured by a variety of magical beings, in his quest, he follows the path created for him by his young wife. Yes, she is stereotypically beautiful and also engages in textile activities that represent "a symbolic process of domestication" (Ivleva 288). Nonetheless, without her wit and resourcefulness, neither Fedot nor the entire fairy tale would have been possible. Victoria Ivleva says it best in her "Functions of Textile and Sartorial Artifacts in Russian Folktales": "The magic ball of yarn that they [female characters] give to heroes embodies their psychic skills and wisdom of foresight while their thread directs not only the heroes' destinies but also the plot of the tale" (294). Thus, despite their seemingly marginal roles in the Russian fairy tale, female characters are more multi-faceted than the much-praised docility and obedience of their characters. It is also not for nothing that such a central image of the Russian folklore and belief system as the Mother Damp Earth, revered by the Russian peasant dependent on agricultural fertility, is of feminine gender.

Even though the fairy tales discussed above by no means exhaust the variety of the Russian folklore, they are, nonetheless, representative of some of the genre's most prominent characters and literary features. When reading these new tales, students should have no difficulty in pulling from their personal literary experiences with fairy tales to identify already familiar elements. They will, however, need more direction in interpreting culturally-specific phenomena.

It will be beneficial thus to start with an introductory lecture covering not only literary but also historical aspects of Russian folklore. No doubt the students' background knowledge of the Russian culture, or rather what they perceive to be such, will factor into future discussions and, if addressed thoughtfully, will yield even deeper critical insights. They might be tempted to interpret Emelya the Simpleton and Ivanushko the Fool as humorous depictions of the national character, with laziness and come-what-may attitude as some of its major attributes. They might look past the ritualistic significance of the villain characters and their vital role in the heroes' rite of passage. They might not even think that female characters are truly empowered in their spinning abilities. They might not all agree on their idiosyncratic perceptions of the characters at hand and the cultural reality of the nation in question, but their individual contributions and reflections, steered by a knowledgeable instructor, will allow for a fruitful discussion that will paint an even bigger picture that, like the magic carpet woven by the dove-maiden from "Go I Know Not Whither," "let[s] a view of the whole [Russian] kingdom be embroidered, with towns, villages, rivers, and lakes" (Afanas'ev 506). There's a tale for you, and a crock of butter for me.

Works Cited

Afanas'ev, Aleksandr. *Russian Fairy Tales*. Trans. Norbert Guterman. New York: Pantheon, 1973. Print.

Connor, Ulla. *Intercultural Rhetoric in the Writing Classroom*. Ann Arbor: University of Michigan Press, 2011. Print.

Croft, Lee B. "People in Threes Going Up in Smoke and Other Triplicities in Russian Literature and Culture." *Rocky Mountain Review of Language and Literature* (2005): 29–47. *Humanities International Complete*. Web. 2 Feb. 2014.

Grădinaru, Olga. "Myth and Rationality in Russian Popular Fairy Tales." *Caietele Echinox* (2009): 315–322. *Humanities International Complete*. Web. 2 Feb. 2014.

Haney, Jack. "Introduction." *Russian Wondertales II—Tales of Magic and the Supernatural: Volume 4 of the Complete Russian Folktale* (2001): 3. *Literary Reference Center*. Web. 2 Feb. 2014.

Heller, Dana, and Elena Volkova. "The Holy Fool in Russian and American Culture: A Dialogue." *American Studies International* (2003): 152–78. *Academic Search Premier.* Web. 2 Feb. 2014

Ivanits, Linda J. *Russian Folk Belief.* Armonk, NY: M.E. Sharpe, 1989. Print.

Ivleva, Victoria. "Functions of Textile and Sartorial Artifacts in Russian Folktales." *Marvels and Tales* (2009): 268–99. *Humanities International Complete.* Web. 2 Feb. 2014.

Onassis, Jacqueline, ed. *The Firebird and Other Russian Fairy Tales.* New York: Viking, 1978. Print.

Prewencki, Cliff. "Ivan the Fool." *Magill's Literary Annual 2008* (2008): 1–3. *Literary Reference Center.* Web. 2 Feb. 2014.

Propp, V. *Morphology of the Folktale*, 2d ed. Trans. Laurence Scott. Austin: University of Texas Press, 1968. Print.

Wigzell, Faith. "Chapter 4: Folklore and Russian Literature." *Routledge Companion to Russian Literature* (2001): 36–48. *Literary Reference Center.* Web. 2 Feb. 2014.

Making a Case

Robin M. Murphy *and*
Macy McDonald

It's no secret that, when we sat down with a novel as children, we often became one of the characters in our imagination or felt their emotions. I, Robin, can distinctly remember crying uncontrollably, first while Billy buried Old Dan and, soon after, when Little Ann died from sadness as she lay across Old Dan's grave in *Where the Red Fern Grows*. Gut wrenching. I also learned from Billy's experiences, and as a child subsequently wrote many a story about enduring the death and maiming of my animal friend, Ringo. I also think I learned to respond to death or recover from tragedy in the same way Billy was comforted by the red fern: good comes from the bad. In many ways, the books we read as children teach us to live as adults. We think this is how it goes with young adult (YA) literature.

Theory agrees with us. Martha C. Nussbaum, in *Love's Knowledge: Essays on Philosophy and Literature*, uses the Aristotelian question "How should a human being live?" to establish the basis for her ethical analysis (25). Aristotle's ethical question is contemporary and general enough to use in our case, in terms of adulthood and YA literature. Following that, Sheila Murnaghan's article "Classics for Cool Kids: Popular and Unpopular Versions of Antiquity for Children" argues that children's literature uses mythology in order to help children develop into young adults (340). We'd like to argue here that studying YA lit that alludes to or adapts stories from classical mythology could boost the effectiveness of a college rhetoric course.

In our case, with YA literature, we strive to instill an "appreciation of antiquity" and other adult values (Murnaghan 340). One strong example of YA literature that promotes adult values is Rick Riordan's Percy Jackson series, specifically *The Sea of Monsters*. Our work here will focus on values as ethics, specifically its connection to citizenry, within YA literature. Using *The Sea of Monsters,* the second in the Percy Jackson series, we hope to show how to include common ancient rhetorical concepts and techniques from the likes of Aristotle and his contemporaries in a higher education modern rhetoric classroom curriculum.

Summary of the Novel

The Sea of Monsters deals with the shocking revelation that 13-year-old Percy has a half-brother, Tyson, who is a Cyclops (Riordan 65). Percy is already friends with Tyson when he discovers their shared parentage, but Percy has trouble adapting to the idea of Tyson being a monster *and* his brother. This is compounded by Percy's friend Annabeth who literally went to hell and back with him. She continues to quest with him, despite her reservations about Tyson, on his way to the Sea of Monsters (107). The only problem is it is not Percy's quest. The real hero of the quest is his Ares-born rival, Clarisse, who will stop at nothing to secure the Golden Fleece and save the camp all on her own (92). The fleece will function to save the magic tree, which is actually a daughter of Zeus named Thalia who was transformed as she lay dying (86–87). Thalia's tree protects the camp's borders from monsters and even the weather (86–87). After much trial and error, and help from Tyson, the young heroes manage to recover the fleece and send it back to camp with Clarisse (235–36). The fleece heals the tree, but perhaps does its job a little too well (278–79). Throughout the story, this book asks the reader to question what a "monster" really is. Monsters are often literary manifestations of human fears and can be used to expose a culture's tendency to stigmatize a certain group; however, in our case, these monsters offer an opportunity to teach tolerance to readers.

The major struggle of the novel is ethical: Percy accepting his Cyclops half-brother. As monsters, Cyclops are deeply distrusted by demigods. It's actually Percy's duty as a demigod to slay monsters. However, Percy reluctantly agrees to live with Tyson after Percy's father formally claims Tyson as his own in front of the entire camp (65). It's one of the many ways that the series works to humanize a number of inhuman beings. Finally, the ethical code expressed in *The Sea of Monsters* includes heroism, personal responsibility, forgiveness, and efficacy which correlate easily with Aristotle's definition of ethical actions as just, virtuous, and noble. This kind of ethical behavior makes Percy a better human and therefore a better citizen of his world. The citizen-based struggle with how to define humanity also preoccupies this text: a main character is transformed into an animal of some kind—and in Percy's case, it's a guinea pig (177). This concept of transformation recurs through the series, possibly a parallel to the transformations that occur in adolescent years.

Connections to Ethics and Myth

Quintilian says a human should see taking part in civic life as a duty and that an ideal citizen/orator should be a "good man speaking well," or a human who speaks for or educates about just purposes or fairness or truth. If we adjust this quote to more contemporary times, he might say a "good man *acting* well" or, for our case here, learning to act for just reasons or truth. This role of acting well is tightly bound to being a good citizen and can be seen clearly in the ethical actions in the characters of *The Sea of Monsters*.

These ethical actions are clearly represented at the beginning of the book when Percy has to deal with bullies at his mortal, mundane school. They steal a picture of Annabeth from him and, even though he wants to "pulverize" them, he reminds himself that he has "strict orders from Chiron" to save his skills for the monsters (13). As a demigod, Percy has battle skills; since he is the sea god's son, he can even control water. He is certainly capable of taking on a middle school bully, but he has to consciously make the ethical decision not to harm the weaker mortals. He, thereby, controls his intentions because of the responsibility inherent in his position.

Percy feels this responsibility toward his mentor as well, which is very Aristotelian of him. When Chiron is falsely accused of poisoning Thalia's tree, Percy defends him. Those protests fall on deaf ears, and he bides his time until he can prove that Chiron is innocent. When the moment comes, he fulfills the role of the proper citizen by speaking and acting well. He tricks Luke, the villain, into admitting his part in the evil ploy to poison Thalia in front of the entire camp (238–41). This forces the director to reinstate Chiron and clears his name; thus, because of Percy's ethical actions, justice is served.

In his storytelling, Riordan clearly uses classical mythology to foster an appreciation of ethical behavior that "syncs" with the central Aristotelian question of how humans, or, in this case, children, should live and also shows how the presence of myth affects ethical representations. While myth lends its authority to the discussion of ethics, myth also makes discussing ethics more enjoyable. A book on the value of philosophy will almost certainly not be of interest to many children; however, if you throw in a sphinx and a near-death experience, the reading suddenly becomes relatable. Myth makes learning about ethics fun.

Myth also gives readers an opportunity to identify with "other"ed individuals as well. The ethics don't apply just to friendly monsters like Tyson; the stories also show the many struggles super human characters go through to live in the mortal world. Demigods like Percy and Annabeth have ADHD and dyslexia (8). These traits help when fighting mythical monsters, but they make mortal world classroom learning a challenge. The mythical creatures have a number of physical attributes they have to hide from the mortals as well. Chiron, a centaur, must conceal his horse half with the help of a magical wheel chair, and satyrs like Grover use crutches to cover up how differently they walk from humans (50). These adaptations help humanize very powerful characters, and they teach readers not to underestimate someone for struggling or being different or "other." Who knows? That person could be a powerful half-blood or monster. We don't know what monkeys people carry on their backs.

Much YA fantasy literature, though written with varying intentions, has a common trait in their depiction of ethical issues and quandaries—and their use of monsters. The monsters are a particular area of focus, and their alternative humanism is applicable to ethics. We also believe that ethics are more effectively expressed in literature when myth is also present. Mythology's special status as both a pop culture phenomenon and former religion lends authority to the story and guides the reader.

It also helps that the characters are easy to identify with in this novel. It's doubtful that any readers have literal Cyclops for brothers, but it is also likely that they consider their siblings or family members to be "monsters" and that many could relate to issues present in a blended family. Reading about how Percy deals with accepting Tyson as his brother could be as heart-breaking or moving as events in *Where the Red Fern Grows*. The implications could go even further than sibling problems to more complex social issues, like homelessness in Tyson's case or bullying in Percy and Tyson's case. The text supports that violence is not the answer to bullying or other problems, even if it is the answer to a monster trying to kill you. As characters work through these complicated situations with ethical reasoning, readers, too, can learn to negotiate similar situations and as a result grow into stronger citizens.

Myths help us make meaning of the world, and this is why recognizing their influence is important. Authors, like Riordan, who allude to or adapt mythological figures or tales are appealing to classical mythology's inherent authority as a former religion and a frequent source of worldly wisdom. If myth is being used to create a code of ethics, like we see here, then it needs to be considered critically so that readers can understand the possible ramifications. With Percy Jackson, the difficulty of making ethical decisions is emphasized as a major struggle. The texts recognize that ethics are ultimately ideals and that the world is essentially varying shades of gray, without clear "good" and "bad" decisions. In fact, the struggles of the characters are what gives them character, or ethos, and what fosters their ability to become better citizens of their world. A focus on responsibility promotes a code of ethics that includes not only responsibility to friends, but also personal responsibility and a civic life, which fits nicely in the curriculum of a rhetoric course.

Curriculum Connections

In a typical rhetoric course, whether it be a speech or writing class, several options can be considered when it comes to curriculum. If an instructor wants to stay true to the rhetorical canon, the divisions of invention (to discover the means of persuasion), arrangement (to select and assemble an effective argument), style (to present a cogent and eloquent argument), delivery (to use voice, gestures, text, and image), and memory (to speak extemporaneously) make sense (Cline). Employing the branches of rhetoric, deliberative (exhortation or dissuasion), judicial (accusation or defense), and epideictic (commemoration or blame) (Burton), also makes sense as guides to organizing curriculum. However, including citizenry (or the more modern notions of service learning or activism) and its connections to ethical behavior within the curriculum not only keeps the ancient notions of rhetorical practices alive, but it also allows for a depth in rhetoric classes beyond the canonical. Including YA literature as a mechanism to add that depth is a logical move since in our case here, and in many cases, the role of ethics is a major component of YA literature. Furthermore, with the movement away from literature and toward the use of more informational texts in secondary standardized curriculum, this mix of the canonical ideas of ancient rhetoric with popular fiction is timely and useful.

Reading literary fiction can actually improve a person's ability to read people. This is a crucial skill in our society, and the implications could change the way that literature is considered. YA literature can open up a venue for the discussion of ethics in an uncertain world. Such literary works can also acknowledge that bad things do happen to children and adults; such acknowledgement makes the connection of ethics to rhetorical traditions that much more necessary. If reading literary fiction actually makes us better able to empathize with others, then it follows that reading myth-based texts with ethical themes would improve an individual's ability to understand ethics and to act in more civic-minded ways, as service learning and activist curriculum require, in the real world.

According to Nussbaum, all works of literature demonstrate both conscious and unconscious decisions about what is valuable in life (7). The question of how a human being should live is central in Aristotelian ethics, and Nussbaum suggests that, if we, as readers, analyze the "empirical" evidence in the literary text, we will be able to see the ethical values its promoting (25). To identify "empirical" evidence in the text, Nussbaum suggests readers investigate and discuss what the text says "about human life, about knowledge, about personality, about how to live," as well as how these issues are addressed in the "form" of the writing (35). A spoonful of sugar certainly does make the medicine go down, as we are all more likely to learn an ethical lesson from a story than we are a stern lecture or boring treatise. The "reader's identification" with the text is also emphasized as a major part of the ethics, since we are more likely to see ourselves in likeable characters and therefore learn from them (35). This identification could also extend to a constituent in a service learning endeavor and make the experience more valuable for all stakeholders.

Many instances of Nussbaum's idea of "empirical" evidence appear in *The Sea of Monsters*, but one of our favorite blatant examples comes from Tyson. In order to recover the Golden Fleece, the young heroes must battle with the infamous Cyclops Polyphemus who trapped Odysseus. After an intense battle that breaks several of Annabeth's ribs, Percy finally has Polyphemus at his mercy (Riordan 215–20). However, just before he can take the swing that will turn Polyphemus into monster dust, Polyphemus starts to cry (219). The sobbing and begging causes Percy to pause. He realizes that Polyphemus, like Tyson, is also a son of Poseidon, just like Percy (219). Percy relents and agrees to let Polyphemus go (219). However, the evidence becomes more obvious once Polyphemus betrays Percy's deal and attempts to kill him anyway (220). Tyson appears and stops Polyphemus with a well-thrown boulder and an equally well-aimed rejoinder of "Not all Cyclops are as nice as we look" (220). This action acknowledges that not everyone is to be trusted (an important consideration especially for young adults when negotiating the cyberworld, for example) and that poor choices can lead to negative consequences.

Ethics hold a fascination for society because we don't always agree on what even counts as ethics, much less what defines the major rules we do happen to agree on. When humans are looking for answers, they tell stories and try to learn by example and through experience. This makes a discussion of ethics via myth not only appropriate but pleasing to audiences—a culturally approved way to discuss the Aristotelian question of how we should live. It's even more pleasing for these stories to appear in young adult literature in which children are the ones who are supposed to learn lessons and who are encouraged to think autonomously and solve their own problems. It's not hard to see how these applications could be useful in a higher education rhetoric course, where storytelling could be analyzed as a rhetorical technique and stories could be analyzed through the lens of rhetoric.

As Aristotle argues in Book II of the *Nicomachean Ethics*, a good citizen is a human who possesses excellent character, who does the right thing, in the right moment, and in the right way. Bravery and the correct regulation of one's bodily appetites display the proper type of character or virtue. Aristotle says explicitly that we must begin with what is familiar to us (*NE* II.1095b2-13), and, for today's higher education students, that familiarity can come in the form of YA literature.

Both of us recognize the value of fiction and have used or experienced it in the writing classroom. It's no large leap to extend those standard practices to YA literature, especially in terms of the rhetoric classroom. Though rhetoric is only taught in a writing or debate class in secondary education, if it's taught at all, many colleges and universities teach it as its own course. It's clear to us that a YA novel, like the one discussed here, would only strengthen a rhetoric course, by adding depth and maybe even whimsy to course content.

Works Cited

Aristotle. *Nicomachean Ethics*. Book II. 1095b2-13. *Google Book Search*. Web. 5 April 2014.

Burton, Gideon O. "Branches of Oratory." *The Forest of Rhetoric. Silva Rhetoricae*. Brigham Young University, 2007. Web. 12 Oct. 2014.

Cline, Andrew R. "Canons of Rhetoric." *Rhetorica*. Wordpress, 2014. Web. 12 Oct. 2014.

Murnaghan, Sheila. "Classics for Cool Kids: Popular and Unpopular Versions of Antiquity for Children." *Classical World* 104.3 (2011): 339–53. *EBSCO E-Journals*. Web. 29 Mar. 2013.

Nussbaum, Martha Craven. *Love's Knowledge: Essays on Philosophy and Literature*. Oxford: Oxford University Press, 1990. Print.

Riordan, Rick. *The Sea of Monsters*. New York: Disney Hyperion, 2008. Print.

Quintilian. *Institutes of Oratory*. Ed. Lee Honeycutt. Trans. John Selby Watson. 2006. Web. 5 April 2014. Print.

Graphic Language (Devices) in the High School Classroom
Jesse Stallings

My course on graphic texts (comic books, graphic novels, newspaper strips, web comics) began as a three-week unit within the English III class. It arose out of my simple desire for my students to look at language devices and techniques in a new light: it is one thing to point out the sublimity of nature motif while reading *Frankenstein*, quite another to experience the paisley visual motif that illustrates the sublimity of love and holiness in *Blankets*—the latter is simply more immediate for students.

I found later that, after such study, my students were less likely to have difficulty answering when I asked why it was appropriate that Claudius poisoned (rather than stabbed) the king, or why Victor's creation should be kind to the poor family before the murderous rampage: they could envision the author's choices as *choices*, rather than an inevitable part of the story. The shift from a short unit to a complete course has required some changes: the students in the Graphic Novel course come to me with a working understanding of the medium and may have composed in the medium, themselves, previously. They want to *make* comics; I want them to analyze literature. We do find common ground, though. The consumption and composition elements of the class occur simultaneously, resulting in immediate application (not simply through analysis) of the terms and techniques presented. By the end of the course the students have a printed anthology of their works and a respectable ability to analyze the structure and content of others' works.

The Cycle

The first few weeks of the course are devoted to reading *Understanding Comics* by Scott McCloud, as it provides a common vocabulary and exceptionally cogent presentations of comic devices and techniques. I supplement this text with connections to literary devices and techniques. We develop a few things during this time:

- an understanding of the devices and techniques that occur within graphic novels,
- connections between these graphic devices and other literary devices,
- application of these terms to texts the students are reading, and
- the creation of short, new comics that apply their understanding of these devices.

Index Card Comics

On the second day of class the students create their first comic. I do not prepare them for this or provide any hint as to the goal of the exercise (pedagogy through obscurity is a thing), as I want a raw baseline upon which to build. This "throw them in the deep end" approach also relieves the stress that students may have in creating their first work. I pulled the idea from a party game but later found a variation on the website *Drawing Words and Writing Pictures* (a goldmine for comic educators) called "jam comics." We call them Index Card Comics (their name is better). The goal is simple: the students collectively create a six-panel comic in 12 minutes. They are given a stack of six index cards and a marker (Sharpie or other felt tip works best, as it forces a simple design and unifies the style across panels). I set a timer for two minutes and they begin the first panel, filling the first card (lots of adrenaline here). After the two minutes is up, they pass the stack of cards to the left. I begin the timer again, and the second student continues the story where the first student left off. This is a bit frenzied, but they soon find a rhythm. The time limit and constraints of the exercise (creating only one panel initially, following the story of the previous panels) actually alleviate initial anxieties; I will ask them to create a complete story by the end of the session, but for now they take it one panel at a time. By the end of the exercise each student has an original comic that we discuss as a class using a projector.

During this first discussion my question is "Which comics work?" which they understand in a number of ways: perhaps the comic with a mundane story and an unexpected punchline (a structure mirroring standard newspaper strips) appeals to some; perhaps the story of an interesting character or one who embarks on an interesting journey appeals to others; perhaps the artistic style established by the first author (I was pleasantly surprised by their immediate grasp of the importance of visual continuity) is appealing, even if the story does not go anywhere. Regardless of the immediate appeal, this gives me an opportunity to model the analysis I expect of them and anticipate McCloud's terms. Many comics in this first round do not "work" in a traditional sense, but, because I am trying to help them articulate the elements of a successful story (to analyze it), this is a wonderful position to be in. I get to illustrate story structure, devices and techniques, and McCloud's terminology in works with which they have an intimate connection, while providing them constructive feedback. This is also their introduction to analysis as an explication of an author's choices—after all, they made them only a few minutes earlier.

Graphic Detail

Chapter Two of McCloud's *Understanding Comics* helps me reinforce their understanding of literary detail. This device is too often overlooked because high school students have a difficult time recognizing that an author has created each bit of the story being told. There is no logical need for King Hamlet to appear to his former guards in full armor, but, because he did, because Shakespeare chose to have him presented so (coupled with Claudius's weakness), we read the character in a different light.

In Chapter Two McCloud describes a graph of abstraction within comics. Triangular in shape, it lays out a continuum of detail from visual verisimilitude to abstraction, and from photorealism to written prose. This gives the students stylistic context for the works they are reading; even though there are no absolute points here, it is beneficial for them to see the possibilities an author has when creating a graphic or prose work. (How does the chiaroscuro of Frank Miller's *Sin City* and Mike Mignola's Hellboy comics influence the tone of the works? What if shadows were not so stark?) The students apply his continuum to the works they are reading, discussing the influence visual detail has on the narrative.

An interesting conversation came out of this the first time we discussed McCloud's explanation of detail: visual detail/realism does not necessarily promote or ensure narrative realism. It was surprising to students to recognize that a story may represent a "slice of life" while being conveyed through cartoonish characters. Chris Ware's work is cartoonish (bold outlines, geometric characters) and clean (straight or curved lines of similar weight throughout, very simple shading), while maintaining a depressive tone and realistic technique.

Graphic Syntax

When McCloud describes the types of panel transitions in Chapter Three, he shows the students the importance not only of the detail being presented but the juxtaposition of the narrative elements within panel transitions, focusing on the amount of "closure" each transition requires of the audience. He recaps this information succinctly in *Making Comics*, as well (McCloud, *Understanding* 74–80; McCloud, *Making* 15–8). For our purposes we look to the influence a few of these transitions have on the reader's experience of time and juxtaposition within the story, and I use the process to draw connections to similar choices available to a novelist or poet. The connections are not perfect or absolute, but the discussion allows us to think about the devices as choices rather than something to be labeled.

Action-to-action and subject-to-subject transitions are the most frequently used in Western comics (McCloud 74–76). They act as the baseline against which other transitions diverge, representing either movement or dialogue within a scene. We contrast the rhythm of dialogue within a scene from *Hamlet* with the dialogue of *Rosencrantz and Guildenstern Are Dead* or *Waiting for Godot*; *Hamlet* is even and regular whereas the others are staccato. Comparing the transitions from Seth's *It's a Good Life If You Don't Weaken* with those from any superhero comic will lead to similar results: the baselines vary significantly.

An author using "moment-to-moment" transition, in which the panels are very similar to one another with only a slight change in position of character or setting, relies on repetition to slow time down within the graphic story, amplify the emotional tone of a scene, or emphasize the subject. It is analogous to rhetorical figures of repetition, and students often recognize this transition from cinema's slow-motion or the slow zoom in/out. When Rick wakes up in the opening page of *The Walking Dead* series, confused as to why he is alone in a hospital, the artist uses this transition to emphasize his disorientation. Ralph Ellison uses a similar technique when the hero of *Invisible Man* recounts the death of his friend Clifton:

Here are the facts. He was standing and he fell. He fell and he kneeled. He kneeled and he bled. He bled and he died. He fell in a heap like any man and his blood spilled out like any blood; *red* as any blood, wet as any blood and reflecting the sky and the buildings and birds and trees, or your face if you'd looked into its dulling mirror—and it dried in the sun as blood dries. That's all. They spilled his blood and he bled. They cut him down and he died; the blood flowed on the walk in a pool, gleamed a while, and, after awhile, became dull then dusty, then dried. That's the story and that's how it ended [456].

Scene-to-scene transitions provide a visual juxtaposition of temporal/ spatial distances. Similar to sequence transitions, they move the audience across significant time or space. In his (very) short story "Instructions on How to Wind a Watch," Julio Cortázar uses a lengthy sentence covering widely divergent scenes to emphasize the passing of time: "Now, another installment of time opens, trees spread their leaves, boats run races, like a fan time continues filling with itself, and from that burgeon of air, the breezes of earth, the shadow of a woman, the sweet smell of bread" (25).

Aspect-to-aspect transitions, in which the artist frames various elements of the setting or characters in a series of panels, most directly illustrate the author's use of detail within a comic. Students recognize that the way in which an author presents various elements of the scene contributes directly to the overall tone of the passage. This is often used at the beginning of scenes to establish setting. We look to paragraphs from the beginning of (nearly every) chapter of *East of Eden* wherein the author establishes the tone through a listing of detail: "That year the rains had come so gently that the Salinas River did not overflow. A slender stream twisted back and forth in its broad bed of gray sand, and the water was not milky with silt but clear and pleasant. The willows that grow in the river bed were well leafed, and the wild blackberry vines were thrusting their spiky new shoots along the ground" (331). Interestingly enough, this example is also analogous to the "establishing shot" used in many comics. Mike Raicht combines the two in opening *The Stuff of Legend* with a wide establishing shot followed by aspect-to-aspect transitions that frame the quiet neighborhood in which the protagonist peacefully sleeps. This provides a contrast to the evil emanations from the boy's closet.

I try to break the categories listed above by following all of this with a shocking scene from Chris Ware's *Jimmy Corrigan*, in which a man dressed in a superhero costume (cape and primary colors) jumps from a building after waving to Jimmy on the previous page (16). The two large panels on the page are identical but for the man who is at the top of the tower in the left panel and is on the pavement in the second. The small difference in panels would suggest a moment-to-moment transition, but the emotional weight of the scene relies on the abruptness of the change. Additionally, the temporal leap between the two panels would suggest an action-to-action shot. Regardless, it gives me an opportunity to ask the students how we could screw up its emotional gravity. "By providing more detail" is usually the answer we fall upon. They have read enough comics and seen enough movies depicting defenestration to know that the camera usually follows the person, or that there is at least a middle panel/shot displaying the man's terror. Any addition to this scene, though, would shift the center of emotion from Jimmy to the man. In this scene the man's death is about Jimmy (and his issues with abandonment by father figures and their weaknesses) and not the caped suicide himself.

Pacing, Diction

We cover the rest of McCloud's work in a similar manner: they read the chapter, I make connections to literary works, we discuss examples from their chosen comics, and we create Index Card Comics. Here are a few highlights:

Chapter Four of *Understanding Comics* is devoted to the influence of dialogue and panel size on the reader's perception of time passed. Much dialogue or a wider panel conveys a larger amount of time than a series of shorter panels and brief dialogue. This is directly analogous to sentence length within a prose piece, and I provide examples for comparison. (See the *Invisible Man* quotation above for a way an author can break this.) The Index Card Comics for this round rely on their understanding of this—rather than relying on the size of the cards to determine panel size, we divide a few with a marker to create empty, smaller panels. The students are given free rein to divide two of the cards (the other four provide a baseline for contrast). Some cards are divided into thirds (anticipating a rapid exchange or moment-to-moment transition), others are split with a jagged panel (implying a split-screen, electronic exchange between characters) or along an asymmetrical divide. Now when they begin writing their comics, they must apply their understanding of pace in order to provide content that suits the panel size.

"Living in Line," Chapter Five of McCloud's work, demonstrates the tonal influence of this most basic element of visual representation in graphic works. The obvious connection here is to diction, and we spend some time looking at random short stories pulled from anthologies and individual panels from the works they are reading. Rather than creating an entire Index Card Comic this time, students choose a work from the anthology, pin down the tone of a section, and represent it on an index card. They are welcome to use any pen or pencil they have available in order to craft the tone to the best of their ability. These panels occasionally germinate complete stories when a student is inspired to take the panel home.

Maus

McCloud's work provides the students with an understanding of the various choices an author can make. For the midterm, they apply this understanding to Art Spiegelman's *Maus*. I use this work despite its age because of the amount of academic writing available on it. Joe Sacco's *Palestine*, Chris Ware's *Jimmy Corrigan*, Alison Bechdel's *Fun Home* and *Are You My Mother?*, Craig Thompson's *Blankets*, Robert Kirkman's *The Walking Dead*, Alan Moore's *Watchmen*, even runs of a single author or superhero would serve the same purpose. We spend a week reading and discussing *Maus* with the goal of addressing the following prompt:

> Using your own understanding of the medium, McCloud's work, and at least two scholarly articles germane to your thesis, identify a major theme within the studied work and provide an analysis of the means by which the author presents it.

More simply: What is the author saying? The students' journal of their independent readings comes in handy at this point, and our daily discussions center on things that stood out to them from the work. A student may notice the novel's epigraph, "'The Jews are undoubtedly a race, but they are not human.' Adolf Hitler," and the fact that Spiegelman chose to represent the various races in the work as animals. Another may notice the harsh words Vladek gives his son in the prologue, noting that this tone continues in his interaction with his second wife, Mala (Spiegelman 11). A third might question the author's motives in light of Artie's promise to his father not to share "such private things" as those he just did (23). I ask the student to analyze how the author has conveyed the noted aspect and how it could contribute to his message. The student who noticed the epigraph and cartoonishness of the author's representation of real people could present an analysis of line in comparison with historical "animal funnies," placing the imagery on McCloud's continuum, or tackle research into postmodern representation. The student who recognized the oddity of Artie and his father's negative interactions may analyze how the author uses detail, transition, framing, and pacing to heighten the emotions of those events and convey the repercussions of the emotional trauma the father endured and inflicted. The student questioning the author's choice to not only go against his father's wishes and publish a private conversation but also to publish the conversation *about* that promise is in for a real treat (and by that I mean more postmodern research).

Regardless of topic, the students are immersed in the application of their renewed understanding of literary devices. Their papers are in some ways more difficult than those written in my other English courses, but time and again I hear that this assignment was the first major paper in which they understood what they wanted to write about from the very beginning. They tell me that the evidence is more "obvious" in a graphic work. Partly, I imagine, this is due to the immediacy of the medium—there is more to decode per page in a novel—but it is also due to their practice in the previous weeks of learning, applying, and analyzing the devices that an author uses to craft his or her message.

Why We (They) Are Here

We devote the final section of this course (the last six weeks) to creating complete graphic works. Many come to the class already having created some stories, while a few have only created characters but have yet to find a world or a story. We have two threads running through this section of the course: narrative composition and visual layout. I begin our discussion of what they want to write about by asking each to tell the story contained within the last graphic work they read. I take notes and project them after they are finished. They clarify plot points that I misunderstood and contribute details they had forgotten. We go around the room like this, recounting tales and recommending titles. This facilitates the shift from analysis to creation, and allows me to get a feel for those who may struggle with detail (too much, too little) or characterization in telling their own stories. The following day I drop Joseph Campbell on them. (Actually, many have had me in class before and see what is coming, but the next bit is cool for all nevertheless.) I lay out the general steps in the hero's journey on the board ("departure, initiation, and return," recite the veterans) and the analogous steps in the story arc ("exposition, climax, denouement," intones the class). Next, the students match up my notes over their stories to the three steps. I present a fleshed-out hero's journey, as well ("call to adventure, refusal, aid, crossing of the threshold...," remembers no one). They apply their plot points where possible. It is interesting how closely the superhero stories suit Campbell's monomyth; they may be the closest we have to myths nowadays.

We enjoy another round of Index Card Comics here, this time tied to the hero's journey. Seven cards make five steps and a title: title, call, crossing, temptations, trials, boon, return. The sense of accomplishment after we've finished these is unlike any we had achieved before. Students recognize that the basic parameters of a story need not be too limiting; once they are comfortable with them, they can lean on the steps to craft an original work.

Some students have a story in mind; they simply fill in the gaps against the hero's journey to find their bare outline. Others may have a message they want to share but no story. I ask them to imagine the person who needs that message but doesn't have it. What would a person need to go through to understand? Boon: check. Road of trials: check. The rest writes itself. A third group of students may have a visual style in mind or a location but no characters or plot. For them I take a page (64) from McCloud's *Making Comics* and recommend that they imagine the kind of person who would live in that environment: does she have siblings? A pet? What does he want to be when he grows up? Whom does he love? This kind of questioning removes the weight of crafting a story and allows the student to think freely about the kind of person he or she wants to live with for the next few weeks.

One year, the Index Card Comics exercise above called the students to ask about previous creations—would they fit the journey? I was skeptical, but dug out the piles of comics we had created in our previous attempts. Many (more than I thought would) comics suited the hero's journey nicely, so we crossed those out, while a couple were mere exposition. With these the students decided to try another round. This time I provided a large stack of cards in the middle of the table and projected the six panels of the incomplete story on the board. Round one: the students each took a card from the pile and continued the story. Round two: they passed the drawn card to the left and took a blank one from the pile. As they progressed, a few were tempted to resort to breaking the fourth wall—a trying habit that plagued the earliest rounds—but most recognized that "going meta" without good reason is no boon to a story. If a student wrapped up the story, the completed story was returned to me and that student sat out the next rounds or helped those still working. After all finished, we reflected again on "Which comics work?" adding, "Are they better this time?" and "Is the hero's journey really *always* necessary?"

The students then take a few days in class outlining the basic plot of their original works. After this, we dive into layout. Frank Santoro of *The Comics Journal* website published a series of guides on visual rhythm and layout that I pull from heavily when introducing the students to these concepts. The punch line is this, though: students should layout their pages on a page larger than the finished product (usually around 6" × 9") at a 2:3 ratio. I provide them with ledger-size pages (11" × 17") with a 1" margin on the top and bottom and ½" margin on the sides. They then insert a grid within the resultant 10" × 15" rectangle (each rectangle at vertical orientation equals a single page) and begin drawing. The students present their work to the class daily, where we provide feedback on panel sizes, transitions, overall tone, and dialogue.

Once the works are completed, we scan them into the GNU Image Manipulation Program (GIMP), where they are cleaned up and colored (if desired). There are great resources at dw-wp.com, the website curated by the authors of *Drawing Words and Writing Pictures*, about how to clean up a page nicely. Once finished, we send the works to an online press to be bound in our anthology.

This course grew out of a desire to help my students in required English courses to better understand the basic elements of literature and their contribution to an author's overall message. It became much larger than that, though. It became an opportunity for the students to find their voice as authors themselves, to apply their understanding of communication to tell their own stories. The course has bled back into my other English classes: we now write very short, twelve-minute fiction when discussing the elements of a novel we are reading (but we don't use index cards), and my students contribute regularly to our school's literary journal. In all, this process has demonstrated to me the importance of providing the students an opportunity to create as well as consume and analyze when learning within the English classroom. When they have made choices as an author, they are able to recognize those same choices in the work of others.

Works Cited and Additional Resources

Bechdel, Allison. *Are You My Mother? A Comic Drama*. Boston: Houghton Mifflin Harcourt, 2012. Print.

Beckett, Samuel. *Waiting for Godot*. New York: Grove Press, 1994. Print.

_____. *Fun Home: A Family Tragicomic*. New York: Mariner, 2007. Print.

Billy Ireland Cartoon Library and Museum. Ohio State University Libraries. 2013. Web. 26 Apr. 2014. A large collection of newspaper comics from the turn of the century onward. Most helpful to an overview of early American newspaper strips: *Katzenjammer Kids*, *Hogan's Alley* (the Yellow Kid), *Mutt and Jeff*, and *Little Nemo in Slumberland*. Search at https://cartoonimages.osu.edu/.

Campbell, Joseph. *The Hero with a Thousand Faces*, 21st ed. Princeton: University of Princeton Press, 1973. Print.

Cortázar, Julio. "Instructions on How to Wind a Watch." *Cronopios and Famas*. New York: New Directions, 1999. Print.

Ellison, Ralph. *Invisible Man*. New York: Vintage International, 1995. Print.

Heer, Jeet, ed. *A Comics Studies Reader*. Jackson: University Press of Mississippi, 2009.

Print. An excellent collection of articles on graphic works. I use Harvey's article when presenting a brief history of comics and Hillary Chute's analysis of *Maus* when we begin reading that work.

Internet Archive. 2014. Web. 26 Apr. 2014. Contains complete runs of *Little Nemo in Slumberland* and McCay's animated *Gertie the Dinosaur*, seminal works in the development of the medium and truly decades ahead of their time.

Kirkman, Robert, writer, and Tony Moore, illustrator. *The Walking Dead, Vol. 1: Days Gone By.* Berkeley: Image Comics, 2006. Print.

Madden, Matt. "Activity: The Jam Comic." *Drawing Words and Writing Pictures.* First Second. 7 July 2010. Web. 26 Apr. 2014. Provides an example of the timed comic exercise I employ in class. The website (dw-wp.com) contains many excellent resources for a comic educator (visit "How to use this site" at the top of the home-page and select the "Educator" category). Their goal is primarily creative rather than analytical, but it is worth a look regardless. The site also contains detailed explanation of the use of photo editing software for cleaning up.

McCloud, Scott. *Making Comics.* New York: HarperCollins, 2006. Print.

_____. *Understanding Comics.* New York: HarperCollins, 2004. Print.

Miller, Frank. *Sin City.* Milwaukie, OR: Dark Horse, 1992. Print.

Mignola, Mike. *Hellboy, Vol. 1: Seed of Destruction.* Milwaukie, OR: Dark Horse, 2004. Print.

_____. *Hellboy, Vol. 2: Wake the Devil.* Milwaukie, OR: Dark Horse, 2004. Print.

_____. *Hellboy, Vol. 3: The Chained Coffin and Others.* Milwaukie, OR: Dark Horse, 2004. Print.

_____. *Hellboy, Vol. 4: The Right Hand of Doom.* Milwaukie, OR: Dark Horse, 2004. Print.

_____. *Hellboy, Vol. 5: Conqueror Worm.* Milwaukie, OR: Dark Horse, 2004. Print.

_____. *Hellboy, Vol. 6: Strange Places.* Milwaukie, OR: Dark Horse, 2006. Print.

_____. *Hellboy, Vol. 7: The Troll Witch and Other Stories.* Milwaukie, OR: Dark Horse, 2007. Print.

_____. *Hellboy, Vol. 8: Darkness Calls.* Milwaukie, OR: Dark Horse, 2008. Print.

_____. *Hellboy, Vol. 9: The Wild Hunt.* Milwaukie, OR: Dark Horse, 2010. Print.

_____. *Hellboy, Vol. 10: The Crooked Man and Others.* Milwaukie, OR: Dark Horse, 2010. Print.

_____. *Hellboy, Vol. 11: The Bride of Hell and Others.* Milwaukie, OR: Dark Horse, 2011. Print.

_____. *Hellboy, Vol. 12: The Storm and the Fury.* Milwaukie, OR: Dark Horse, 2012. Print.

Moore, Alan. *Watchmen.* New York: DC Comics, 2014. Print.

Raicht, Mike. *The Stuff of Legend Book I: The Dark.* New York: Villard, 2010. Print.

Sacco, Joe. *Palestine.* Seattle: Fantagraphics, 2001. Print.

Santoro, Frank. *The Comics Journal.* Fantagraphics Books. Web. 2 July 2014.

Seth. *It's a Good Life If You Don't Weaken: A Picture Novella.* Montreal: Drawn and Quarterly, 2003. Print.

Shakespeare, William. *Hamlet.* New York: Simon & Schuster, 2003. Print.

Spiegelman, Art. *Maus.* New York: Pantheon, 2011. Print.

Steinbeck, John. *East of Eden.* New York: Penguin, 2002. Print.

Stoppard, Tom. *Rosencrantz and Guildenstern Are Dead.* New York: Grove, 1994. Print.

Ware, Chris. *Jimmy Corrigan.* New York: Pantheon, 2003. Print.

Steppin' Out
with "Jabberwocky"
Mike Turvey

The ability to express oneself is a skill that is recognized in behavioral research as contributing significantly to the reduction of stress and frustration, two conditions that are frequently cited as dominant in people whose responses to conflict turn quickly to aggression, fighting, and other violent ways of expression.

The Initial Success

As a high school English teacher, I made it one of my goals to arm my students with an expanded vocabulary through weekly vocabulary tests and strengthening their ability to express their thoughts on paper by beginning each class meeting with a timed journal writing. I placed on the board a suggested topic with a number of minutes next to it. They were free to use that topic or one of their own choosing, just as long as they didn't stop writing until I called "time."

My clock started when everyone was in the room and writing. The daily writing and weekly tests consistently produced students who, by the end of the first quarter, were able to write non-stop for 10 minutes with ease, and with an expanded vocabulary. It also prompted them to "one-up" each other, both in my classes, and, according to other teachers, in other classes.

The Desire

I was pleased with the effect these two teaching methods had on my students, but I wanted them to gain something more. I wanted them to exit my class at the end of the year knowing more than just the mechanics of communicating. I wanted them to *own* the ability to write creatively, to be practiced in making use of their skills of expression, to know how to reach inside themselves with confidence, and to put their ideas in front of others clearly and creatively. I came up with a series of exercises that, over a six- to seven-week period, led my 11th and 12th grade English students to write creatively. I decided they needed to be able to create an original poem of at least twelve lines. I knew the focused exercise of writing their own poem would provide them with conviction that they could make productive use of their feelings, insights, and perspectives through their writing. This experience would give them a chance to gain a firm grip on writing for expression beyond the classroom. To accomplish this goal, I knew I needed to design a process that would lead them by simple steps, patiently, one completed step at a time, to that level of creativity. I had to find a way to nurture them into becoming confident writers and let them prove to themselves that they understood how to use their vocabulary to move images and feelings from their minds to the minds of their readers. If successful, the process would leave them with the new feeling that it was no big deal to write creatively, to share their thoughts, to become as familiar with expressive communication as they were with the ultra-concise, lazy technology of texting. What follows is the creative writing process I used for over 20 years that allowed all but two of the over two thousand students I had during that period to do what they believed they could not do: write an original poem that shared with the world what they saw as noteworthy.

In my experience, students possess a broad range of degrees of reluctance in becoming creative writers, and that reality is based on a myriad of reasons, from their personalities to the everyday expectations of conformity imposed on them by the system. I had to design the steps of the lesson in a way that showed them it was safe to express their tenderest thoughts and feelings. The lesson I came up with usually took around six weeks to complete, plus or minus a week depending on the beginning writing skills of the class. What they eventually produced were poetic themes and messages that were not just original and creative but awe inspiring, and in many cases so touching as to be cathartic, for them as well as their readers. They surprised me, themselves, and each other. It was a milestone in advancing their ability to express themselves with confidence.

The Process

Since the first comments students always made in response to my announcement that we were going to write our own poems were things like

"I can't write" and "I don't even like poetry" and "I don't have any 'creative' ideas," I determined that the first step had to be to get them to realize how much they already knew about communicating in general, and expressing images in particular. I needed them to drop their individual limits or experiences in vocabulary and writing training and enter what would appear to them all as an unfamiliar arena. This was necessary so that everyone would be equally forced to focus beyond the word meanings and on the structure of the poem. This approach put them on a level playing field and enhanced their buy-in during the first step of the overall lesson. I chose to begin with Lewis Carroll's 1871 nonsensical poem "Jabberwocky." It contains words Carroll made up, spoken by characters he created, behaving in ways that made no sense on their face, but still communicated a clear flow of actions. This negated any vocabulary advantage an advanced student might have over the others and brought them all evenly to the starting line. We were all in Carroll-land now, with me as their guide. They had no choice but to suspend their vocabulary knowledge in favor of exploring the poem in other ways.

On the first reading I walked expressively and slowly through without stopping to comment or explain. I challenged the class to explain all of what we had just read. I needed them to balk at being able to explain the meaning, to state that no one was able to make sense of this nonsense. I gave them time for as many as possible to balk. This was perfect for my purposes as I had no expectation of them gaining any knowledge of the poet's message through commonly used words, since there are no commonly used words in the poem (except "chortle" [line 24] and "galumph" [line 20], which eventually made it into the English language).

As we made our way through the poem the second time, I could elicit from them, with increasing ease, the identity of the characters, the actions those characters took, and the emotions communicated by those actions. I began to ask them questions to show them how much they had learned without realizing it. For instance, we started with the opening lines: "Twas brillig, and the slithy toves / Did gyre and gimble in the wabe / All mimsy were the borogoves / And the mome raths outgrabe" (lines 1–4). I asked them in what kind of atmosphere the action of this poem was happening. Since it is not possible to know from the words alone what action is being described, they were forced to instead pay attention to the syntax and context Carroll uses. They would take a moment, study it, and someone would say, always in the form of a question "brillig?" I'd affirm it. They could all now see that the atmosphere was "brillig." The poem said so, clearly. Then we'd proceed to discover that the toves were "slithy," that the toves were in the "wabe" acting in a "gyre and gimble" way, that the "borogoves" were being "mimsy" while the "raths" at least the "mome" version of them, were busy being "outgrabe"—and what all that means didn't matter. What mattered was that they got the message. I also asked if anyone got hurt, and if they could tell if someone had feelings about that. This question allowed them to begin to understand the heroism of the "beamish boy" who had slain the dangerous "Jabberwock" with "jaws that bite and claws that catch" using his "vorpal blade" and how it made the poet "chortle in his joy" at such courage.

Every student had broadened his or her view to take in the actions being described through Carroll's uncommon nonsense words. It was always fun at this point to say, "I told you you were smarter than you thought." I conceded to them that these were made up nouns, with made up verbs, adjectives, and adverbs, but added that I wasn't all that concerned about the poem's meaning at this point. I just wanted them to discover that they already had a handle, at their age, on how to get a message across in a poem. They had already internalized the process of syntax and context years ago and that allowed them to get a handle on the message even if the words made no known sense. I told them that all we needed to do now was to pick our own images and messages that were worth other people's time to read and put them in our own poems. I assured them I could show them how and that it would be easier than they thought.

They had begun the process of giving themselves permission to create, and they slowly began to realize how their vocabulary knowledge and the rules of syntax and context that they already understood might be enough to be useful. Then came their next concern: how distasteful it would be to have to do it in a stodgy boring p-o-e-m. It was time for Step Two.

Step Two was another chance for me to strengthen my credibility as leader of this adventure in creative writing. I would convince them that they already liked poetry, more than they knew. I announced that our next class period would be spent listening to their favorite songs. I said anyone could bring a CD or provide me with an Internet address that I could use to access their song and play it for the class through my laptop. The rules were that I would choose which songs to play (it had to be classroom appropriate, and anyone who thought I hadn't heard their song before had to give me time to preview it). They each had to bring a verbatim copy of the lyrics for their song to be eligible to be played. Many students brought me CDs and Internet addresses the very next morning. By the time the class met again, I had been provided a long list of songs. As we finished our journal writing at the beginning of our next class, I played about 20 minutes worth of their music, stopping to read the lyrics aloud after each song. After 20 minutes, I stopped and asked them to tell me the difference between the lyrics to their favorite song and a poem. Most comments focused on the topics of their music being so much more relevant to their life than "some poem about flowers." I assured them poems could be on any topic imaginable and that what is written about didn't limit poems any more than it did music; in fact when I read the lyrics, wasn't it just a poem until the music was added? Needless to say, they now had no choice but to admit that they all had a favorite poem, since songs were just poems set to music. And it was on to lesson three.

The class was now beginning to recognize that writing poetry might be less intimidating or boring than they had first presumed it to be. It might require them to be more thoughtful, more precise, less assuming, and, if they were open to discovering new concepts, writing a poem might be fun, which as it turns out, is exactly where their minds needed to be to start writing creatively. Step Three was to use my freshly manufactured credibility to free them from what they thought were the rules of poetic writing and energize their creative engines. Rules like "poems must use rhyme" were banished by reading and discussing stanzas of Walt Whitman's *Leaves of Grass,* such as, "Have you reckon'd a thousand acres much? have you reckon'd the earth much? / Have you practis'd so long to learn to read? / Have you felt so proud to get at the meaning of poems? / Stop this day and night with me, and you shall possess the origin of all poems" ("Song of Myself, II" lines 22–25). Then we abolished the rule that "poems are always about flowers or love" by pointing out that we had agreed that the lyrics to their favorite songs were poems, and none were about flowers. I included an exposure to limericks with a short assignment of writing their own limerick as part of this lesson, too, so that those who wanted to use rhyme could see it was a bit harder to do but acceptable. This also gave all of the class practice in recognizing and creating rhythm in a poetic line since limericks all use the same five lines of rhythm.

Step Four was added to give them practice expanding their vision by taking simple sentences of no more than three words and "blowing them up" into ridiculously long descriptive sentences that filled up to a half page. I gave them several sentences like "The boy ran" or "She knew them" and had students add descriptors until an intricate picture emerged such as "THE tall well muscled BOY with flaming red hair and dark menacing eyes, watched his friends' faces slowly reflect panic as they backed away from the edge of the wreck he crawled out of before he turned and RAN like a full force hurricane in the opposite direction." The longer they could sustain the sentence and continue creating new pieces of the picture, the more expansive their conceptualizing became.

When they completed "blowing up" five sentences, I continued stretching their vision skills by having a short review lesson on the difference between metaphors and similes and assigning them the task of creating five new similes and ten metaphors. They were allowed to work with each other, but no two students could use the same examples. As soon as they finished making up metaphors and similes, I handed them a list of prepositions to use in describing their daily journey from waking up in their bed at home and coming all the way into their classroom at school, using only prepositional phrases. This really exercised their imagination and made them slow down to describe the images in their mind's eye. When done correctly, it would read like "up at 7; out of bed; across the room; into the shower; out of the shower, beside the sink; with a towel over my body; into my clothes; down the stairs; over the lawn; into my car; along the street; in the school parking lot; out of the car; through the doors; into my 1st hour class." No one's assignment was considered complete if they skipped any necessary steps along the way, for instance, no one could get "into my car" and be "at the school" without driving from home to school. No magical maneuvers were allowed.

Young writers, like mine, were so full of hormones and so used to taking communications shortcuts and speeding up their speech, that making them slow down and ponder was essential to their accessing the mindset with which they could communicate creatively. The next to last exercise in the process emphasized this by taking them to an open space, outside or in a gym, where I could separate them to prevent them from visiting or helping each other and giving them 30 minutes to record all of whatever was going on around them, using all five senses to describe everything they saw, heard, smelled, tasted, or touched. After the half hour, we would go back to class where I would gather their writings, mix them up, and read each one aloud to the class without saying whose writing I was reading. Writers could identify themselves if they wished, but only after the class had critiqued how complete the writing was in describing the scene. I gave some sort of public praise to each writer, and those who chose to identify themselves were almost always praised by the class. They were often surprised that others had seen things they had missed.

The last exercise before we began writing was to practice listening and to show them how successful the previous year's class had been. They most always knew the authors who sat in the same desks one year earlier. This was due to the fact that I published a school wide literary anthology each year, containing poems, short stories, and essays written during the first three quarters of the school year. The top three in each category received monetary awards given by a panel of teachers and other adults in the school. This is the anthology from which I read; I made sure to mix in some of the more moving and intense poems (one about a mother who abandoned her kids, one describing a delicate morning alone in the snow during Christmas break) with those that were hilarious (an athlete describing his love for his pickup) or were written on unusual topics (a poem about how much one boy hated writing poetry). This served to emphasize that others, just like they, had created poems with and without rhyme, on a myriad of topics, expressing personal pain and deep loyalty, the confusions as well as the funny aspects of being a teen, and all with no more experience than they had. As a final assurance to them that it was safe to let themselves write about whatever moment or experience moved them, I informed them that all their poems were eligible to be submitted to the school anthology where they could compete for the cash awards and that anyone who chose to could sign their poem as "Anonymous" as long as I knew who they were so I could give them credit. They spent the rest of the classes after this writing, bringing their work to me to suggest what areas needed work, how to proceed if they were stuck, and how to polish up their imagery or clarify their message. When 80 percent to 90 percent had finished, we went back to the curricula, and the remaining students took their poems as homework, using their journal time to check with me until they too were finished.

And that's how we began with the nonsensical poetry of Lewis Carroll's "Jabberwocky" and ended up a few weeks later with a classroom full of empowered teenagers writing some of the most moving poetry I've ever read.

Works Cited

Carroll, Lewis. "Jabberwocky." *Through the Looking Glass and What Alice Found There.* Literature.org: The Online Literature Library. Knowledge Matters. 1996. Web. 3 April 2014.

Whitman, Walt. "Song of Myself: II." *Leaves of Grass.* Bartelby.com: Great Books Online. 2014. Web. 3 April 2014.

Composing a Work That No One Hero Could Compose Alone

SARA N. BEAM *and*
HOLLY CLAY-BUCK

On the "Letters" page of Issue 001 of Kieron Gillen and Jamie McKelvie's run of the Marvel comic *Young Avengers,* where the author/artists/creators typically interact with fans, Gillen provides a writerly, reflective epilogue about rebooting *Young Avengers*: "The only way I could do this is cut it to the core and then rebuild everything around it. And the core, means the heart. Its optimism. Its intelligence.... *Young Avengers* in its first incarnation was about being sixteen. This *Young Avengers* is about being eighteen." The choice to situate the comic in that specific age of eighteen, that borderland age, was deliberate on Gillen's part. "At eighteen," he says, "it's about being in the adult world whether you want to or not," and it's about "meeting people your age who are entirely amazing and suddenly your peers are your hero figures." The Issue 001 "Letters" page sets the scene and tone of the run as much as the panels of 001 do; there, Gillen whirls around the topics of young adulthood, interdependence on peers, heroism, and the importance of openness and determination in the face of whatever "perfect, life-affirmingly doomed endeavor" the reader might also be taking on. The text is made to be read and re-read and offers readers a complexity in form and content that they recognize and can decode using familiar tools—connection-making tools that, if recognized for what they really are, can be useful in the composition classroom. Examining Keiron Gillen and Jamie McKelvie's spin-off *The Young Avengers* reveals that dynamics between groups of heroes parallel and are enhanced by interaction between creators and their audiences. This illuminates how collaboration among fictional heroes and among author, artist, and fandom offers a model for composition that piques the interest of 21st-century first-year writers.

Collaboration, Comics, and Composition

The literary tradition is packaged and presented to students in the form of collections of texts by individual authors, giving the impression that works of literary merit are produced by singular great minds. Writing students often seem to have the impression that, if they cannot produce greatness by their lonesome, then they cannot produce greatness at all. However, thinking broadly, collaboration has always existed between writers, editors, publishers, and readers; therefore there is no reason to devalue coauthored works or coauthorship or to think of them as lesser than works purportedly authored by a single, solitary writer. At the present time, when many works are created using digital publishing technologies, collaboration, sharing, openness, and remixing are regular practices. As Douglas Rushkoff notes, "digital technology is biased in favor of openness and sharing" because it was created by people who shared openly as they were creating (118). As writers navigate the spaces between print culture and digital culture, ideas of ownership and ownership of ideas shift and the everlasting plagiarism crisis finds new tinder to burn. However, amid all the tension and debate, we sometimes forget that collaborative writing has been going on for a very long time. To name a few examples, 19th-century authors, such as the Shelleys, Brownings, "Michael Fields," etc., wrote together and/or edited each other's works. Also, as children, the four Brontë siblings created worlds together—these texts, referred to as their "juvenilia," have recently been collected in scholarly editions and made available for study, since they are now considered academically valuable. Last, writer/illustrator pairs, such as Sir Arthur Conan Doyle and Sydney Paget (*The Strand*), together created the thrilling, enduring Sherlock Holmes persona and tales for serial publication. Part of re-thinking authorship (is there an author? asks Post-Modernism) is recognizing the communities that make texts, the different audiences those authors/creators may create for, and the different media the collaborators make use of.

Comics are, by their nature, collaborative efforts. Marvel revolutionized the creation process of comic books and, in turn, created the intensely collaborative nature of the media that has come to be associated with comics and comic culture. Instead of being fully scripted down to panel layouts and colors by an author, then handed off to an illustrator who simply followed directions to the letter, the Marvel Method integrates all parts of the process, giving more freedom of interpretation to all those involved in the process (Edelman). In the Marvel Method, the author first writes a script that can range from a skeletal outline with suggestions for the illustrator to an almost prose-like script of internal motivation and scene suggestion (Edelman). Depending upon the relationship between the author and illustrator (known as the penciller, as s/he generally works in pencil for ease of adaptation as ideas progress), the process can involve many levels of dialogue to create a unified vision. From there, the collaborative process continues as the product is sent to the inker, who solidifies the illustrations into more three-dimensional and print-friendly panels and who must determine, interpret, and emphasize the most vital parts of the sketches. The work then goes to the colorist, who makes decisions about color and shading. In comics, color is crucial to the identities of the characters, and the colorist's interpretation creates iconic images—think of Kate Bishop's signature shade of purple or Teddy/Hulkling's distinct green skin tone. Finally, the images are sent to the letterer, who creates and fills in the dialogue balloons and boxes. The letterer must make interpretations about placement and also emphasis. What is bolded, italicized, and broken into segments from the dialogue and exposition is up to the letterer (Larson). Therefore, the finalized product is less a vision of one person and more a highly stylized game of Telephone, wherein the vision changes with interpretation and mirrors the highly interpretive style of the oral tradition.

Also like the oral tradition, comics have a history of audience interactivity. From the beginning, they have included feedback from fans within the texts themselves with the "Letters" pages, where fan letters and writer/artist responses are shared. Further, Marvel began enfolding fan feedback into the stories themselves with the creation of the "No Prize." This is a faux honor given to readers who supplied, in the "Letters," retroactive continuity that explained away mistakes or plot holes. As technology and fan culture grew, so did the interactivity between the creators and consumers. Comic conventions have grown in size, allowing comic creators to interact directly with fans who give unprecedented feedback.

"Cosplay," the art of dressing up as characters from a book, movie, comic, etc., translates the characters into real-world interpretations. The interpretations are not static and do not always bind themselves to accurate reproduction. Concepts like "Rule 63" (gender-swapped characters), race-bending, culture-bending, and steampunk bring each individual cosplayer's experiences and expectations to those set forth by the established canon. Creators tend to react very positively to these displays. The *Captain Marvel* series boasts a dedicated fan base known as Carol Corps. Issue #17 is known as the "Carol Corps" issue, and features many Captain Marvel cosplayers on the cover. The purpose of this, according to the creators, was about showing appreciation for the engagement of the fans. Kelly Sue DeConnick, former writer of the series, says, "I'd like to think it was more of a thank you than pandering." Instead of seeing fan engagement as something to be wary of or to exploit, many comic creators see it as a high honor. Gillen goes so far as to actively encourage fan works of the most hotly contested kind: fan fiction. On his Tumblr, Gillen writes, "Ever since our work on *Phonogram*, Jamie [McKelvie] have [*sic*] strove to make our comics—for want of a better phrase—slash-fic-able. If you're working in certain heroic fantasy genres, that's part of the emotional churn." "Slash fiction" or "slash" is a sub-genre of fan-created works that focuses on pairing two characters romantically. These characters are often both male (Salmon). Gillen and McKelvie's openness to the sexualization of the characters they work with and create is a new frontier in fan engagement, where such works are often derided, ridiculed, or even met with legal resistance. In comics, however, and especially in this series, sexuality is seen as simply another facet to explore and as valid an interpretation as the multitude of variations on cosplay. What we have in the *Young Avengers* series is a text that pushes the limits of our definitions of writing, ownership, and collaboration by laying out every step of the process and asking the audience to contribute, even if that contribution is not what the author(s) intended.

Classroom Application: The Marvel Method

The writing process is and should be a community effort. In fact, the comic creation process could easily be paralleled to a collaborative class project that emphasizes the steps of the writing process and helps students identify and specialize in these steps. First, you should explain the comic creation process (perhaps using a *Young Avengers* sample excerpt from http://marvel.com/comics/series/17647/young_avengers_2013) by way of example. Have the students identify the contributions of the

Writer
Illustrator
Inker
Colorist
Letterer

Next, show how these jobs correlate to steps in the writing process:

Writer → Creates thesis and main points/sub points
Illustrator → Finds appropriate examples and research
Colorist → Integrates and explains/contextualizes research
Letterer → Does the "prose" portion of the paper, makes it flow

Finally, discuss fan feedback and criticism in the form of the "Letters" page.

Ask students to identify how the letters make the comic better in the future. Make sure they take note of both positive *and* negative responses. Then, ask the groups to share their works in pairs and compose peer review responses to each other in the form of a fan letter.

Social Media in/and Young Avengers

If comics as an art form have always been especially accepting of fan interaction, social media has exploded this phenomenon. As of this writing, the dominant forms of social media are Twitter, Facebook, YouTube, Tumblr, Instagram, and Pinterest. While these will inevitably change (remember Myspace? Friendster? Xanga?), the culture they have created is a permanent part of our social landscape. As such, comic creators have many more chances to interact with, respond to, and engage fans—and they do. Gillen currently maintains active accounts with LiveJournal (blog), Spotify (music sharing), Tumblr (another blog site that focuses on sharing items), Goodreads (book review and blog), Instagram (photo sharing), and Twitter (a short-form social media site). McKelvie maintains WordPress (blog), Twitter, Instagram, and Tumblr accounts. As you can see, Gillen and McKelvie maintain many social media accounts; they use them to interact with fans, supplement their material, and even provide primary resources for analysis of their works. While their LiveJournal, Goodreads, WordPress, Instagram, and Twitter accounts are primarily "one way" communication (meant for updates, etc.), Gillen and McKelvie's use of Tumblr and Spotify are highly interactive and crucial to understanding their works. On Tumblr, Gillen began the lead up to the release of his *Young Avengers* run by writing and sharing in-depth character analysis of the team under the tag "Meet the Team." These sketches provide insight into Gillen's background ideas, perceptions, and intentions. All of the characters had appeared in previous series (some in the first *Young Avengers* run, others in other series), so Gillen's objective seemed to be to contextualize his own interpretations for his readers. Therefore, the interpretation and analysis of characters and their traits began before this series was even *written*. Further, Gillen integrates YouTube videos of songs he associates with his characters within these posts. This engages readers on multiple levels, making analysis of the characters in *Young Avengers* accessible to many learning styles, including auditory, linguistic, and visual.

By providing the reader with tools to begin his/her own interpretive analysis, Gillen demystifies the creative process. In addition to character analysis, Gillen posted "Writer Notes" after the publication of each issue. These notes break down Gillen's thoughts, influences, and ideas. Additionally, they deconstruct which parts of the page were inspired by each team member. For example, in the writer notes for 014, Gillen writes of page 18, "Laurie (aka Transonic) orange dress and blue skin, with red hair is a daring choice, fashion wise—Jordie's [Bellaire—guest colorist] call, I believe. Annie [Wu—guest illustrator] doing a proper punk rock Kid Gladiator (and doesn't KID GLAD-IATOR! Sound like a band?) is also a joy." Gillen also provides links to other primary sources and even secondary sources. For example, his "Young Avengers" tag contains a link to an interview with Matt Wilson, one of the series' colorists, where Wilson deconstructs his process of choosing coloring and even gives advice for beginning colorists. The tag also contains links to fan analysis, such as Hazel Robinson's (a.k.a. piratemoggy) 8,000+ word commentary on the last issue and her in-depth critique of the rest of the series. Beyond simply fleshing out "behind the scenes footage," these notes become a primer for deconstruction and analysis. Readers are led through the process of asking themselves, "What is each person's influence on this text? What is *my* influence on the text?" They also lay out the process in clear form with examples from each step. Thus, the text becomes less a mystical work of cohesive art and more a series of potentially reproducible steps.

Gillen also uses Tumblr to interact with his fans. Fans send "Asks" (ranging from praise to critique), and he answers them honestly and publicly. Fans are able to question the material and receive explanations that either answer directly, in the case of one character's sexuality ("She [Miss America] is a lesbian. I have to say that any reading of YA that argues otherwise is performing Demiurge-level reality warping"), or vaguely enough to give room for personal interpretation. In the following exchange from May 5, 2014, Gillen essentially says his own reading of his work is no more valid than any others':

> **avenger-dave asked: Does a piece of art ever belong more to the audience than the artist?** [Emphasis here and following is in the original text.]
> [Gillen responds,] It certainly doesn't belong to the creator.
> But Art doesn't belong to "an audience."
> It belongs to *you,* that audience of one.

This, it seems, is at the heart of not only *Young Avengers,* but comic creation as a whole. Because the characters have been through so many artists and incarnations, individual interpretations are not a luxury but a necessity. Through Tumblr, Gillen models fan interaction that mimics well-researched literary analysis and broaches arguments of influence, context, and author's intent.

Another social media component integral to the *Young Avengers* run is Spotify, a music sharing and radio service. In Spotify, users can follow one another, create playlists from millions of songs found on the server, and share playlists. Essentially, users are all DJs. Because music is so important to *Young Avengers*, Gillen created a playlist of songs mentioned in the series, songs that reflect characters' personalities, songs that "spoil" major plot points (for example, Prince's "I Would Die 4 U" aligns chronologically with Billy/Wiccan contemplating sacrificing himself in order to save the rest of the team), and songs that were inspirational to Gillen during the writing process. This crosses over with both Tumblr and the series itself. Gillen made sure his audience was aware of the playlist and referenced it frequently, going so far as to answer questions about how specific songs related to specific scenes and characters. In the two-part final issues, the team attends a New Year's party. On the "Letters" page, the creators publish a "playlist" of songs appropriate to the party. Essentially, they ask the reader to join them in soundtracking the work, underlining the importance of inspiration and personalizing the creative process. Gillen and the *Young Avengers* artists demonstrate that whatever gives the creator a sense of place and direction is a valid form of process.

The series also integrates social media into the text itself. Most of the recap pages, created by the editorial team, are in the style of "Yamblr," a pastiche of Tumblr. The recap pages review what has happened in previous issues and remind readers of the characters by using the post and tag style of other social media. Each "post" is by a different character from the Marvel universe, none of whom appear in the comic itself. This transforms the recaps from static, objective reviews to interpretive pieces. The "tags" on the posts provide commentary on what is being stated, providing levity and emotional context. The recaps also poke fun at the series itself and the comic genre as a whole. For example, on the recap page for Issue 015, a post by "ManicPixieDreamGirl" (the character Pixie) explains the resolution of a romantic subplot. The tags read, in part, "#so much love drama #what teen movie is this? #answer: all of them." Another post, this one by "MoHunk" (the character Kallark) recaps the reappearance of a character who disappeared early in the run after a brief cameo. The tags for this read, "#who's this guy? #No idea #totally forgot about him." Millennials are genre savvy and hyper-aware of clichés. By acknowledging these clichés and laughing at itself, the series makes it "safe" to enjoy the kitsch inherent to the story.

A final use of social media is in the text itself, where social media provides exposition. In Issue 007, the writer conveys a three month time jump through a series of images and commentary that are implied to be Loki's Instagram account. The images show stylized snapshots of various adventures the team had during that time with time stamps and commentary from the characters in the form of comments on the pictures with appropriate aliases (music-loving alien Noh-Varr is INTERGALACTICPLANETARY, conflicted Billy/Wiccan is BILLYKAPLAN666, and the ever-dignified and self-assured Kate/Hawkeye is simply KateBishop). In Issues 006 and 011, David/Prodigy and Noh-Varr, respectively, are seen using instant messaging to communicate with antagonists, and in 011, David/Prodigy texts for backup in the final confrontation with The Mother. The presence of social media, in these cases, actually makes for much better storytelling. Instead of clunkily having characters talk about their shared experiences or fabricating ways characters who are far away could communicate with the leads, the writers can use technology to streamline the details, keeping focus on the characters and their development. In a culture where every form of media is scrutinized in excruciating detail for the smallest mistakes, social media itself closes some of the biggest plot holes.

Classroom Application: Social Media

Social media's use in comics provides an excellent opportunity for classes to discuss both interpretation and primary vs. secondary sources. Have the students read one of Kieron Gillen's "Writer Notes" and a fan critique of the same issue. Have them take note of the differences in interpretation and what is/is not answered by the author. Open the discussion: how much does the author's intention matter? Gillen himself says that the text belongs to each individual reader, so how much of our own ideas are we "allowed" to bring to the table? Is it different if the author does *not* give audiences this permission?

Then, have the students find both primary and secondary sources on an assigned topic. Have them also compare these sources and discuss how their view of legitimacy of the sources differs. Are primary sources *always* best? What are some exceptions?

Visuals as Text

To show students that "text" is more than the inert, printed word on a page is to open up their understanding of composition. Illustrated works like the *Young Avengers* comics count as writing, may be read, and may inspire critical thought. As author Seth Godin recently asserted, discussing his abecedarium for adults, *V Is for Vulnerable: Life Outside the Comfort Zone*, writing and publishing have changed:

> We type something, or we design something, and it can be seen by hundreds of thousands or millions of people, if it spreads. That's a whole new way to think about how we make things. So why bother making a book, ever again? What's the point,

if can reach ten times as many people with a blog post as will ever read one of my books?.... If I'm going to make a book, there'd better be a reason experientially [qtd. in Popova].

Godin means that, since writers can reach large audiences without having to publish in print, they may now feel like they need a special reason to publish in print. That reason might be how the experience of handling a physical book, owning the book, sharing the book, smelling its pages, seeing it on one's shelf, etc. can complement the content, the ideas, in the text. The relevance of Godin's project to this discussion lies in his book's conscious employment of genre (children's literature) and textual materiality (i.e., the book as an object). He specifically chose the style and form to appeal to his audience's senses of playfulness and gravitas—the cover and pages are colorful and illustrated in a rudimentary kind of way, the letters reminiscent of *School House Rock* cartoons, but the captions that augment each image add layers of gentle, nuanced, serious ideas about what it is to compose and create, about what risks a writer-creator must take in order to create something meaningful. The interplay of words and the feel of the book in a reader's hands create the overall effect. The *Young Avengers* project, we will argue, effectively employs the same tactics.

The panels and pages of *Young Avengers* are, like those of most superhero comics, varied and dynamic. The reader moves from character to character, from narrative to narrative, between past and present, from interior experience to exterior experience, across and between realities. Some of the panels are "quiet" or wordless, relying on the image to create the emotional impact. For example, in 001, Teddy hugs (a being who he thinks is) his mother, somehow returned from the dead; later he finds out she's not who she seems to be. The image is outside of panel series, takes up more than the bottom half of page, is centered, and shows only the top halves of their bodies. The intense embrace of mother and son is drawn toward the reader, outside of the rest of the narrative taking place in the panels. Everything else is gone, and only the embrace matters. Words can do nothing to enhance the moment.

Next are panels where what is said contradicts what's happening visually. On the second-to-last page of 001, in the second-to-last panel, Jeff reacts to Teddy's mother's negative statements about their sons' relationships; he begins to stand, right hand hitting the table for emphasis, and asks, "We're happy that Billy and Teddy are happy. What kind of a parent **are** you?" Mother responds terrifyingly, "The better kind," her eyes all white; she's smiling eerily, and her right hand reaching toward the viewer and just beginning to liquify and extend. Her words do not fit with the image; they emphasize that something has gone deeply wrong. She is not who she seemed to be, and the *it* that she is is able and eager to do harm.

The image in the final illustration carries over from that moment. In 001, the final, full-page illustration is of Teddy/Hulkling's "mother" infecting Billy/Wiccan's parents. The full-color visual is set in Billy's foster parents' (Rebecca and Jeff Caplan's) kitchen around their kitchen table where they sit in bathrobes with cups of coffee (the father's now tipped over toward him and spilling down his front). The point of view is behind and above Billy's parents, about eye-level.

Teddy's mother, at this moment, is revealed as some sort of monster, her eyes white and her right arm outstretched, forked, and grotesquely extended and latched to the faces of Billy's parents. Again, the words contrast the image, heightening the frightening moment; what kind of parent is this monster? "The kind that knows best." These words imply a kind of parental authority that can be dangerous to young adults—an authority that does not listen to its subjects, that tries to control/manipulate their actions, that denies them autonomy, that actively seeks to hurt.

Another example of text-image relationship is the point at which the text interacts with the visuals. One of the most strikingly effective storytelling visuals occurs in Issue 004 on pages 5–6, in the two-page spread depicting Noh-Varr's dramatic rescue of Miss America, Wiccan, Hulkling, and Loki, who have been captured by Mother in a nightclub. The visual is cinematic, architectural, fragmented, and orderly, all at once. Centered on the page crease and taking up most of the spread is an overhead view of the dance club. In miniature, multiple Noh-Varrs take out the bad guys from all different angles. The tiny fight scene snapshots are numbered one to twelve, and a key is provided in a small box on the far left. Triangle-, parallelogram-, and trapezoid-framed, numbered images zoom in on certain details of the fight scene. The text in the key box shows Noh-Varr's thoughts and meta-commentary on the action: phrases like "(1) Dramatic entrance," "(11) My shoes are ruined" (he has just stepped in exploded liquid flesh goo of a Mother creature), and "(12) Dramatic exit" add a level of humor and self-consciousness to the character.

Three of the six pull-out details in the shapes outside the main image add another layer to the fight scene: in three of the images, Noh-Varr carries on an inner monologue about his relationship with Kate/Hawkeye that begins on the page before the fight scene. After Kate tells him to call her Hawkeye when they are "in the field" and after Noh-Varr notes that she is his "favorite Hawkeye," Noh-Varr remembers "another" Hawkeye. This moment of reflection/memory, rather than being interrupted by the fight scene, flows into the fight scene. Those three of the six detail images feature Noh-Varr's thoughts about "another" Hawkeye, the images and monologue in what McCloud would call "parallel combination," where "words and pictures seem to follow very different courses—without **intersecting**" (154). "We didn't make love," Noh-Varr thinks in image number one, as he shatters through a glass window, weapons blazing and face set in an aggressive expression. "He was a man," and "Also fond of Purple," muses Noh-Varr in images numbered eight (backflip with arms outstretched, perfectly aimed weapons firing) and twelve (flying punch at the remaining Mother creature), respectively. Notably, the image numbered twelve features a light purple-colored background, significant because it highlights the color mentioned in the text box, the signature color of the Hawkeye identity, as well as a color associated with LGBT activism (see, for example, the tradition of wearing purple on "Spirit Day, an opportunity for individuals, organizations and public figures to stand up and show support for LGBT youth and bullying prevention") (McCarty).

The final layer in the scene is the song that Noh-Varr, whose love of American pop music is well established, chooses and places on the DJs turntable mid-scene: according to the key, "(7) 'Young Hearts Run Free'—Candi Staton." The song enters the physical and mental action at a crucial moment; one of the six pull-out detail images, Number Seven, zooms in on Noh-Varr's hands delicately placing a record on the turntable and moving the stylus into place. The choice of song is telling. The anthem immediately brings to our minds the moment in Baz Luhrmann's *Romeo and Juliet* when Mercutio, dressed in drag, leads the party to a crescendo by lip-syncing a remix of the song. However, other readers will remember (or soon discover, thanks to Kieron Gillen's Spotify playlist or YouTube) the original tune from 1976. The song underscores sexual freedom, exploration, and identity. Noh-Varr, readers remember from Issue 001, is an alien; he has sexual interest in humans of both/all genders, making him pansexual. The tune accentuates action/moment Number Eight, the backflip beneath the spotlights with perfectly aimed laser shots from the weapons in both of Noh-Varr's hands, and Noh-Varr's heroic acrobatics, as well as the revelation that this young superhero is genuinely and thoughtfully engaged in sexual- and self-discovery.

Classroom Application: 1,000 Words = 1 Picture

Considering visuals as text has many applications in the classroom, such as making inferences and analyzing non-written communication.

First, have your students analyze selected sections of the series where the visuals play an important role (e.g., this art preview: http://kierongillen.tumblr.com/

post/37350814188). Have them write out what is going on to make it more concrete. Does it work? Why or why not?

Next, introduce your students to a piece of text with an unreliable narrator or an implied thesis. This can be a work of fiction or a biased essay or article. Have them tease out what is "true" and what is "not true" and what the audience is meant to gather from this. What is not being said? Have them write out, explicitly, what is not being said and *why* it is not being said.

Last, bring the two descriptions and analyses sets together: ask students to notice how the images in the first fill in gaps. Have them brainstorm what sorts of images might serve to "fill in" gaps, implied ideas, or unreliable narration in the second text.

Allusions in Young Avengers

From its first issue, the *Young Avengers* run alludes to other works about popular superheroes or epic tales that are part of the contemporary pop culture imagination. In 001, Hulkling disguises himself as Spiderman. Later in 001, Teddy makes a reference to Tolkien's *Lord of the Rings*, saying to Billy, "You have **two** sets of parents. Your actual mom is **the Scarlet Witch**. That's like discovering you're Galadriel's kid and you're a magical elf child." In his January 22, 2013, "Meet the Team: Hulkling" entry on Tumblr, Gillen explains Teddy's character using *Lord of the Rings* references, actively engaging curious readers in a bit of education about how texts can interact and play, how readers can explain themselves using texts other readers are familiar with, etc. The links between the Tumblr discussion of LOTR and Spiderman and the references to them in the text are rich with meaning. Readers can understand Teddy's character and his relationship to/with Billy that much better. By obliquely elaborating on the references, Gillen's text becomes inclusive—anyone who wants to invest the time and who has Internet access is invited to find all the hidden Easter eggs and share in the community.

The text further links itself to the literary tradition by referencing Shakespeare. The work directly alludes to *Hamlet* in 005 when Loki says to himself, "Of course I'm not real. I'm a guilty conscience, Hamlet! And aren't **you** the tragic little prince?" and "Aw, diddums! Poor you! Well, can't make a Hamlet without breaking a few eggs." Split in two, one material form and one ethereal form, Loki plays the trickster to himself. Summoning the story/character of *Hamlet*, the writers/authors emphasize that Loki is a larger-than-life character; they also illuminate that even an immortal trickster has an interior life.

While the text further links itself to the literary tradition by referencing

Shakespeare (*Hamlet* in 005), the run is also rife with allusions to pop music, including, for example, Loki referring to Prodigy as "Mr. Young, Gifted, and Black" in 007 (see Nina Simone's "To Be Young, Gifted, and Black"). The most obvious and striking allusion to pop music is the Ronettes' "Be My Baby" frame. Page Three of 001 features Noh-Varr loading a record and dancing joyfully, then saying coyly, "Kate, I come from a dimension where there is transcendental peace and universal enlightenment. But there are no close harmony girl groups. How could **anyone** leave a world that makes things as wonderful as this?" After the reader's curiosity about the music is piqued (it appears in several panels and the two characters obviously love it), the issue "Credits" page reveals that the song Noh-Varr played was The Ronettes' "Be My Baby." The song adds layers of meaning to the first few pages and creates a cinematic feel—the audience of this work loves a good soundtrack and a good music video. The post-coital glow, view of outer space from the bedroom window, Kate's gaze over Noh-Varr's dancing body, and the overall well-captured snapshot of sexuality as it matures are then interrupted by an alien attack—if only the late teen years could go smoothly. Much later, in 015, the run winds down with a dance party. Noh-Varr, who is trying to get over Kate, whom he left a few issues ago, is handed a record by the robotic DJ: a remix of "Be My Baby." The return to the tune and Noh-Varr's return to the dance floor signal not only nostalgia but also the ability to move on and to accept the events, as well as oneself.

One of the most powerful and resonant allusions in the work is the character Loki—actually, the references are more than just a simple one-time allusion or name choice. The character is actually *the* Loki. A figure from Norse mythology, Loki is a "master of fire," a "trickster," who could move between/among worlds and who could transform himself (Barndon 99). The myth of Loki's misbehavior and punishment by the gods are a bit parallel to those of Prometheus in Greek mythology. In *Young Avengers*, from time to time Loki will directly reference his mythological past. For example, when readers meet Loki in 001, he is in kid-form, arguing with the waiter about paying for his meal. Loki says to waiter at Joe's Diner, "Please, sir. I'm the **actual** god of mischief! Asgard variation! Haven't you heard of me?" Here, Loki clarifies for the server (and for the audience) that he is not just in "cosplay" but is the actual mythological figure. He even points out which version of the trickster he plays. Of course, as a *Young Avengers* character, Loki acts like a trickster. The others are distrustful of him, with good reason. He manipulates them and their reality. He is, after all, the character who convinces Billy/Wiccan that he may have used his reality-warping powers to fabricate his relationship with Teddy. Loki never lies—this *is* in fact possible and almost certainly something the chronically insecure Billy would have thought of. Like Billy, Loki warps reality, except Loki warps perceptions instead of matter. A final key moment in this character's development and the intertwining of the *Young Avengers* story with the Loki mythology appears in 015, when Loki says to Prodigy, "I'll play this part for as long as I can. I'm a story. I just have to be the best story I can be." At this point, Loki has changed to a more mature physical form (he now looks closer to the age of his peers rather than an adolescent); his words and his appearance suggest that, though he cannot change who he is, he can be conscious and reflective. He has to play the role of a trickster, but he can flavor or add nuance to that role. He is an actor in a story that will go on through many permutations, through many ages.

Classroom Application: Allusions

At its heart, allusion is reference. By making allusions, we draw on the works of others to give our own work clarity, weight, or relatability. To use this in the classroom, talk about references and allusion. Have your students identify allusions in one of the comics (like this one: http://kierongillen.tumblr.com/post/402055 89301) and have them discuss what those allusions do—what is their purpose? How do they change the text? Why do you suppose the author chose them?

Next, have your students read a piece of researched work. Ask them the same questions. How are citing a source and using an allusion in fiction the same? How are they different?

Finally, ask your students to keep a log of allusions they make in their everyday conversations, with an explanation of each. How is their everyday use of allusion the same or different from the types you discussed before? Do they use allusion more like fiction does or more like research does?

Conscious Collaboration, Conscious Text

In the end, the takeaway from this text is that there is value in conscious collaboration, conscious texts, and personal reflection because there is value in managing the emotional labor of invention and creation. The *Young Avengers* text repeatedly speaks to/about itself. For instance, in 011 Loki states, "[Leah] has allies. Our exes. Mainly Marvel Boy's. Admittedly, but some of ours. Plus the Patriot, who is abstractly ... **Kate's**? Have I got my continuity right?" Readers should also remember the 004 spread and the labels "Dramatic entrance/exit" in its key. Last is the two-page spread near end of 013 where, empowered by love, Wiccan as the Demiurge "walks" over the images of the story, rearranging the narrative to put things in their proper place. "It's like cradling all reality in my arms," states Wiccan, while readers watch over his shoulder as he winds his way over the pages and panels, musing on his role and responsibility. This spread is also an example of a character reflecting about himself. Wiccan muses to himself about his choices, his narrative, his reality. Like Kate's interior monologue that begins the run in 001, Wiccan's strategy of putting his thoughts and feelings into words is a technique that aids his personal development.

In addition to a text talking about itself and characters talking about themselves are authors/artists who talk it out. The "Letters" pages are the most immediate examples of creators reflecting as they write/draw. In the 001 "Letters" page, Gillen highlights the collaborative nature of the project and the project's characters: "So, basically, [this project]'s a gang of people doing a book about a gang of people." Another poignant example is in the final issues of the run, in which the creators each take a turn talking to readers in the 015 "Letters" page. There, editor Christian Ward declares, "[*Young Avengers*] IS the super hero book of the tumblr generation"; Mckelvie says, "I also had my own team"; and Gillen writes, "Being a super hero is amazing. Save the world." These glowing final words, which follow the resolution of the action, tie all the threads of reflection together.

Thus, this project acts as a model for writers: students can talk out or write out their problems understanding a text, their problems communicating about a text, and/or, by extension, their problems understanding or communicating about *themselves*. Though it may be easy to assume that the 2013 *Young Avengers* re-boot, one more fantastical story about superheroes told in an often undervalued illustrated medium, is simplistic, redundant, or shallow in content, the text has much to offer young writers and their writing teachers. The work means a lot to us personally; it reminded us of what it's like to be on the verge of adulthood, and it offered us comfort as we continue to develop as young adults now in our mid–30s. To be honest, Gillen and McKelvie's enthusiastic reflections on invention and presentation helped us write this paper, and we know the message that "PROCESS > TERROR" (i.e., "Process is greater than, or stronger than, terror"), our new motto and reminder to take a project one step at a time and to remain flexible, will be useful to all lifelong learners. To read more about the process of writing this paper, see our chat transcripts (PROCESS > TERROR origin story!), look at our outlines, ask us questions, and generally learn more or waste some time: check out the Tumblr we created to archive and supplement this essay: NoOneHeroWrites.tumblr. com. There, we share with readers and our own writing students how writing this piece was a collaborative and reflective effort.

Works Cited

Barndon, Randi. "Myth and Metallurgy: Some Cross-Cultural Reflections on the Social Identity of Smiths." *Old Norse Religion in Long-term Perspectives: Origins, Changes, and Interactions.* Ed. Anders Andren, Kristina Jennbert, and Catharina Raudvere. Lund, Sweden: Nordic Academic, 2006. 99–103. Google Books. Web. 29 May 2014.

Brontë, Anne, Charlotte Brontë, and Emily Brontë. *Tales of Glass Town, Angria, and Gondal.* Ed. Christine Alexander. Oxford: Oxford University Press, 2010. Print.

DeConnick, Kelly Sue. Email to Holly Clay-Buck. 11 April 2014. MS.

Edelman, Scott. "So When EXACTLY Did the Marvel Method Begin?" *Scott Edelman.* 28 December 2013. Web. 5 June 2014.

Gillen, Kieron, writer, and Jamie McKelvie, artist. *The Young Avengers.* Pencillers Mike Norton and Kate Brown. New York: Marvel, 2013–2014. Print.

Gillen, Kieron. *Another Way to Breathe.* Tumblr. Web. 6 June 2014.

Larson, Devin. "Overview of the Comic Creation Process." MakingComics. 16 January 2014. Web. 6 June 2014.

McCarty, Maureen. "Four Years of 'Going Purple.'" HRC Blog. Human Rights Campaign, 15 October 2013. Web. 12 June 2014.

McCloud, Scott. *Understanding Comics.* New York: HarperCollins, 1994. Print.

Popova, Maria. "Seth Godin on Vulnerability, Creative Courage, and How to Dance with the Fear: A Children's Book for Grownups." Brainpickings. 20 May 2014. Web. 2 June 2014.

Rushkoff, Douglas. *Program or Be Programmed: Ten Commands for a Digital Age.* Berkeley: Soft Skull, 2011. Print.

Salmon, Catherine, and Don Symons. "Slash Fiction and Human Mating Psychology." *Journal of Sex Research* 41.1 (n.d.): 94–100. *Literary Reference Center.* Web. 17 June 2014.

The Truth About
Native Stories

SALLY EMMONS

Oklahoma has a rich Native American cultural history that extends back 30,000 years. (What is now Oklahoma included the homes of Plains Apache, Arapaho, Caddo, Comanche, Kiowa, Osage, and Wichita peoples.)

This history was enriched significantly in the 19th century when dozens of tribes were forced to move to what was then called "Indian Territory" (Oklahoma is now home to more than thirty federally-recognized tribes) so that their homelands could be used by white settlers. Many accounts detail this tragic period of American history which crippled and nearly destroyed the tribal peoples of this country.

That isn't the focus of this examination, however. Instead, as a resident of Oklahoma, a professor of Native American literature at a regional Oklahoman college where 18 percent of the student body is Native, and a Choctaw woman, I wish to examine how teaching Native American children's literature in academia can serve as an important gateway into tribal life to college students who are only somewhat familiar with the history of their state, country, and the peoples from whom they often share ancestry.

Several years ago the writing faculty in my department—admittedly spurred on by my very loud urging—opted to teach a Native American novel in every section of Composition I. This novel was written by Pawnee writer Anna Lee Walter. *Ghost Singer* is a contemporary Indian novel that explores the mysterious happenings occurring at the Smithsonian museum and the eventual realization that spirits of Natives haunt an exhibit because their artifacts were robbed from their graves many years ago. Published in 1994, just four years after the passing of the Native American Graves Repatriation Act, the novel was exciting, informative, and mysterious. I imagined the freshman students being shocked and outraged at the idea that the graves of Native peoples had been desecrated in this country; after all, how would *they* feel if such a thing happened to a family grave in Oklahoma? I envisioned the novel opening doors to an American history that they were largely unaware of and introducing them to a culture outside of the mainstream. And sadly, because so few college students actually enjoy reading for pleasure in today's society, I anticipated that the students would enjoy the novel; after all, it has *ghosts* in it. How could they *not* be interested in that?

You no doubt have already anticipated where this is going.

The novel was a calamitous failure. Yes, the students were horrified that graves were deliberately dug up to acquire not only the valuables inside of them but also the skeletons of the dead; yes, they were interested in learning about the Native American Graves Repatriation Act and what this meant for real places in Oklahoma that they had visited. But, no matter how passionately I lectured to them about the deeper significance of the novel and its literary value, they were resoundingly confused by the narrative structure of *Ghost Singer* (Walter), which is circular in nature; they also found the magical realism in the plot to be unbelievable. So much for my foray to extend my knowledge and love of contemporary Native American literature to a mainstream audience, I thought.

However, I also teach an upper-level Native American literature course both on campus and online. The students who enroll in this class are typically interested in the subject matter and opt to take the class as one of their electives or because it satisfies a core requirement of their academic degree. Many of the students who take the class are Native. A small number of the students are very connected to their culture and may even speak their Native language, but most of the students know very little about their tribal cultures and enroll in the class because they wish to connect to and learn about their heritage in a meaningful way. Many of the students share that their families have denied or hidden their Indian ancestry because they do not want to be discriminated against, or they feared what might happen to them if it were learned they were Native. Not surprisingly, this is a common narrative in Oklahoma, where so many Indian people were forcibly moved generations ago after enduring horrific hardship and near extinction and others lost lands they had thought they owned in Oklahoma after being "removed" here.

Teaching this class is tremendously rewarding but also a large undertaking, for one cannot understand and appreciate the literature without also having an appropriate historical context for this literature. Moreover, the subject itself is complicated. In order to appreciate the deeper significance of many of the stories, one must not only be able to engage in some rather sophisticated literary analysis but also understand that Native American literature is frequently tribally specific and that it features worldviews and life ways that may be radically different from the mainstream. Yes, a reader can appreciate the written quality of Leslie Marmon Silko's (Laguna Pueblo) *Ceremony* without having knowledge of the Laguna belief system and traditions, but the novel is far more complicated, meaningful, and significant if one reads the novel from *within* its point of view rather than from an outside, mainstream point of view. And it is increasing the ability to understand, appreciate, and analyze this differing perspective that is so difficult to teach. Complicating this discussion further is that contemporary Native American literature also reflects American culture; thus, it can be rife with popular culture and other allusions; it can both condemn and celebrate America; it can make fun of the stereotypes surrounding the "Indian" in America while also affirming attributes of the stereotype; it can include its Native language while being written mostly in English (and may also feature other languages, too); it represents different Native experiences in this country so one "authentic" pan–Indian experience can never be identified (although there are certainly scholars who attempt to do so).

And it is a new literary canon. Its renaissance is commonly recognized as beginning when N. Scott Momaday's (Kiowa-Cherokee) *House Made of Dawn* won the Pulitzer Prize in 1968; yet, it is also centuries old and conveys features of oral storytelling although it is a written medium.

Sheesh. Where does one begin?

This is where contemporary Native American children's literature comes into play. After many years of experience teaching this class, I have found that one of the best ways to introduce my students to a differing worldview is through the lens of children's books. Not only is the literature familiar to them because they had picture books when they were children, but it is also more accessible to them for the very same reason. Additionally, we can cover several picture books in one class period, allowing me to cover a large number of discussion points quickly, all of which will ultimately resonate with the novels that we will eventually tackle, which I constantly remind them of during class discussion. The genre of Native children's books continues to expand, yet I tend to find myself using a combination of the same picture books when I teach, perhaps because these are books that I have read to my own son:

1. *The Good Rainbow Road*, Simon Ortiz
2. *Jingle Dancer*, Cynthia Leitich Smith

3. *Crossing Bok Chitto*, Tim Tingle
4. *A Coyote Columbus Story*, Thomas King
5. *Saltypie*, Tim Tingle
6. *Shi-shi-etko*, Nicola Campbell
7. *Shin-chi's Canoe*, Nicola Campbell
8. *The Good Luck Cat*, Joy Harjo
9. *Less Than Half, More Than Whole*, Kathleen Lacapa
10. *Trickster: Native American Tales—A Graphic Collection*, multiple authors

The thread that ties all of the books together is they are all books that present accurate, authentic representations of American Indian communities. This is vitally important because today's society is egregiously guilty of misrepresenting Native peoples and upholding ridiculous stereotypes. When I am reading a book to my class, I do so the way I would to a child: slowly, with animation and gestures, assigning different voices to different characters. I take my time, allowing the story to unfold and making sure that I emphasize vocally any elements that I want my students to really notice. After I've finished reading a book, we discuss it as a group. I usually reserve *Trickster* for last because it consists of multiple stories by different authors, and it is the only book on this list that I ask my students to purchase. With *Trickster*, my students become active participants in the storytelling process with me because I assign specific parts and characters to them. They not only rise to the challenge of playing the parts of rabbits, wolves, crawfish, and princesses, among others, they seem to enjoy it. We spend about two weeks with children's books and manage to cover a variety of important topics that are essential to their understanding and greater appreciation of contemporary Native American literature. Although not comprehensive or exhaustive, important points that I make sure we cover include the following:

1. One of the most important topics that we address in class is that books written by Native authors typically reflect a differing worldview. This is a subject that we return to repeatedly in the course. I remind the students that every tribe has its distinct culture, traditions, language, dress, and beliefs. While there is some crossover among tribes, especially those that share a linguistic stock, it is important to be knowledgeable in the author's specific tribe to better understand the meaning of what he or she is writing about. This, of course, is not an easy task because there is not a pan–Indian belief system that is common to all tribes. To truly understand the nuances of a literary work, one must

become immersed in the worldview represented. I also tell the students that if they are not willing to do this, they really have no business in interpreting Native American literature, a difficult lesson to hear. The diction used by scholars to describe this worldview should be organic and fluid; this is one of the reasons why it is so easy to tell when a non–Indian scholar is analyzing a Native text: they not only misunderstand the significance of the text, but the tone and diction they use for literary analysis tends to be rhetorical and inert.

2. An important element of much Native literature is the idea of interconnectedness: that humanity, nature, and animal kind all share equally in the delicate balance of maintaining the well-being of the universe. There is no hierarchy, as is seen in the Western tradition; humanity is not better than animals or nature. Instead, all serve an important purpose in maintaining the health of all life and restoring the balance when an out-of-balance occurs (such as depicted in *Ceremony*—more on this later).

3. Sacred spaces are of preeminent importance in much Native literature, and this spirituality is complicated, is tribally specific, and must be respected as being holy and equal to all other spiritual systems. Much misunderstanding occurs when non–Indian readers read Native literature and attempt to understand spiritual moments by superimposing Christian motifs upon them. Other misunderstandings occur when a non–Indian reader encounters a "magical" moment in Native literature and discounts it as being supernatural, superstitious, or, even worse, dismisses it as just not real. These attitudes lead to blatantly wrong interpretations of events and are derogatory. I tell my students that the sacred is often connected to a specific landscape; thus, specific locations may be invested with spiritual significance and power. I also remind them that the belief systems of American Indians vary widely, just as they do with all people. Some adhere strongly to their Native religions, while others are Christian. This myriad depiction of belief is reflected in the literature and should be respected. One of the ideas we discuss quite a bit when we discuss the sacred is the idea of balance, and that one must live in harmony with the natural world, other people, animals, and the universe or this gentle balance can be disrupted. This is a difficult concept to grasp for Judeo-Christian thinkers who interpret spirituality as being an individual relationship with the sacred rather than a community-oriented relationship.

4. Contemporary Native literature participates in the oral tradition. Oral stories are dynamic and fluid. They are frequently not in chronological order and feature repetition and circularity (mirroring the cycle of life); important details of the story may change depending upon the audience, the environment, and the storyteller. The stories are frequently didactic in nature. Thus,

even a story for children may impart a lesson about appropriate and inappropriate behavior, or a spiritual belief, so that the tribal worldview is reinforced. Though didactic, the stories are typically conversational in tone and frequently feature humor and other entertaining elements to maintain the interest of the people. (If you have been a savvy reader, then you will also have noticed that I've used many of these storytelling elements in this essay.) These are all elements that will be frequently encountered in contemporary Native novels. One of the problems the Composition I students had with the novel *Ghost Singer* (Walter) is that it is not linear, as is the Western storytelling tradition; instead, it is circular in nature, and most students were unable to make the transition to a different way of a story being told. One of the best comparisons of the oral tradition in contrast to the Western storytelling tradition is Thomas King's *The Truth About Stories*, a book that I often have my students read in conjunction with the children's literature.

5. Sovereignty is emphasized. Communities, past and present, are presented, but I remind my students that one of our roles as a reader of Native American literature is that we be able to assess whether the communities are presented both accurately and respectfully. Knowledge and experience certainly make this judgment easier, and the students typically lack in one or both areas; they make tremendous strides during the course the more literature they read. Also, though they may lack in the mechanics to identify specific features of the literature at first, all of the students *are* capable of determining and articulating whether characters in a text are depicted with multi-dimensionality and believability, or whether they reflect a stereotype.

6. Native American writers typically stress community and familial ties above the individual. This in particular resonates with my students because a large number of them are first-generation college students from rural areas. They tend to feel a connection to the places they were raised—to the open Oklahoma landscapes, the hills and prairies and lakes, the farm animals one usually sees—and most have deeply rooted ties to their families.

7. A variety of Indian experiences will be encountered because the experiences of American Indians are radically different: some are urban Indians, some reservation Indians; some live deeply connected to their tribal community, while others don't. One experience is not better than or more Indian than another. We see this great variety of experiences even in the children's picture books that we read together. This helps to prepare the students to expect that they will encounter a variety of Indian experiences in the novels we later cover in the class.

One of the children's books that aids in introducing my students to many of the above concerns is Simon Ortiz's *The Good Rainbow Road*, a story which depicts hard times being thrust upon a community because of drought. The story unfolds with characteristics of the oral tradition, yet the book's epilogue reveals that the tale is not a contemporary reworking of a tribal story, but instead a new invention. This is an important point because it emphasizes that stories are not static and relegated only to the past (which unfortunately is one of the stereotypes of Native people: that their cultures and peoples exist only in the past); instead, contemporary Native storytellers continue to create both oral and written stories. In this case, we have a new story that has the feeling of an old oral story.

In Ortiz's story, animals and plants used to be plentiful, but there is now scarcity and the people are worried and hungry. Ortiz states that the people in the community "felt helpless and very sad. Because they were no longer happy, they grew angry and argued among themselves. Without any reason except their helplessness, they blamed each other for the bad times" (page numbers not provided). The people are distraught, leading them to bicker with each other; they don't understand why hard times have fallen upon them, and they don't know how to make things better. This is of course very reflective of the human condition, for we frequently ask "why me?" when bad things happen. Finally, an elder, described as "an old woman no one had noticed," speaks up: "it is time to go to the west, to the home of the Shiwana and seek their help. It is time to go and ask them for help. We have forgotten we must ask for help."

This is a pivotal moment in the story. The elder gently reminds the people that they have broken with their traditional ways and that this has caused the out-of-balance which has resulted in the drought. She tells the people that they must select two brothers to make the journey across the mountains to ask the Shiwani, the spirits of rain and snow, to return to the people. At this point, the story unfolds as a traditional journey. The boys must overcome hardships and obstacles on their way, and are ever mindful of their greater goal—to ask the Shiwani for help. When the task seems insurmountable, and one brother starts to cry in desperation, he notices an old, blind woman has suddenly appeared and is about to walk off the side of a cliff (this is a good moment as a class for us to discuss magical realism, since inexplicable and magical elements often emerge in Native literature). The boy saves the woman's life and confesses his fear and inability to help his people by seeing his task through; in return for his help, she magically aids the brothers in creating a "rainbow road" in the sky upon which they can walk, crossing the deep caverns that are full of lava down below them, safely. The story ends with a brother on the road, saying, "Thank you for helping me, beloved grandmother, so that I may help the people and the land. I will always remember you." Although we don't see animal and plant life return to the community, the inference is that, because the boys have completed their journey and have demonstrated respect and caring to an elder, balance will be restored.

This picture book is an excellent gateway into Leslie Marmon Silko's complicated novel *Ceremony*, one of the novels we read and discuss in class. Not only does an out-of-balance occur when Tayo, the protagonist, curses the rain while he is a POW during World War II—causing a drought back home— it is reinforced when Tayo returns home from the war, suffering from post-traumatic stress syndrome and suffering from the feeling that he does not belong anywhere because of his mixed heritage. Tayo suffers from an identity crisis, which is magnified by the atrocities he both witnessed and committed during war.

In the old times, a warrior underwent ceremonies to remove the horrors of war before he/she was allowed to reintegrate with the tribe. In modern warfare, a bomb kills thousands of people without the soldier ever seeing the physical devastation or automatic weapons gun down civilians as collateral damage, and soldiers are too often expected to be able to return home and automatically reintegrate with society without intervention of some kind. Tayo and many of his fellow soldiers return home broken and turn to alcohol and drugs as ways to cope with their memories. Silko's narrative criticizes white medicine for not being able to help Tayo and others like him. Tayo's family turns to the help of traditional medicine man to help Tayo. His ceremonies only partially work; the criticism in the novel is explicit that old ceremonies must adapt in order to be effective in helping soldiers who endure modes of modern warfare. Tayo then undergoes several ceremonies (including a traditional sand painting ceremony) conducted by a second medicine man, Betonie, a mixed-blood like Tayo. By the novel's close, Tayo is healing but the process is not 100 percent complete because witchery ("bad medicine") has been working to maintain the out-of-balance in Tayo—and the larger community.

Ceremony resonates with almost every item in the above list. Immediately, the reader notices the different narrative structure at work when the novel opens with a series of poems invoking traditional stories and ceremonies. The novel's structure is complex; Tayo's story is told in the present-day, with many flashbacks to his boyhood and his experiences in the war, but it is accentuated with traditional stories told in poetic form that show individuals/animals/beings undergoing experiences similar to Tayo's and echoing different elements of his controlling storyline. In the poems, we see out-of-balance that must be healed, just as an out-of-balance in Tayo and in his community must be healed in order for wellness/balance to be restored. In the poems witchery works to interrupt the balance—in a dark twist, witches are depicted as creating white people in a competition to see which of the witches can generate the worst evil; realizing the horror that has just been unleashed, the witches ask the winning witch to take back his spell, but he says it cannot be undone now that it has been set free. This is certainly a teachable moment in class as we discuss the history of Indian and white relations in America—seeing in them the problems that affect current Natives just as witchery works to keep Tayo figuratively and literally sick in the present. The structure of the novel and its worldview are different from the prevailing western view that my students are largely accustomed to, but the difficult structure and concepts are easier for them to grasp because they have already been introduced to similar ones in the children's books. Moreover, the novel offers the students a glimpse into a specific contemporary Native experience that most are unfamiliar with: that of the mixed blood Indian who straddles two worlds, the traditional and white, as he is both discriminated against by Indians and whites for his Native ancestry, and also that of a veteran who is trying to readjust post-war, after having found a modicum of equality in the military because he defended his country.

Contemporary novels that dovetail well with the children's books listed include

1. *Ceremony*, Leslie Marmon Silko
2. *House Made of Dawn*, N. Scott Momaday
3. *Tracks* and *Love Medicine*, Louise Erdrich (Ojibwa)
4. *Flight*, Sherman Alexie (Spokane/Coeur d'Alene)
5. *The Truth About Stories*, Thomas King
6. *Winter in the Blood*, James Welch (Blackfeet)
7. *The Sharpest Sight*, Louis Owens (Choctaw)
8. *The Grass Dancer*, Susan Power

A variety of themes and subjects emerge in the literature, and the settings and characters differ substantially. All, however, present real Native Americans in past and present communities facing challenges that are sometimes distinct to Native peoples but more frequently speak to the human condition. An important task in my class is for my students to be able to assess whether the Native communities are presented accurately and respectfully and to also articulate what literary themes reoccur in the texts and why. We accomplish this through class discussion and guided written and research assignments.

While I have found a student body hungry for knowledge about their heritage and Native America, I have also ironically discovered many of them are quite ignorant of their personal histories, their state's history, their country's history. Oklahoma is rich in its Native presence: Native symbols and murals adorn many structures; many Native American museums appear in larger cities; place names are frequently Native names; pow-wows are regular occurrences; the news reports on Native issues and tribal governments; there are sovereign tribal nations with tribal governments; Indian tacos and fry bread are commonplace. Contemporary Native America is complex; consequently, it's easy to misinterpret, especially by inexperienced readers. Although I've certainly taught a number of Native American literature courses without using children's literature as a preamble to the material we will be covering, I've found that I have more success when I start the course by reading and discussing some of the picture books listed above.

Children's books serve as a gateway into subject matter and themes that are difficult for students to grasp when they are first introduced to Native American literature. It is much easier for us as a class to discuss how differing belief systems and worldviews exist in *The Good Rainbow Road* before the students tackle a difficult and multifaceted novel like *Ceremony*. *A Coyote Columbus Story* introduces students to the complexity of white–Indian relations in America in a whimsical, oftentimes funny storyline, yet also hints at the destruction this relationship eventually caused to tribal people. And, yes, it also shows Indian people being shipped off as slaves. There is *that* element of history to be discussed, too, as well as all of its serious consequences. *Less Than Half, More Than Whole* tackles the issue of blood quantum and what it means to be a "real" Indian in today's world; *The Jingle Dancer* depicts a modern Indian girl who clearly inhabits the modern world, yet also celebrates her heritage; Nicola Campbell's stories introduce students to the days of Indian boarding schools and their effects on families and communities.

In instance after instance, the books serve as vehicles which allow us to discuss important historical and cultural moments that will emerge again in the novels in the class. Children's literature not only handles these difficult themes on its own but also offers an entrée to the multitude of literary adult offerings from Native American authors. Thankfully, just as a renaissance of literature has emerged in Native American fiction, the same is true of Native American picture books, with more offerings published every year.

Works Cited

Alexie, Sherman. *Flight*. New York: Black Cat, 2007. Print.

Campbell, Nicola I. *Shi-shi-etko*. Toronto: Groundwood Books, 2005. Print.

_____. *Shin-chi's Canoe*. Toronto: Groundwood Books, 2008. Print.

Dembicki, Matt, ed. *The Trickster: Native American Tales: A Graphic Collection*. Golden, CO: Fulcrum Books, 2010. Print.

Erdrich, Louise. *Love Medicine*. New York: Bantam, 1984. Print.

_____. *Tracks*. New York: Perennial, 1988. Print.

Harjo, Joy. *The Good Luck Cat*. New York: Harcourt, 2000. Print.

King, Thomas. *A Coyote Columbus Story*. Toronto: Groundwood Books, 1992. Print.

_____. *The Truth About Stories*. Minneapolis: University of Minnesota Press, 2005. Print.

Lacapa, Kathleen. *Less Than Half, More Than Whole*. Flagstaff: Rising Moon, 1994.

Momaday, N. Scott. *House Made of Dawn*. New York: Harper & Row, 1968. Print.

Ortiz, Simon J. *The Good Rainbow Road*. Tucson: University of Arizona Press, 2004. Print.

Owens, Louis. *The Sharpest Sight*. Norman: University of Oklahoma Press, 1992. Print.

Power, Susan. *The Grass Dancer*. New York: Berkley Books, 1995. Print.

Silko, Leslie Marmon. *Ceremony*. New York: Penguin, 1977. Print.

Smith, Cynthia Leitich. *Jingle Dancer*. New York: Morrow Junior Books, 2000. Print.

Tingle, Tim. *Crossing Bok Chitto: A Choctaw Tale of Friendship & Freedom*. El Paso: Cinco Puntos, 2006. Print.

_____. *Saltypie: A Choctaw Journey from Darkness into Light*. El Paso: Cindo Puntos, 2010. Print.

Walter, Ann Lee. *Ghost Singer*. Albuquerque: University of New Mexico Press, 1994. Print.

Welch, James. *Winter in the Blood*. New York: Penguin, 2008. Print.

Shifting Perspectives

HUGH FOLEY

The use of American Indian imagery in popular culture has increasingly become headline fodder. Due to social media and a carnivorous twenty-four-hour news cycle, Native people have been able to communicate their message that derogatory words, such as "redskins," and stereotypical caricatures, such as Major League Baseball's Cleveland Indians mascot, Chief Wahoo, are no longer acceptable as contemporary representations of American Indian people.

Teachers may have a rough time explaining why these images and mascots are acceptable to some Native and non–Native people, but not acceptable to other Native and non–Native people. One way of helping students understand how many contemporary images of Native Americans are still stuck in antiquated and stereotypical mindsets is comparing modern children's literature with American Indian themes by Native authors with antiquated and romanticized depictions of Native American people by non–Indian authors in children's literature. Then we as teachers can begin to demonstrate how images of American Indians have changed in children's literature—but not necessarily in wider American popular culture, as exhibited in commercial products, popular media, and athletics wherein stereotypical depictions of American Indians are pervasive.

The depiction of Native Americans in popular children's literature from the 19th century through the present day has had an important impact on the impressions of American Indians formed by mainstream American youth. In turn, those same impressions provide a catalyst for non–Indian and, in some cases, Native American acceptance and promulgation of stereotypical depictions of American Indians. Ultimately, by viewing a few children's books by recognized Native American authors, or at least by vetted non–Indian authors, one can provide a more truthful view of American Indians for young people who will hopefully carry those impressions into their own maturity.

Before launching into a lecture on the inaccurate stereotypes of American Indians in children's or any other literature, teachers would be wise to consult Robert F. Berkhofer's *The White Man's Indian: Images of the American Indian from Columbus to the Present*. Along with discourse on the origins of the term and European concept of "Indian," Berkhofer devotes five essays to "Imagery in Literature, Art, and Philosophy: The *Indian* in White Imagination and Ideology." Of particular interest to the focus of this essay, readers will want to review "The Indian and the Rise of an American Art and Literature," "The Western and the Indian in Popular Culture," and "From Stereotype to 'Realism' in the Literary Indian."

Subsequent to those readings, teachers may pursue any number of leads on the depiction of American Indians in children's literature (Seale), and keep current with the website specific to this subject, *American Indians in Children's Literature*, active since 2006: the website has a stated goal of providing "critical perspectives and analysis of indigenous peoples in children's and young adult books, the school curriculum, popular culture, and society."

In a college classroom, students should at least be peripherally aware of Mark Twain's *Adventures of Tom Sawyer* (1876) in which the primary villain of the novel is "Injun Joe," who is evil because of his "Indian blood," a concept founded in European discovery narratives and furthered by authors such as Laura Ingalls Wilder in her *Little House on the Prairie* series from the 1930s and 1940s.

Teachers with enough knowledge of both Native American stereotypes and the history of American Indians' interaction with the United States government and white settlers of the 1860s will interpret some of what happens in *Little House on the Prairie* within the context of individual characters' contextual understanding of Native people of the period. Even with a historically critical review of the text, however, readers should be prepared to encounter American Indians described as "wild men with red skins" and other characters who repeat a phrase often credited to General Philip Sheridan, "The only good Indian is a dead Indian."

Teachers may also want to research images depicting Native Americans that accompanied various publications of J.M. Barrie's *Peter Pan*, originally a play in 1904 and then a novel in 1911. The story's primary Native character, Tiger Lily, is often highly sexualized; other characters fit all of the negative stereotypes of Native Americans as primitive savages who talk in the "ugh" monosyllabic language of multiple cartoon and Hollywood characters of the 20th century.

One of the most helpful and readily available texts with images on the subject of perpetuating Native stereotypes is the cartoon "Injun Summer" (*Best*) first published in 1907 in the *Chicago Tribune*, but continuously anthologized at least through the 1960s, and contemporarily available in color on any number of websites, including one linked in the John T. McCutcheon entry in *Wikipedia*. Within the cartoon of only two frames, a grandfather is talking to his grandson about why late autumn is called "Injun Summer" (McCutcheon). The grandfather tells the boy that "Injun Summer" is when "all the homesick Injuns come back to play." Avoiding any real stories about interactions between the U.S. government and tribes that ultimately ended in forced removal, relocation, war, or death by disease and exposure, the grandfather tells the boy not to be "skeered" because "hain't none around here now, leastways no live ones.... They all went away and died, so they ain't no more left." After spinning an elaborate yarn about "corn shocks" really being "Injun tents," and a pile of burning leaves actually being the "campfires a-burnin'" and "pipes a-goin" of the "Injun sperrits," the grandfather also says the leaves turning red in autumn is just another "sign o' redskins. That's when an old Injun spirit gits tired dancin' an' goes up an' squats on a leaf t' rest" (McCutcheon).

"Injun Summer" was still being anthologized as late as 1960, at least, in collections such as *Best in Children's Books*. In fact, I found it taped on my son's elementary school wall in 1999. Not only can a skilled teacher use this cartoon to indicate the real history that is left out of this narrative, but one can also use it and other previously mentioned texts to reveal erroneous or stereotypical writing by non–Indians that was extremely popular and that shaped many young 20th-century minds regarding what Native people are and are not.

Additionally, these texts and images can provide the foundation for exploring the counterpoint of contemporary children's books written and illustrated by Native authors. Those books provide authentic tribal stories and illustrations that more accurately depict the diversity of tribal entities and variability of experiences of Native American people of North America. Two broad categories exist of what might best be considered acceptable or appropriate texts about Native Americans for children: books with stories and images by Native people or books with stories and/or images that, while they may not be composed by Native Americans, have a verifiable or vetted integrity, according to Native communities.

While American Indian authors have been published since 1881 and have often provided counterpoint text and imagery to less flattering depictions of American Indians, their works have not been nearly as popular nor as influential on American popular culture as those works by non–Indians with faulty and inaccurate portrayals of Native people (Reese 136). In addition, since 1990 numerous works by Native authors have been published that are set in contemporary environments, as well as those which detail traditional stories or histories of individual tribes.

Cherokee author Gayle Ross tells a traditional story in *How Turtle's Back Was Cracked,* a work richly illustrated by Cherokee painter Murv Jacob. This work exemplifies the American Indian storytelling tradition of teaching basic life lesson through tales. Another book itself may be too big for little hands, but serious readers to children will want to explore the anthology *The Telling of the World: Native American Stories and Art.* Edited by W.S. Penn, Nez Perce/ Osage, the compilation includes traditional stories on multiple life cycle subjects: creation, adolescence, family, marriage, children and community, old age and elder wisdom, and death.

Teachers seeking a modern perspective of American Indians may want to look at Turtle Band of Chippewa author Louise Erdrich's *The Range Eternal* or *Grandmother's Pigeon,* both of which are set in the modern era; characters are not dressed in the pre–European contact clothing but are clearly working within the memory realm of Native peoples' experience. Muscogee (Creek) author and poet Joy Harjo mines similar territory in *The Good Luck Cat,* in which a young Native girl recounts the close calls her cat has in the settings of relatives going to powwows and playing bingo. Prairie Band of Potawatomi author Marty Kreipe de Montaño also provides a contemporary view of a traditional coyote trickster story in *Coyote in Love with a Star,* in which Coyote goes to modern New York City in search of work and a friend. While placing a traditional story in a modern context, the book also includes a historical explanation of the coyote as trickster, as well as historical photographs and background of the Potawatomi. Readers get an opportunity to learn a traditional story in a modern setting and, in addition, authentic images and facts about the author's tribe. Abenaki author Joseph Bruchac has authored several books that might be used to illustrate accurate depictions of historical figures, including *Crazy Horse's Vision* and *Squanto's Journey: A Story of the First Thanksgiving.* Bruchac also has works of traditional storytelling, such as *A Boy Called Slow* and *Fox Song.*

Teachers may want to tread carefully in the area of children's books written about American Indians by non–Indians. The previously mentioned website for American Indian Children's Literature is a go-to resource for determining whether or not a book is appropriately written and/or illustrated authentically. Typically, if an author is a member of an enrolled tribe, that fact will be stated in the author's biographical note, usually included somewhere on the book's jacket or on a back page. While a book may be well-intended, and an author may claim some close affiliation with a tribe, members of that same tribe may or may not endorse the version of the story being told, which brings up additional issues regarding intellectual property, rights of authorship, and verifiable and vetted sources for the story.

Of course, exceptions may exist, as in the case of *The Trial of Standing Bear* written by former Oklahoma governor Frank Keating and illustrated by noted, but non–Indian, artist Mike Wimmer. The story of Ponca Chief Standing Bear's 1879 trial is one of the most important American Indian history stories for children (and adults) to read, hear, and see. In very plain language by Keating and beautifully illustrated by Wimmer, the book tells the story of Ponca Chief Standing Bear's 1879 trial. In this trial, a Federal judge determined that an American Indian *is* a "person" and entitled to all protections and rights under United States law. The judge did not say an American Indian is a caricature, but affirmed he/she is a person. Adept teachers should be able to incorporate these children's works into at least one lesson about not only the changing perspective of American Indians in children's literature but also the changing status of Native people in American history.

By examining romantic and caricatured depictions of American Indians in 19th- and 20th-century children's works, teachers and students can gain a better idea of how the stereotypes of American Indians ossified into American popular culture consciousness. Furthermore, by teachers reviewing and sharing authentic American Indian authors' writing about their own tribes from their point of view, learners can gain valuable insight into the real stories that make American Indians a unique people. Last, if teachers choose non–Indian authors carefully (by validating either their background in American Indian communities, scholarship, or activities, as well as confirming the sources used by non–Indian authors), these additional valuable texts can further elevate students' understanding of American Indian life-ways, history, and concerns.

Works Cited

American Indians in Children's Literature. 2006. Web. 12 Aug. 2014.

Barrie, J.M. *The Annotated Peter Pan.* Ed. Maria Tatar. New York: Puffin, 2011. Print.

Berkhofer, Robert F. *The White Man's Indian: Images of the American Indian from Columbus to the Present.* New York: Vintage, 1979. Print.

Best in Children's Books. New York: Doubleday, 1960. Print.

Bruchac, Joseph. *A Boy Called Slow.* New York: Philomel, 1994. Print.

_____. *Crazy Horse's Vision*. New York: Lee & Low, 2000. Print.

_____. *Fox Song*. New York: Philomel, 1993. Print.

_____. *Squanto's Journey: The Story of the First Thanksgiving*. New York: Voyager, 2007. Print.

de Montaño, Marty Kreipe. *Coyote in Love with a Star*. Washington, DC: National Museum of the American Indian, 1998. Print.

Erdrich, Louise. *Grandmother's Pigeon*. New York: Hyperion, 1996. Print.

_____. *The Range Eternal*. New York: Hyperion, 2002. Print.

Harjo, Joy. *The Good Luck Cat*. Orlando: Harcourt, 2000. Print.

"John T. McCutcheon." *Wikipedia*. 17 Mar. 2014. Web. 12 Aug. 2014.

Keating, Frank. *The Trial of Standing Bear*. Oklahoma City: Oklahoma Heritage Association, 2008. Print.

McCutcheon, John. T. "Injun Summer." *Tom's Place*. 2014. Web. 12 Aug. 2014.

Penn, W.S., ed. *The Telling of the World: Native American Stories and Art*. New York: Fair Street, 1996. Print.

Reese, Debbie. "Native American Children's Literature." *The Oxford Encyclopedia of Children's Literature*. 2006. Print.

Ross, Gayle. *How Turtle's Back Was Cracked*. New York: Dial, 1995. Print.

Seale, Doris, and Beverly Slapin, eds. *Through Indian Eyes: The Native Experience in Books for Children*, 4th ed. Los Angeles: American Indian Studies Center, 1998. Print.

Twain, Mark. *Adventures of Tom Sawyer*. 1910. New York: Oxford University Press, 1996. Print.

The Story, Myth, Legend of Jumping Mouse

David Newcomb

Around the fall of 2000, I was teaching at a regional university in the American southwest. There I met a student named Joan Candy-Fire. Joan was a member of the Cheyenne-Arapaho tribe; as a child she heard the story of Jumping Mouse. Jumping Mouse is a Native American myth, story, or legend that covertly advocates pro-social and pro-psychological values, such as sacrifice, patience, compassion, and, particularly, transcendence. At least four versions of this tale exist.

Joan was interested in working in the chemical dependency field and believed that the Jumping Mouse story could be useful in that area. By her junior year she had identified certain mythic truths in the story that seemed to apply to someone struggling with overcoming addiction and that could contribute to prevention efforts. By her senior year she had developed a presentation based on Jumping Mouse and made her presentations at a juvenile detention center, public schools, and at recovery groups in the Tulsa, Oklahoma, area.

The Role of Stories, Fairy Tales, Myths, Legends

We will probably never know who the first human being was to tell a tale or story to others, or where and when storytelling began. Before human beings developed writing some five thousand years ago, knowledge and information transfer was limited largely to physical gestures and verbal exchanges. Early humans living in small groups would have had considerable, if not constant, face-to-face interaction. Basic, agreed-upon behaviors or norms would have

111

been essential for them, as it is for our society. Storytelling can be a means of informally promoting coded values of the social group. This may also be true for the earliest humans and even pre-humans. It seems that, as small social groups evolved into complex societies, informal socialization of "right and wrong" became insufficient, and formal laws emerged to promote social control. Perhaps due to our ability to think symbolically, at some point in time, moral tales began using animals as stand-ins for human actors. *Jumping Mouse* is such a tale. Though certainly old, even ancient, the story's moral seems most contemporary. *Jumping Mouse* is about transcendence, not transcendence as goal but transcendence as the outcome of compassion, sacrifice, and risk.

Transcendence

Transcendence refers to evolution from one state or stage to another. Our individual physical transcendence includes going from infancy to crawling to standing to running; it also includes the transition from total dependence to total independence, as reflected during the progression from childhood to adulthood. Our individual mental transcendence also begins early in infancy and continues through adolescence into the stages of adulthood. Socialization, as a process, may be an ultimate form of transcendence. I believe that it was early sociologist Emile Durkheim who noted that, at birth, we are born animals and must be socialized, or taught, to be human. Socialization reflects transcendence from animal state to human state and includes mental positions such as values, beliefs, and world views. Of particular importance is the role of social interaction throughout the socialization process. Both the early socialization phases and the adult life phases too can have difficult challenges. The myth of "Jumping Mouse" reflects personal evolution.

Social scientists contributing to an understanding of transcendence include psychologists, mythologists, and philosophers. Carl Jung's analytical psychology holds that we humans are unconsciously motivated to achieve wholeness or unity. This is accomplished by transcending both the physical and mental states by unifying consciousness with the unconscious.

Viktor Frankl's logotherapy, more than other forms of psychotherapy, promotes the importance of human transcendence. For Frankl, transcendence is a fundamental human task. Human suffering is unavoidable but can be transcended by redefining or finding the lesson suffering has to offer us. Transcendence is also possible by reaching out to the world or to others, thinking of and acting for the good of others, thinking less often of self.

Mythologist Joseph Campbell demonstrates how, throughout human existence and across cultures, myth has provided the model, through the archetype of the hero, for how we can be better than we are. The message is often that, by transcending our suffering and challenges, we can become the hero in our own lives.

Philosopher John Hanwell Riker argues that ethics can be defined in terms of maturity and that maturity comes from transcending unconscious aspects of our selves. All four of these thinkers in some form promote individual transcendence that involves going beyond one's social group and experiences, as well as sacrificing for the good of others.

Application of Jumping Mouse

During the spring semester of 2014, students from two upper-division university classes were introduced to the Native American story of Jumping Mouse (Candy-Fire, "Native," "Jumping"). Both classes watched Joan Candy-Fire's presentation of the tale on *YouTube* and were given a printed, but different, version as well. A single class period (75 minutes) for each class was devoted to discussion. In one class, students were asked to respond to one question on a test by applying the story's context to social ethics. Students in the second course, a social and behavioral sciences internship class, were asked to apply the story's context to their individual internship experiences. I had assumed that responses written by the ethics class would be more detailed and in depth, in part because of the numerous classes devoted to ethics. I was wrong; the responses from the internship class were better developed and more thoughtful and showed applications of the story. The aspect of *application* of ideas or ideals (including compassion, suffering, sacrifice, love, etc.) to individuals and work may account for deeper meaning and understanding. Curiously, none of the responses dealt with or mentioned transcendence, perhaps suggesting that transcendence may be a more difficult concept than the others. My results, though not an experiment, still seem to suggest variation in outcomes might be due to the difference between thinking about pro-social values versus thinking about applying pro-social values.

Mouse Transcendent, *a Retelling of* Jumping Mouse

To transcend can suggest going beyond the limits of something or exceeding something. The main character of this tale, like many heroes in ancient myths, must transcend not only himself but his community as well. Both internal and external forces drive him. Paradoxically, internal and external forces can both aid and hamper him. First known as Little Mouse, after his first transcendence of community and self, he is renamed Jumping Mouse. After manifesting compassion, sacrifice, suffering, and love, he experiences an ultimate transcendence, from mouse to eagle.

The following adaptation of "Jumping Mouse" is an amalgamation of the three versions from the Candy-Fire, "Native," and "Jumping" sources.

As the story begins Little Mouse is struggling to understand a roaring sound in his ears. Members of his community, who do not hear anything, conclude that something must be wrong with him. In effect he has been evaluated, judged negatively, and stigmatized. The process of defining him as an outsider has begun, and he himself has moved towards accepting this label. He does not yet know that his desire to discover the source of the unidentified sound is the beginning of a quest. His first challenge is to break free from the limited thinking or collective consciousness of his mouse community. The other mice, consumed with simply finding a means to exist, focus on community-established norms and physical survival. Little Mouse does not accept the collective limits of his community's reality. This represents the beginning of Little Mouse's transformation as he leaves comfort, security, and community to enter the unknown. Little Mouse must sacrifice the safety and security of home in his quest. Mystic or epic tales often involve the need for the hero to leave his or her home. Symbolically, Little Mouse is breaking with the past and consciously going into a new and uncertain future.

Little Mouse is driven from within and hindered by the external. Yet the hindrance may actually be spurring him to find his own answer. In addition to Little Mouse's internal motivation to seek and find answers, it is internally that he experiences fear and doubt. In the external world Little Mouse finds rejection and danger, yet there he also finds aid and encouragement.

Different versions of this story have different details of what happens on his journey and whom he encounters. All versions agree, though, that his first encounter is with Raccoon. Greetings of "Hello, Brother Mouse!" and "Hello, Brother Raccoon!" are exchanged. These greetings reflect the Native American belief that all living beings comprise a "family," sharing life. The concept of "brother," in this context, seems to imply commonality or equality despite species differences. Mouse and raccoon are of different species, but both are equal members of nature or life. Little Mouse explains the purpose of his wandering to Raccoon, going outside of himself for help and answers, reaching out to another, as the hero is aided in his quest by others or by natural forces.

What seems essential is that Little Mouse is transcending his own social world, limited reality, and limited understanding. This transcendence leads to his learning of the Great River. Although he wants to begin the journey and reach the Great River immediately, it is, as Raccoon counsels, a moment for patience. Little Mouse begins thinking of returning and vindicating himself with his former community, telling them the noise that he hears is the noise of the river. However, at the river, Raccoon tells Little Mouse that, if he wants to gain additional knowledge, even beyond the knowledge of the Great River, he must open his heart and attain wisdom. Little Mouse asks Raccoon to return with him to his mouse community to prove to the other mice that the roaring sound is real and caused by the river. Raccoon declines: if it is to be done, Little Mouse will have to do it alone. Though often the hero will be aided at times, some tasks must be accomplished or attempted by the seeker alone. Raccoon's last action is to introduce Little Mouse to Frog, who will be the most important external source for knowledge for Little Mouse.

Little Mouse is mystified by Frog's dual nature, living on land and in water; thus, Little Mouse continues to expand or transcend his previous understanding of the world. Eventually Frog asks Little Mouse if he would like some medicine (or power), which means roughly an aid or something helpful. Little Mouse's response is "Yes," and he is instructed to squat down as low as possible and then to spring upward as fast as he can and with all possible energy. He does this, going way up, then falling back to earth. When Frog asks Little Mouse what he sees at the height of the jump, he responds "the Sacred Mountain." Frog renames him Jumping Mouse. The value of the power or medicine Frog bestows on Little Mouse is in the openness to new possibilities that Little Mouse now possesses. Because of this new attitude, Little Mouse has manifested his potential for jumping. The real magic can happen when we allow for the possibility of the impossible. In jumping higher than he ever had, Little Mouse sees farther than he ever had. He is able to see so far that he sees the Sacred Mountain. Little Mouse has transcended on several levels. He has gone beyond the understanding of his community by learning that, though it is dangerous, one can navigate safely through unknown environments. He understands the river and knows of other (species) family members or Brothers and, presumably, Sisters. He knows he can jump, and he has seen the Sacred Mountain. He is a new mouse so he has a new name: Jumping Mouse.

After thanking Frog, Jumping Mouse begins his long journey home. Motivated by a new understanding and eager to enlighten his former mouse community, he returns to his former residence to tell of the river, of Frog, and of the Sacred Mountains. Jumping Mouse is disheveled, worn, and wet when he arrives. The mouse community cannot get beyond his appearance; they don't even hear any of the wonderful things he talks of. They focus instead on how he looks to them, concluding he is not one of them, that he is an outsider, an outcast.

Though excluded from the group, Jumping Mouse feels a need to remain with them, at least for a while. Perhaps he has doubts about all that he had seen and experienced, since all of those that he has known for so long doubt him. There do seem to be times when, to believe in ourselves, we need others to believe in us first. Too, he may have considered accepting the collective definitions and positions in exchange for the safety and security of the group. If these are the thoughts that haunt him, he finds a solution: he must seek out the Sacred Mountain.

For a second time, the hero must reject the community that has rejected him by leaving home in quest for knowledge and experiences. Though Jumping Mouse may not be conscious of it, the break with his past (community) is necessary in order to experience his broadening future. There are times when the community that we have always been a part of has defined and scripted us in a way that does not allow change or growth. His break is needed to move from "what he was" to "what he can be." His first encounter after leaving home for the second time is with Old Mouse. Jumping Mouse greets Old Mouse with "Hello, Grandfather," the term "grandfather" conveying respect and connection. Although Old Mouse had also desired to visit the Sacred Mountain, he chose safety, abundance, and ease—"what is" over the uncertainty of "what might be." His ideal, his dream, his quest ended; he has settled. He has become old, not only in name or in age, but by accepting the old way of community thinking concerning the necessity of safety and ease. As he did with his own community, Jumping Mouse must part company with Old Mouse to complete his quest. This is the second time Jumping Mouse has been tempted with safety but instead has chosen adventure and pursuit of knowledge.

When Jumping Mouse meets Great Buffalo, we see quite a contrast between a very small mouse and a very large buffalo. Yet it is the buffalo that is in greater need; he is dying. He confides to Jumping Mouse that he could be healed by "eyes of a mouse" but says everyone knows that there is no such thing as a mouse. Jumping Mouse, deeply touched by Great Buffalo's need, sacrifices his mouse eyes and heals Great Buffalo. In gratitude, Great Buffalo takes Jumping Mouse to the foothills of the Sacred Mountains and leaves him. The journey is particularly dangerous and frightening for Jumping Mouse who runs under Great Buffalo as he thunders across the plain. Though he is safe in one way, protected from birds of prey, the trip terrifies Jumping Mouse because Great Buffalo might step or fall on him. At the foothills, Jumping Mouse finally tells his fear to Great Buffalo, who responds that there was no danger for Buffalo is a creature of the plains, knowing his own abilities and aware of and connected to the land. This seems to be a reminder that at times our fears are baseless. Although Great Buffalo takes Jumping Mouse to the Sacred Mountain foothills, in another sense it is Jumping Mouse's compassion and sacrifice that "takes" him.

Jumping Mouse, alone and blind, encounters Gray Wolf, who has lost all sense of self-identity and memory due to his vanity and pride. Vanity and pride has often resulted in a lost sense of identity as human beings. Jumping Mouse meditates on Grey Wolf's issues; again sacrifice is demanded, this time a nose and sense of smell. Gray Wolf is healed. One lesson that can be learned from a selfless act that we benefit from may be that we have appreciation; we can see things that we otherwise could not. Gray Wolf offers to guide Jumping Mouse, now sightless and without a sense of smell, to the High Magic Lake at the top of the Sacred Mountain. There he leaves him. Again, the hero may repeatedly receive aid from others in his or her quest, but certain tasks must be accomplished alone.

There alone, frightened, and doubtful, Jumping Mouse once more turns within through meditation and prayer. Frog appears and instructs him to jump high, "as high as you are truthful." This instruction seems metaphysical. Jumping Mouse's success seems dependent on how truthful he was in pursuit of knowledge, how truthful as measured by sacrifice, compassion, and trust. Because he was truthful, as he jumps, he goes high and is transformed into an eagle. So ends a saga equal to any other classical myth. A small, insignificant field mouse wonders what the source of a sound is that he hears. Seeking the answer, he both is rejected by his community and rejects his community. Fate places him in situations where only his compassion, sacrifice, and suffering will heal others. In acting as he does, he transcends himself and his community. He is freed from being earth-bound as Jumping Mouse and soars to the heavens as Eagle.

Students' Application of "Jumping Mouse" in Their Internships

During the class, I asked students in the social and behavioral science internship class to reflect on their experiences as interns, especially in relation to the Jumping Mouse story. Some revealing examples follow:

One student interned with a county adolescent residential facility and said,

> Through the volunteering of my time, it is my wish for the kids (to) understand it is important to give back. When they make something of themselves, hopefully a trust and bond should have developed so they will see that it is not hard to let go and let faith and trust guide them when they are unsure. This example is found in JM right before he turns into Eagle [K.F.].

A student interning at a church with declining membership added,

> I see two life lessons at work. The first is the main character's time spent with the Fat (Old) Mouse in a very comfortable lifestyle. For many years, the church was supported by a local corporation, which provided many educated, affluent people for the congregation. These people were committed to the church and the community, so they made things happen in a way that made the entire congregation become fat and lazy. It was losing the educated, affluent people to death and transfers that caused the church to look at itself and decide to move toward a new goal. The second lesson is the main character taking a blind leap of faith once he was out of options. The church is losing resources and running out of options, so in order for them to survive these new challenges, they are going to have to release the past and take a blind leap of faith into the future. Only by taking a blind leap of faith will the church realize its true destiny or in this case its true mission [J.B.].

Working in a domestic abuse shelter for women and children, a student said Jumping Mouse shows

> the broad picture of being a student intern who makes sacrifices along the way. Sacrifice shows compassion which is a main contribution in the Jumping Mouse story when the mouse gives away his eyes to the buffalo and sense of smell to the wolf in need.... Also in relation to the JM journey, students will go through obstacles: "it is not a linear journey." ... we should give without expectations. One of the most important factors of the JM story and reality is the interaction with others. Without social relationships, achievements are hard to conquer. Encouragement, advice, and hope from others are what help steer people in the direction they want to go. When comparing the story of JM specifically to my internship site, the women's shelter, it highly mirrors what the women go through. These battered women who leave their abuser or women who just need a fresh start are able to go through the shelter. Although it may be tough for some getting back on their feet after such suffering, it is still a step in the direction when they decide to create a better life for themselves and their children [C.D.].

A student observing a speech pathologist at an elementary school commented that

> [Jumping Mouse] relates to my internship because I am on (a) journey where I am at the bottom like Jumping Mouse, at my internship. We have to give first before

we can receive. If you expect to get things in return after you do something good then you aren't doing it for the right reason. Jumping Mouse took a leap of faith. And because he had faith and trust, he leaped into the unknown. I think my internship is a leap of faith, because in life we never know what to expect. Jumping Mouse shows flexibility. My internship teaches me to be flexible because not everything revolves around me [H.W.].

Conclusions

Story-telling in any form (myths, fairy tales, and legends) seems as functional for us today as ever in our species history or prehistory. *Jumping Mouse* is much more than just entertaining and engaging. It's mythic; it's archetypal; it's heroic; it's a coded text promoting sacrifice, patience, compassion, and transcendence. Student comments during class discussions and in written assignments demonstrated how sacrifice, patience, and compassion were related messages of the story, as you can see in students' quotes above. However, the concept of transcendence was not mentioned in anyone's papers despite my brief but repeated class discussions. I believe that, in brief, the use of *Jumping Mouse* in my upper division university class has been most beneficial for students. I will use the story again but experiment further with discussions of the concept of transcendence. I suspect that understanding of sacrifice, patience, and compassion was enhanced by first seeing the tale in story form, then applying the concepts to personal internship experiences.

Works Cited

Campbell, Joseph. *The Hero with a Thousand Faces: The Collected Works of Joseph Campbell*, 3d ed. San Francisco: New World Library, 2008. Print.
Candy-Fire, Joan. "Jumping Mouse's Journey to Recovery." YouTube. Posted by Hugh Foley. n.d. Web. 26 June 2014.
Durkheim, Emile. *A Moral Education*. Mineola, NY: Dover, 2012. Print.
Frankl, Viktor E. *Man's Search for Meaning*. Trans. Ilse Lasch. Boston: Beacon, 2006. Print.
"Jumping Mouse." *YouTube*. Posted by russelljda. n.d. Web. 26 June 2014.
Jung, Carl. *Psychology of the Unconscious*. Mineola, NY: Dover, 2012. Print.
"Native American Legends: The Story of Jumping Mouse." *First People: The Legends*. n.d. Web. 26 June 2014.
Riker, John Hanwell. *Ethics and the Discovery of the Unconscious*. Albany: State University of New York Press, 1997. Print.

Happy Hedgehogs, Happy Students

Gioia Kerlin

Once upon a time in a flowering, verdant garden at the forest's edge, a young hedgehog named Tino lived and dreamed. He understood the curative powers of plants and was intimately familiar with all the different species of animals that called the garden home. He was a quiet, sensitive hedgehog who lived a solitary life with his more practical, earthy grandfather, Tarek. More than anything else, Tino loved to spend his time observing the natural world around him.

One day grandfather Tarek stumbled upon Tino reclining in his garden, daydreaming while watching the clouds float by. The elder hedgehog brusquely chastised his grandson, decrying the lack of motivation evident in modern youth and admonishing the young hoglet to go in search of something useful that would bring him happiness in the future. So Tino gathered a few belongings and left the safety of his garden in search of fulfillment.

While wandering through the meadow, Tino met several animals that taught him lessons about happiness: a turtle who was training to become the fastest, most famous turtle in the world; a hare that attended school hoping to become the most intelligent hare in the world; a weight-lifting badger whose goal was to become so strong that he no longer needed to fear anyone; and a colony of ants that was too busy working to take heed of anything else. After observing the lives of these creatures, and trying them on for size (although failing to become fast, smart, or strong), Tino realized that he had always been happy at home with his medicinal plants, and so he returned to his garden. He found grandfather Tarek, feeling a bit under the weather due to a cough, and offered him a special tea that cured the older hedgehog's symptoms. As he sipped the medicinal tea his grandson had prepared for him, Tarek realized how much his grandson understood about healing, and he began to appreciate Tino and his garden.

At the best of times, introducing undergraduate university students to textual analysis is a delicate balance between pushing them to uncover the multiple layers of meaning in a literary work and simply allowing them to experience the joy of reading. And, sometimes, this joy of reading is absent from students' experience with literature; every semester in the third-year Spanish classes I have taught, there are a few students in class who openly state that they dislike studying literature and who candidly admit that they don't like to read books. Add to this scenario the fact that, in the case of third-year literary analysis classes, they're learning about literature in Spanish (which for the overwhelming majority of these students is their second language), and the challenges multiply. In order to bring students gently into the world of literature and literary analysis, in my *Introducción al análisis literario* classes I use a children's book, *El erizo feliz* (*The Happy Hedgehog*) as the first reading. Students find themselves engrossed in the challenges Tino the hedgehog faces in this juvenile *bildungsroman*, and this connection facilitates my efforts to inspire them to think about many important aspects of understanding literature: the artistic categories of literary works; the relationship between author, text, and reader; the setting of a text; and the text's narrative voice.

Of course, before we begin discussing what such terms as *el arte con fin docente* (the instructive art), *la trama* (the plot), *la exposición del asunto* (the exposition), *el desarrollo* (the development), *el suspenso* (the suspense/dramatic tension), *el punto decisivo* (the decisive point), *el clímax* (the climax), *el desenlace* (the denouement), or *el ambiente* (the environment/the setting) contribute to the story, students learn some essential literary vocabulary. Then, in order to make this vocabulary relevant to our course, we begin to discuss Tino's story, using these literary terms as our tool. One of the first topics we discuss is how literature is akin to any other form of human communication. There is a relationship between speaker, message, and listener. In the case of literature, the speaker can take the form of the author, the narrator, or the characters; the message can be understood in terms of the text (whether it be narrated events, a character's thoughts and words, or direct commentary); and the listener can take the shape of the actual reader of the work or the implicit recipient of the message.

With respect to *El erizo feliz*, we discuss the speaker in terms of narrative voice, author, and translator. Since the work we are reading is a translation into Spanish from the original *Der Glückliche Mischka*, we discuss the ways in which a translator's voice can affect a message. This topic is of special interest to the students, given that nearly all of them are learning Spanish as a second language and are faced daily with choices about how to express themselves in a language that, in most likelihood, didn't give birth to their thoughts. We also consider who narrates the story, asking whether the narrative voice is the same as the author's voice or whether "someone else" tells the story. We ask if the narrator has any role in the story other than simply recounting events and whether his/her perspective is trustworthy or calls into question his or her authenticity (as is common in the autobiographical genre of the picaresque novel, which is one of the genres we study throughout the semester). We discuss how the work might have been different if Tino himself had told his story, rather than an anonymous third-person omniscient narrator. We discuss what the dialogue between Tino and his grandfather Tarek tells us about the personality, thoughts, values, and opinions of the protagonist; even though Tino tries to convince Tarek that he is in reality accomplishing something useful by learning about the plants in his garden (which demonstrates a degree of self-understanding on his part), he's unassuming enough to be receptive to his grandfather's advice. One could say that Tino is mature beyond his years and that he is introspective and humble. We also consider Tino's interior monologue and personal thoughts after each unsuccessful encounter with one of the forest's creatures. Tino observes and tries to imitate the animals he meets along his way, but time and again he fails. Tino consistently reflects verbally and mentally on what he has learned in each case, which informs the reader about the lessons the hoglet is absorbing. Concerning the recipient of the message, we discuss who might be the intended *narratario*, versus ourselves. Can a message be understood differently by different listeners? Does the listener or recipient of a message have any role in the creation of meaning? How can we know that our understanding of a message is solid?

After grappling with the complexities of interpersonal communication, we discuss certain basic questions of genre and artistic categories of literature. We first discuss three overarching categories: *arte por el arte* (art for art's sake), *arte con un fin docente* (instructive art), and *arte comprometido* (art with a commitment). To what degree can we characterize a work within any or all of these categories? What are characteristics of each type of art? Does any certain type of literature fit more readily within one of these categories more than the others? Is there ever any overlap? And what about the general literary genres we're studying this semester? Does *El erizo feliz* fit best within the genre of the narrative, poetry, theatre, or the essay, and how do we know that? If it fits most within the narrative genre, what sort of narrative is it? Are all narratives (like the epistle, the novel, the short story, the memoir, etc.) characteristically the same? If not, how do they differ? And finally, how do we know if a written text is in reality "literature"? Are all texts "literature"? Can written communication like text messages be considered "literature"?

Students also learn about plot development in terms of *la exposición o planteamiento del asunto* (the exposition), *el desarrollo* (the development), *el suspenso* (the suspense or rising action), *el punto decisivo* (the turning point), *el clímax* (the climax), and *el desenlace* (the dénouement). In the exposition of *El erizo feliz*, we learn that Tino lives on the edge of a forest and tends a garden of medicinal herbs and other plants. He enjoys observing nature and quietly thinking in solitude. His mother and father are absent; Tino lives with his grandfather, who is much more practical than Tino in his approach to what it takes to lead a useful life. We see a tension, or suspense, developing between Tino and Tarek concerning the former's bucolic tendencies and the latter's drive for productivity. Students discuss whether or not they have experienced a similar conflict between themselves and an elder family member and are asked to answer questions about that situation. What was the conflict about; how was it resolved? To what extent can we say that the conflict between Tino and Tarek represents a universal lack of understanding between generations that transcends geographical, social, or ethnic barriers? How does Tino react to his grandfather's criticisms? Can we say that Tarek's critical estimation of Tino's relationship with nature forms the impetus for Tino to embark upon his path of learning and growth? The tension between these two fictional hedgehogs culminates in Tino's departure from his home and his impending journey of self-development.

The turning point in Tino's exploration comes as he reflects on the other animals he has met during his travels and the failures he has suffered while trying to be more like them. After a futile attempt at communicating with a colony of ants that is so busy laboring that not even one of them responds to Tino's greeting, the young hedgehog begins his return journey home. He ponders whether or not he wants to live such a life. He remembers the words of his grandfather: "*Es absurdo que pierdas el tiempo mirando el pasto y oliendo las flores. Debes aprovechar que eres joven y empezar a hacer algo importante que en el futuro te haga feliz*" [It's absurd for you to waste your time looking out over the pasture and smelling the flowers. You should take advantage of your youth and start doing something important that will make you happy in the future] (Pfister). Tino realizes that his grandfather was right but concludes that even though the other animals are indeed busy achieving their goals, they don't seem to enjoy life.

This realization on Tino's part marks the story's turning point. From this moment on, he will think for himself and value his own abilities. The story climaxes when, upon returning at last to his garden, Tino expresses his new worldview in a telling interior monologue:

> No. Yo no quiero ser el erizo más fuerte.... [n]i el más inteligente, ni el más rápido. ¿Qué sentido tiene vivir una vida miserable para ser feliz en el futuro, si yo ya soy feliz? A mí me gusta ser como soy ahora; aquí, en mi casa y mi jardín.
>
> [No. I don't want to be the strongest, nor most intelligent, nor fastest hedgehog. What sense does it make to live a miserable life so that I can be happy in the future, if I'm already happy? I like how I am right now; here, in my home and my garden] [Pfister].

The dénouement of the story occurs immediately after Tino comes to realize the value of the life he has always been living. Tino hears a hoarse cough and sees the cougher is his grandfather. The youngster has matured and has learned to speak up for himself. With self-assurance, he offers Tarek a special, honeyed tea that Tino says will help alleviate the ailment. Tarek is taken somewhat aback, but Tino continues to inform him about many other medicinal plants and herbs that can cure headaches, twisted ankles, etc. The grandfather is surprised to find out how much his grandson knows and how much there is to learn in Tino's garden. A more comprehensive level of understanding is reached between grandfather and grandson, and the reader is lead to believe that this understanding will define the future of their relationship.

After discussing the mechanics of plot development in *El erizo feliz*, students are divided into small groups and are tasked with analyzing the story's discourse. What is the tone of the narration? How is the story organized and presented? What rhetorical devices are used and what do they contribute to our understanding of the narration? How does the author develop his characters? The students come to understand that dialogue and description are two of the primary methods of character development used by the author. The story is set in a forested area, with a nearby meadow and Tino's garden. It's spring or summer, which we know because the narrator describes the flowers that are blooming, and the birds that are singing. This setting is significant in that it forms the backdrop for Tino's travels, as well as provides a glimpse into Tino's personality; Tino is intimately aware of the plants, animals, and insects that call this place home because he spends his time observing and studying them. These are things that bring Tino peace and a sense of purpose in life. Dialogue is another literary tool that the author uses to paint a portrait of his characters. Tarek uses vocabulary such as "*¡Qué barbaridad!*" [What nonsense/stupidity!], and verbs like "*haraganear*" [to loaf or sit around idly] (Pfister).

These words express Tarek's emotional and intellectual state when he finds his grandson lying in the grass and tell the reader much about Tarek's estimation of Tino's activities. After expressing his opinion regarding young people these days, Tarek challenges Tino to go out into the world and find something useful to do. This admonition underlines the grandfather's work ethic and value system. Tino then questions the validity of his grandfather's words, saying to himself that Tarek doesn't appear to be a particularly happy individual. This act of questioning the attitude of his elders and the world around him is what marks Tino's capacity for reflective thought and his intellectual independence. Tino is observant, whether his curiosity concerns a specific plant in his garden or the demeanor and behavior of those around him. Tino's ability to observe and reflect is emphasized time and again in the story by his interactions with other forest creatures. Each time Tino meets an animal who is busily working to achieve a particular goal, he imitates actions. After attempting to do what each animal is doing to ensure happiness in its future, Tino reflects, silently to himself or out loud to other characters, on his experiences. He weighs the benefits and deficits of each activity and formulates his own independent valuation of what is right for him as an individual.

Nowhere is this independent observation and reflection more evident than when Tino meets the young hare who wants to become the smartest hare in the world. Tino follows the hare to his classes where the instructor teaches geography, mathematics, and writing. Afterwards, Tino asks the hare if he has understood what the professor was teaching, and the hare admits that, no, he hasn't. But he quickly adds that he simply memorizes the lesson, presumably so that he can pass the test later. Tino thinks to himself that it's enjoyable to learn new things, but that, for him, it is more important to understand what he's learning, not just memorize formulas and facts (Pfister). This capacity for experiencing the world through the eyes of others, and weighing these experiences against what he believes to be an acceptable outcome, is what marks Tino as an independent evaluator of his life and goals. With Tino's and Tarek's personality traits in mind, students are encouraged to extrapolate the lessons Tino learns into their own lives. How do they learn, and how do they evaluate what they are learning? Should Tino have done anything else to ensure his arrival at adequate conclusions regarding his interactions with the other animals?

El erizo feliz is an engaging children's story to which university students can relate in ways that they often find challenging in other texts. The characters are animals, and the protagonist is a juvenile hedgehog who evokes empathy on the part of the reader. The students care what happens to Tino in the story, and this helps them participate as active readers. Throughout the story, Tino searches for self-fulfillment and understanding, which is itself a process that often marks the real life experiences of college students. This process facilitates student engagement with the text, and of course the more engaged a student is, the more likely she or he is to enjoy and participate in classroom activities. And participation, coupled with engagement and understanding—not simply memorizing literary vocabulary—helps students assimilate their lessons, as Tino discovered after sitting in class with the hare.

Works Cited

Friedman, Edward H., L. Teresa Valdivieso, and Carmelo Virgilio. *Aproximaciones al estudio de la literatura hispánica*, 6th ed. Boston: McGraw-Hill Higher Education, 2008.

Pfister, Marcus. *El erizo feliz*. Trans. Diego Lasconi. New York: Ediciones Norte-Sur, 2003.

*Unwind*ing Ethical Questions

JACQUELINE BACH,
MELANIE HUNDLEY *and*
EMILY TARVER

Young adults, those students in middle school, high school, and college, often question who they are, if they are important, and whether they see their questions and concerns reflected in the world around them. Young adult novels can provide spaces for teachers and students to explore what-if scenarios tied to deeply divisive topics.

One example is Shusterman's Unwind dystology, a series that addresses the value of life. We are huge fans of these books and appreciate the multiple levels of ethical issues which our students uncover. Shusterman's story begins somewhere in the near future, after the conclusion of the Second Civil War, a battle between the Pro-Choice Army and the Pro-Life Army that ended in the creation of Bill of Life—a document hoped to bring about a compromise regarding this contentious issue. This novel does not avoid dealing with the issues raised by the particular stances of each of these groups, and we admire Shusterman's ability to embed contemporary issues within a fictional world. As teachers of college-level courses, we begin our classroom discussions of Shusterman's work with the questions "What is the value of life?" and "How does one determine the value of one's life?" in order to explore critical issues raised by the novel.

While the exploration of larger, universal questions in college classrooms is not new, the integration of a young adult novel that extends a challenging argument to a potentially logical conclusion and that introduces the imagined implications of that conclusion into the lives of the three central characters provides a safe, low-stakes space for students to explore multiple perspectives. Shusterman's series could serve as supplemental reading in a number of general education courses in the humanities and social sciences. In this chapter we focus on how the Unwind series can help students identify and argue for multiple perspectives on complex issues and topics. In each of the following sections, we discuss an ethical question raised in Shusterman's work and provide an activity that we use with our students in the classroom.

Setting a novel after a great war in itself is not novel or unusual. Many young adult novels present the reader with the world *after* a cataclysmic or polarizing event. We see stories of survival, of hope and courage, of growth; in *Unwind*, we see the aftermath of a civil war fought about a person's right to life. A character in Shusterman's 2007 *Unwind* explains how the war was resolved: "The Bill of Life was signed, the Unwind Accord went into effect, and the war was over. Everyone was so happy to end the war, no one cared about the consequences" (224).

The Bill of Life, a set of laws passed to end the war, established specific guidelines for when and how life will be valued. According to these laws, life is sacred from the point of conception until the age of 13. Between 13 and 18, a child may be retroactively "aborted" as long as the child's life doesn't technically end. The process by which a child is both terminated and yet still alive is called "unwinding."

What makes this novel unique is the set of moral and ethical questions it raises as we see the societal repercussions of a peace accord that preserved the sanctity of life by banning abortion prior to birth but identified a period of time in which a person could be "unwound" or recycled for body parts. Technically, life is preserved as that person is not considered dead because his/her body parts, though separated, are alive in other people's bodies. The moral questions raised in this novel provide a unique and thoughtful way for students to consider the value of life, as well as the definition, causes, and value of war. The novel also allows students to consider the moral quandary of new circumstances made possible by scientific advances—for instance, just because science has progressed to the point that something, such as the harvesting of body parts, can be done, does this mean that it should be done?

What Is War? What Is the Purpose?

The majority of young adults in high school and college have grown up during a time in which the United States and its allies have been at war in Afghanistan and Iraq. They have noticed the ways in which the political rhetoric around war, the purposes for war, and the ongoing costs of war have changed. *Unwind* deals directly with these issues; multiple characters discuss the role of war and how wars change society. The Admiral, who oversees the Graveyard, a sanctuary where those teens destined to be unwound can hide, argues that, "a conflict always begins with an issue—a difference of opinion, an argument. But by the time it turns into a war, the issue doesn't matter anymore, because now it's about one thing and one thing only: how much each side hates the other" (223). In Melanie's class, this point of view provides a conversation-starter for students who have been studying propaganda. Emma (a student pseudonym), one of Melanie's students, argued that "The war started because the two sides differed on the idea of abortion, so many people lost their lives in a war about preserving life." The students discussed the idea that war is more complicated than they had originally believed. They focused on ways in which the initial reasons for a war—to preserve life, to protect a people from a dictator, to retaliate against an unprovoked attack, to gain freedom from tyranny, to protect a way of life—are not necessarily the reasons that a war continues.

Unwind shows a society in the aftermath of a brutal war and dealing with the consequences of the Bill of Life. The characters who remember the war talk about it in ways that differ from many poems and novels. The characters do not talk about heroes or great battles; rather they focus on what started the war. The Admiral explains,

> I was right there in the room when they came up with the idea that a pregnancy could be terminated retroactively once a child reaches the age of reason.... At first it was a joke—no one intended it to be taken seriously. But that same year the Nobel Prize went to a scientist who perfected neurografting—the technique that allows every part of a donor to be used in transplant....
>
> With the war getting worse.... We brokered a peace by bringing both sides to the table. Then we proposed the idea of unwinding, which would terminate the unwanteds without actually ending their lives. We thought it would shock both sides into seeing reason—that they would stare at each other across the table and someone would blink. But, nobody blinked [223–24].

This is not a description of a glorious battle or a carefully crafted peace treaty. This is a description of a moment intended to make both sides stop and think; however, this moment didn't do that. Instead, both sides embraced an unthinkable, unreasonable solution as an opportunity to end a war and to satisfy issues which started the war. Melanie's student Simon noticed that "while the Pro-Life soldiers' side fought for the right of babies to be born, they didn't question the unwinding of a teenager." The technicality that the teens are still alive because their divided parts are alive seemed to be enough for the Pro-Life faction to agree. Were they just tired of war, or were the rhetorical moves enough to make them believe they were doing the right thing? The technicalities seem to make the Pro-Life faction accept the compromise. Technically, they win because abortions are illegal and babies have a right to be born. Technically, the teens who are unwound or retroactively aborted aren't actually dead because they are alive in other peoples' bodies. The rhetorical move of renaming retroactive abortion and calling it "unwinding" allows them to see this loss of a singular life as "living in a divided state." The individual as a whole is gone, but his/her parts live on in others. Aly questioned, "Even though the Admiral said the war was getting worse, what could make a group who were fighting to preserve life think that this was an okay solution?"

Equally challenging is the Pro-Choice faction backing a solution that allows parents the choice of unwinding for five years. From thirteen to eighteen, adolescents can be unwound by their parents or by the state. At a time in which children are developing their own identity and autonomy, both can be taken away from them. Another way in which people lose the right to choose specific elements of their own lives is the practice of "storking." In this practice, a baby can be dropped off, abandoned, and the person or family who finds the baby must take care of the baby—unless, as is shown in the first part of the book, the recipients also choose to stork the baby and pass it on to another family.

The lack of choice leads to multiple unintended consequences—a baby passed from house to house with no actual care or attention, teens forced to run away to preserve their lives, children being "tithed" (just as religious families donated 10 percent of their income to the church, the 10th child was donated to be unwound) without a choice on their part. Unwinds are not given choice about whether or not they want to be organ donors. Again, technicalities make this law acceptable to the Pro-Choice factions. Technically, parents have the right to choose whether or not to keep the baby. Emma stated, "While a baby's right to be born is protected, no one seems to be protecting the baby's right to choose her own life."

War and the rhetoric around war and peace provide an interesting discussion focus for students. The comparisons between the war in the novel and its aftermath and the current conflicts in Afghanistan and Iraq are inevitable. Students talk about the purposes for each war, the ideals that made the war seem necessary, how the "talk" around those ideals shifted over the course of the war, and how the unexpected outcomes have consequences that society is ill-equipped to handle.

Activity: Constructing the Argument Using Textual Evidence

The students in Melanie's class participated in multiple layers of argument building in their reading of this text and their discussions about war. In order to prepare for the discussion, using the chart below, students worked in small groups to develop three claims they wanted to make, identify textual evidence to support their claims, and connect with current events.

Discussion Preparation: Claim and Evidence	
Claim 1:	
Evidence from the text (Quotes & Page Numbers)	Connection to Current Events (source)
Claim 2:	
Evidence from the text (Quotes & Page Numbers)	Connection to Current Events (source)
Claim 3:	
Evidence from the text (Quotes & Page Numbers)	Connection to Current Events (source)

After the discussion, the students then chose a claim that they wanted to explore in a more formal academic essay. They used the graphic organizers for the discussion, and the discussion to help them in their planning for the essay.

What Counts as Life? What Is the Value? Who Decides?

The Second Civil War is fought, in part, about life and the value of life. The Pro-Life faction argues that all life has value from the point of conception forward. The quality of that life isn't discussed; the only consideration is that life is valuable. The novel addresses this issue in multiple ways. The three main characters are each slated to be unwound for very different reasons. Risa is being unwound due to state budget cuts. Though she has a musical gift strong enough to be considered above average, her talents are not strong enough to be considered exceptional. Her life has value to the state only if she is someone exceptional; nothing else matters, not her behavior, not her hard work, not her other contributions to the state home. Unlike Risa, Connor has a family, and, unlike Risa, Connor is impulsive and hot-headed. His parents choose to have him unwound rather than work with him to improve his behavior. He is too much trouble to keep, and the parents don't seem to question whether this is a behavioral phase he will grow out of as he matures. Lev is the tenth child in his religious family; he grows up knowing that he will be tithed when he turns thirteen. His life has value not in the living of it but in the sacrifice of it. In each of these three cases, the end and value of their lives is decided by outside forces—money, judgment, religion.

Risa, as a child raised in a state home, recognizes the inequities in the system in which she is raised. She is told, "It looks like your behavior has been exemplary. Your grades have been respectable, but not excellent" (22). The distinction between respectable and excellent is significant. Her value is related to her performance, not her behavior. She is being unwound not because of something she did wrong but because she did not stand out as exemplary. She can be unwound as a cost-cutting measure; her life is not valuable enough to the state to continue to feed, clothe, and educate her. When Risa protests, she is told, "Change is always scary" (23). Risa says, "Dying is a bit more than a 'change'" (22). The lawyer steps in and points out that she's "not actually dying" and that "everyone would be more comfortable if [she] didn't suggest something so blatantly inflammatory" (24). The only way that the people at the state home can make themselves feel better about unwinding Risa is by focusing on the idea that they are not sentencing her to death. Risa has no value to them as a whole person; her parts have value.

Both Connor and Lev are unwound by their families. Connor's parents cite his behavior issues as a reason while Lev's parents have raised him, their tenth child, as a tithe. Connor's life only has value to his parents if he is well-behaved. Lev is valued as a tithe; his family gives ten percent of their income and possessions as part of their religious practice. Lev's value to the family is in the donation of his life. Lev doesn't have a choice, and nothing he does will change the family's intent. Not until Lev has a conversation with another character, Pastor Dan, does Lev even question the way in which he was raised. Pastor Dan says that he has lost his convictions because he can't "believe in a God who condones human tithing" (329). At that moment, Lev realizes that his life's value is not as a tithe or as a sacrifice. He says, "I never knew there was a choice" (329). For both Connor and Lev, their lives are valued not because of who they are but rather because of their role as troublemaker or tithe.

Activity: Multi-Genre Paper

In this activity, students in Jackie's class write a multi-genre paper that explores an ethical question. Romano defines a multi-genre paper as one that "arises from research, experience and imagination" (x). In it, students make individual points that support their argument in a paper comprised of a number of genres and media, including images, recipes, poems, essays, and screenplays. Papers can be digital or print-based. Each portion of the paper works toward addressing a question, an argument, or topic. A student interested in the question "Who decides what makes us valuable to society?" might pull together an obituary, an essay on recent health insurance policies, a letter (in *Unwind*, those destined to be unwound who escaped are asked by one of their protectors to write a letter to someone they love), and a preface introducing the reasons these particular genres were chosen to address this question. These pieces are supported by references to informational texts.

Teachers interested in Romano's approach should consult his book *Blending Genre, Altering Style* for guidance. This approach works nicely with Schusterman's style as the later books in his dystology become examples of multi-genre texts.

Selling the Cause: What Responsibility Does Media Hold?

In Shusterman's second book, *Unsouled*, the media plays an increasingly important role in raising ethical questions about the value of life. Interspersed throughout the novels are public service announcements, advertisements, and news stories.

Activity: Unwind*ing Persuasive Pieces*

In this activity, Emily's students perform close readings of the advertisements included in the novel *Unsouled*. Set apart on the pages of the book, these short pieces of writing resemble actual advertisements for the multiple uses for unwound body parts, many of which are enhancements rather than replacements. In their discussion of the novels, in particular of these additional mock advertisements and new stories, our students often refer to actual news stories that involve similar issues from organ transplant items to corrupt politicians. In this way, students consider the role of the fictional advertisements as supplements to the storyline. In doing so, they may make connections between the way products in *Unsouled* are marketed and the way our society markets products, many of which may come at someone else's expense or may appeal to vanity. For example, students may start with the following advertisement for "Scultptura," a procedure that claims to use "advanced scar-free technology, [so] you can have any major muscle group refit with healthy, strong muscle tissue, guaranteed or your money back" (100); "Thinkfast" which "augment[s] your memory with millions of healthy young neurons harvested from prime Unwinds" (35); or the promotional commercial for Initiative 11 which would allow for the unwinding of "violent offenders" (131).

In a guided discussion, her students analyzed the method of persuasion used in the advertisement—pathos, ethos, or logos. They examined the explicit and implicit messages contained in the advertisements. Students then created their own advertisements using Schusterman's as models.

Conclusion

In order to understand better how Schusterman depicts his world—in order to understand his world—readers must piece together the disparate parts. In the end, putting these parts together demonstrates the connections between the *Unwind* world and our own. Just as the Unwinds in Schusterman's series continue to exist even though their parts are spread out among others so, too, do the questions raised by Schusterman's text. The questions—What is war? What is the value of life? Who has the right to make decisions for others?—play out in our current society, and, as in the dystopia, the unintended consequences of those questions and our responses to them continue to echo long after we have forgotten the initial reasons for our choices. Attending to these kinds of ethical and moral questions in classrooms allows students the opportunity to think critically about choices and consequences.

Works Cited

Romano, Tom. *Blending Genre, Altering Style: Writing Multigenre Papers*. Portsmouth, NH: Boyton/Cook, 2000. Print.

Schusterman, Neal. *Unsouled*. New York: Simon & Schuster, 2013. Print.

_____. *Unwholly*. New York: Simon & Schuster, 2012. Print.

_____. *Unwind*. New York: Simon & Schuster, 2007. Print.

Children's Books
from Serious, Adult Concepts

Laura Gray *and* Gary Moeller

Women in the Literary and Visual Arts (WLVA) is a unique, interdisciplinary, senior-level seminar that combines the study of women's literature and art into one challenging and innovative semester. This co-designed course is team taught by Professor of Art Gary Moeller and Professor of English and Humanities Laura Gray. Without a formal women's studies program, and with few courses focused exclusively on women's history or issues, the depth and breadth of this 16-week course can be daunting. However, in the nearly ten years since it was first created and offered, this course has become very popular and is considered significant enough to have been adopted as a mandatory core course for students completing a Bachelor of Fine Arts, for those completing a Humanities Option in the Bachelor of Arts in Liberal Arts, and for those completing a Humanities Minor.

The Problem

How, then, might a senior-level university course that deals with challenging images from Judy Chicago's *Dinner Party, Eight Women in Black and White* by Ghada Amer, Marlene Dumas's *Dead Girl,* and the literary works of such women writers as Sylvia Plath, Virginia Woolf, and Audre Lorde convert complex concepts of and about adult women into essential ideas? Ideas so important that need to be accessible, perhaps so accessible a child might understand them? A children's book, of course. As counter-intuitive as this might sound, our experience with including the creation of a children's book into this course opens many opportunities to engage in what we value. First, it calls on students to work collaboratively (which is an important feminist value, and one modeled by the collective teaching approach). Second, it engages the talents of the literary and visual arts students enrolled in the course and allows them to produce something (rather than simply read and write about other's productions). This, in turn, offers them the same sense of voice and agency we champion in the course content. In this essay we describe the project and process, and then we offer some thoughts on the value of the learning process and the final function and quality of the resulting projects.

The Project

Included below are the assigned details regarding the Children's Book project.

Women in the Literary and Visual Arts Group Project
A Children's Book

Working within a team, each of you will contribute significantly to the creation of a children's book that focuses on some aspect of women's art, literature, or history. The specific focus will be determined by each group and approved by the professors. Teams (of around 5) should be formed with the following jobs in mind:

1. Story
2. Layout /Art
3. Production/Direction

The specific division of labor should be determined and agreed upon by each group. Some jobs will require more than one person. The key to a successful project, however, is equitable participation across the entire team. Group members will be evaluated by each other throughout the process. Slackers will be penalized. Overly controlling members probably will not do well, either.

Final Length: 15–30 pages (including illustrations)

Final Due Date:_____

Step 1: Select a team. You may wish to continue working with the original groups formed at the beginning of the semester. Or, you may decide to regroup based upon interests and talents. We would like to have these groups set by next week. Everyone must be a part of team. While we hope that you are able to self-select, we will have to make sure that each student is properly placed and that the integrity of the class is maintained.

Step 2: Select a topic, clarify target audience (age group), and assign jobs. The focus of the project should tie closely to the content of our class. Consider the questions, issues, and artists (visual and literary) that we have discussed these past weeks. You are not limited to the materials covered thus far.

Step 3: Once your topic has been approved, begin work on the book. When possible, we will set aside class time for group work. However, please know that you will have to work on this out of class and at the same time that other class material is underway. There will be progress reports and evaluations along the way.

Step 4: Submit and present final book on _____. While we do not expect a professional, glossy finished project, we do expect a complete and appropriately academic project. This means a story with a beginning, middle, and end, and art work to accompany it. We will discuss the technical details throughout the project.

The problem of converting the adult concepts covered in the course to children's understanding is a major learning experience and challenge to the university students. The over-riding subjects of women writers and visual artists studied in the course are often challenging. These creations after all are dealing with the marginalization, sublimation, and objectification of women throughout known history. Specifically, this subject matter can be uncomfortable even for the senior-level students. Images of voyeurism, childbirth, and decapitation and fiction and histories that focus on the sexual abuse of female slaves, rape, depression/suicide, and revolutionary social moments are difficult issues to render down to children's text and images.

Over the semesters, however, students in their groups have managed to find ways to make main ideas work for the assignment. Students faced with this project have often looked at the general concerns and questions of the course as opposed to the heavy specifics as the themes for the books. Ideas such as gender equality in the arts, as well as in life; characterizations of women through the eyes of important women writers and artists; concepts about the questions related to whether women's and men's creative works should be separated (see *A Room of One's Own* by Woolf) or whether space should be inclusive of all genders, races, and beliefs—all are discussed throughout the course and at times applied to the production of the books.

The educational directions, interests of the students, and previous study provided by the course serve to make the results of the student effort more often successful than not.

Backgrounds

The majority of the students in this required course are traditionally-aged Bachelor of Fine Arts juniors and seniors with emphases in Studio Arts, Graphic Design, Photography, and/or Multi-Media. In the minority there are traditional Bachelor of Arts in Liberal Arts (BALA) majors who opt to take the course as part of the humanities option. Both of these demographics also include non-traditional students. Some of the students have children and therefore have an in-house test audience. These facts relate to the Women in the Literary and Visual Arts (WLVA) Children's Book assignment in many interesting ways.

First, many of the BFA and BALA majors, especially the traditionally-aged students, are very much familiar with, and in some cases dedicated to, many disciplines of fantasy arts. Most of the traditional students not only play animated games, watch movies and television programs, and read books and graphic novels of the same genre but have also created examples of this kind of art/writing through assignments and other venues as part of their university work. Therefore, the student should be able to convert known ideas into new contexts and realities. Consequently, the students are not unaccustomed to changing realities in art and writing. In addition and as part of the course curriculum, they all have experience of at least eight weeks of intense reading and art analysis of women's literature and visual works from the Middle Ages to the present day before the children's book assignment is due. This configuration of visual and literary experiences, interests, and preparation is seemingly ideal for this assignment.

The Projects: Challenges

The WLVA course is truly an educational adventure that packs much more than one semester's worth of information and work into the sixteen-week session. From the intensive readings and scrutiny of artworks, common themes arise for the children's books produced by the student groups: specifically, gender equality (books encouraging girls and boys to be valued regardless of interests), girl-power books (books that focus on a female protagonist that finds empowerment), and historically-centered books (ones that teach the reader about some of the important women in history). Of course, these are not mutually exclusive threads; threads often have multiple purposes.

The Children's Book assignment emphasizes cooperative directions toward a common goal. All the cogs in the wheel, each student's attention and expertise, are needed to contribute toward the desired end. It is up to the group to divide tasks. Success is given the best chance when each member of the group carries respective loads in order for the product to show continuity as well as creativity. The book should not be the work of one student or personality. Unfortunately, the nature of group work sometimes becomes part of the challenge.

Students have much to consider when working on a deadline. Which student can do the story, the images, the layout, the continuity, the printing, and the presentation? What forms of communications and decision-making will be employed? Should outside critiques be part of the editing process? How does the group react when all the expectations of individual roles are not met? Is there a plan for that possibility?

The Pitfalls

Some dangers and pitfalls are inherent within such projects—navigating hazards like these is as important to the learning process as success:

1. The over-simplified approach that is not grounded in any true learning from the course. Such productions can be the results of those students unwilling or unable to live up to the true challenges of the course.

2. The missed target—the books that are overly academic or text-based. The easy mistake is to depend too much on the written word to carry the idea. For young children, the images should carry the story, and the words should serve to support the images. Nowhere in the book should there be pages of nothing but text, whereas images can fill a page with few or no words and the ideas of the book can progress.

3. The unsuccessful group—final products will show the lack of coordination and cooperation between members (sloppy productions, mismatched art, disconnect between the story and art). (See the section "What Did the Students Learn from the Children's Book Project?")

The Successes

To our surprise and delight, each semester, even the first, brought to fruition really thoughtful productions. Despite the potential pitfalls outlined above (and committed by several groups), no work was a complete disaster, and several were very engaging and nearly ready for publication. Titles included *Arty and Smarty* and *Be Creative*.

Several groups enthusiastically embraced the opportunity to try something new. Two good (not perfect) productions came in the form of handmade books: *Mattie Learns to Read* (screen print) and *The Knights* [*sic*] *Secret* (pop-up book). Excerpts of two of the most notable examples follow: *Unmonsterly Matilda* and *Aubrey the Kitten*.

Matilda was sad. She only wanted to help make their sneaking and creeping better. But if they wouldn't listen to her, she thought, she would simply try harder to be noticed in a good way. She would not, however, give up her love of knowledge and science.

10

Unmonsterly Matilda (**Kristen Cleary, Gretchen Eagle Chaffin, Hannah Hanley, Francyne Melberg, and Melody Davis**)

Aubrey the Kitten (**Jordan Wong and Erico Zetina**)

The example from *Unmonsterly Matilda*, written and illustrated by Kristen Cleary, Gretchen Eagle Chaffin, Hannah Hanley, Francine Melberg, and Melody Davis, merges whimsical illustration with positive concepts of young girls' aspirations.

In the book *Aubrey the Kitten*, text lines are overlaid on the picture of bats, cats, and bear creature:

> At the bottom of the cliff was a shady, purple grotto, full of jewels, bats and a bear named Otto. "Stop!" exclaimed her brothers, "We can't go in there! It's dangerous!" But Aubrey flexed her claws and said, "We've got to be courageous!" [Jordan Wong and Erico Zetina].

In creating *Aubrey the Kitten*, the group divided the duties of illustration and writing into separate sections, with two students from the larger group working on one section, another set of two working on another section, and a final set working on the last section. This approach to the construction of the piece certainly presented continuity questions, and, in the end, those questions were not completely resolved. On its own, however, this image and text, created for *Aubrey the Kitten* by students Jordan Wong and Erico Zetina, is coherent and presents the concepts of female courage and power in a very creative manner.

The Results

The results find many of the final products of the assignment just a few edits from possible mass publication. The groups have often created pieces that surprise the reader in terms of not only the knowledge of women's art and literature but also of how creatively the group incorporated the ideas in art and storyline.

The students are challenged to re-think the original concepts and implications of the major works studied and translate those to storylines and images to entertain and teach children from toddlers to young teens. This means the students have to fully understand the concepts in order to articulate them clearly.

What Did the Students Learn from the Children's Book Project?

Young children commonly learn the rudiments of language by first seeing pictures and then associating the letters and sounds of words to the images. They also commonly learn by associating the images and words with contexts of what they know of the world. These are often found to have a hierarchy of forms, marks, and colors, each representing and presumably indicating the value of importance each element of the design has on their lives. This is the world the university students must be aware of before attempting this exercise.

Beyond the obvious benefits of working with a group and creating a product to add to portfolios and websites, what is gained from the challenge? By the time the Children's Book assignment is given, the students in the course all have been part of small groups responding to readings and images and reporting their findings to the larger student body. While these groups of four or five elect respective spokespersons in the normal classroom assignments, they have not by that point been in a situation in which each student has a designated important role in the production of a product, the overall grade of which is dependent on the self-discipline of each group member. Students in their groups are asked to critique the groups' effectiveness and the success of the project, as well as how well each member contributed to the end product.

As professors of the arts and humanities, we advocate the value of looking back at process. We also advocate looking back at the value of children's creations. In the visual arts, for example, it is especially obvious that young children's works are fresh, honest, free of many social and cultural restrictions, and creatively essential. These are the exact goals many well-established adult artists desire in their mature work. These also are aspirations we hope to instill in our students, whether in our regular courses or as part of this Children's Book assignment.

Works Cited

Amer, Ghada. *Eight Women in Black and White.* Acrylic and embroidery on canvas. New York: Gagosian Gallery, 2004.

Chicago, Judy. *Dinner Party.* Installation. Brooklyn: Brooklyn Museum, 1974–1979.

Dumas, Marlene. *Dead Girl.* Oil on canvas. Los Angeles: Los Angeles County Museum of Art. 2002.

Woolf, Virginia. *A Room of One's Own.* Eastford, CT: Martino, 2012. Print.

Image and Text in
The Tale of Peter Rabbit
MICHAEL MCKEON

Among the courses I teach in the fine arts is Senior Capstone. At the beginning of every semester, without exception, a student will come to me with an idea for a senior project: a combination of text and image, usually in the form of a graphic novel. Rarely, if ever, do I see success in these ventures. A student is either strong in narrative or a good visual artist, but hardly ever both. Consequently, the project's asymmetry proves fatal, and I am left wondering what models could have best served the student's understanding of the graphic novel. Beatrix Potter's *The Tale of Peter Rabbit* has to be one of the best examples possible.

To make my case, I will elaborate and expand upon six criteria Margaret Mackey treats in her book *The Case of Peter Rabbit* (5–13). These criteria, like the tale itself, are deceivingly simple. Yet they offer, I believe, a way of "reading" the tale as a beneficial, heuristic device for art students struggling to write narrative.

The first criterion is text. As a work of literature *The Tale of Peter Rabbit* is itself highly instructive, not to mention entertaining. Those who have had the pleasure of reading the tale know the lesson of obeying parents is succinctly told. At the beginning of the story, Peter's mother admonishes her children not to venture into Mr. McGregor's garden—but why? Their father "had an accident there," Peter's mother states. "He was put in a pie by Mrs. McGregor" (Potter 10).

Peter disobeys his mother, of course, and his resulting escapades inevitably follow from his refusal to heed her injunction. He surfeits himself on vegetables, making himself sick, and then bumps into Mr. McGregor working in his garden. A chase ensues, during which Peter encounters a variety of animal life in the garden. These creatures express reactions ranging from concern to indifference over his plight. Finally, Peter espies the gate he originally crawled under, and, while Mr. McGregor's back is turned, makes a mad dash for it. He escapes the garden and Mr. McGregor. He rushes home, where he collapses from exhaustion. He is finally put to bed and dosed with chamomile tea by his mother.

Our pleasure reading *The Tale of Peter Rabbit* arises, in part, from Beatrix Potter's unique style of story-telling. Students may be surprised to discover that composing this *apparently* simple tale took nearly ten years of Potter's creative life. From its original conception in 1893 to the standardized text of 1903, she worked tirelessly on the story, revising and editing two private editions (MacDonald 29). Changes to those editions were subtle and mostly of minor detail; nevertheless, they show Potter to be a consummate craftsman. For instance, between the 1893 letter to Noel Moore, wherein we find the original tale, to the story's first private edition, Potter eliminated the line: "After losing them [Peter's clothes] he ran on four legs and went faster" (qtd. in MacDonald 27). A variation of the line is re-introduced in the 1902 publication. However, it is juxtaposed with a different image, and only has reference to Peter's loss of shoes (Potter 35).

Those familiar with the scene know that Peter has become entangled in a gooseberry net; successful escape from Mr. McGregor requires shedding his jacket. Potter cleverly illustrates the scene through depicting a naturally rendered rabbit fleeing capture; that is, Peter is no longer clothed or bi-pedal. The pictorial transition, according to Ruth MacDonald, is a dehumanizing moment for Peter, a "reversion" to his animal nature artistically rendered through nudity and agility (27). Consequently, the picture makes inessential any textual reference to Peter losing his clothes and running faster. Potter's editing the line therefore was a wise choice at eliminating a redundancy found in the story's original telling to Noel Moore (MacDonald 27).

This is one example, among many, showing Beatrix Potter's sensitivity to the most subtle nuances of pictorial and textual meaning. But it is the constant refining and honing of her skills as a writer that prove most valuable to the young art student attempting narrative. Potter's example shifts focus away from artistic inspiration to craftsmanship. Though the original idea may arise from the unfathomable well-spring of human creativity, the written product itself, according to Potter, is always in need of "chastening." She states, "My usual way of writing is to scribble, and cut out, and write it again and again. The shorter and plainer the better. And read the Bible (unrevised version and

Old Testament) if I feel my style wants *chastening* [emphasis added]" (qtd. in Mackey 6).

From the first and second private editions to the 1902 publication, we find Potter stripping away irrelevancies and redundancies, looking for the most concise and efficient use of language. Her style has been called "brisk, spare, sharp, lively, supple and elegant," terms judiciously applied to a style acquired over time, work, and effort (Mackey 5–8).

The second criterion is pictures. We learn by studying models, and, when it comes to visual paradigms, the art of *The Tale of Peter Rabbit* supersedes all others. As already mentioned, Beatrix Potter anthropomorphizes rabbits, ducks, and mice to teach a moral lesson. But is there an artistic precedent for humanizing the nonhuman? One immediately thinks of *Aesop's Fables*.

Aesop's Fables has been a favorite of illustrators from time immemorial. But unlike Potter's tales, the fables originally come to us as written texts based on previously existing oral tradition. When artwork does accompany the fables, it unsurprisingly shows animals engaged in speech acts, often expressing emotions through facial expressions and hand gestures. This imposition of uniquely human linguistic and gestural behavior on the part of animals assumes something we take for granted in art. The convention is as old as the Italian Renaissance.

Renaissance humanists encouraged artists to explore the human soul and its intentions through representing emotion and gesture in realistically "human" ways. This was not a priority in medieval art, and one has to go back to antiquity to find artistic representations of genuine human interaction with the world. The Renaissance revives these aesthetic priorities, and ultimately they find their way, either consciously or unconsciously, into the creative imaginings of Beatrix Potter.

Nowhere is this idea more clearly illustrated than in Leon Battista Ablerti's concept of *Istoria*, which is introduced in his theoretical work *On Painting* (1435). English translator and commentator of Alberti's treatise, John Spencer states, "It [*Istoria* according to Alberti] is to be built around antique themes with human gestures to portray and project the emotions of the actors" (24). Wherein do we see it in the art of *The Tale of Peter Rabbit*?

Well, it is everywhere actually—but at the same time subtle. For instance, comparing two images of Peter shows the full range of Potter's gifts as an illustrator. Clearly depicted on page 25 is Peter's full humanity. He wears a blue Victorian jacket with brass buttons and slippers, which forces him to stand erect and bi-pedal. He is also shown clasping his stomach, a classic gestural sign of indigestion. Clearly the hand gesture and clothing humanize Peter (Potter 25).

Reciprocally, the absence of clothing is a visual clue to Peter's character transformation. That character-change could be enhanced via illustration Potter knew better than any writer and illustrator at the time; moreover, she was up to the task. Peter's visual morphing from human to animal on page 46 presented not the slightest artistic challenge to Potter, since much of her early artistic repertoire was of naturalistic animal life, as evidenced in illustrations on pages 38 and 46 of the text (MacDonald 5–6).

On pages 36 and 50 Peter is shown crying about his circumstances. It appears he is doomed unless he can find some way of escaping Mr. McGregor's garden. He does escape, and, when he finally arrives safe at home, it isn't clear whether he expresses remorse over his disobedience. He is too exhausted to express anything. However, he does lament the forced dosing of chamomile tea by his mother as depicted in the book's frontispiece. At story's end, his siblings dine with relish on milk and blackberries, a feast justifiably earned in contrast to Peter's surreptitious feasting in Mr. McGregor's garden, resulting in his sickness and predicament.

To conclude the second criterion, art students would do well to consider the appropriateness of artistic imagery complementing a text in any form, e.g., the graphic novel. This contemplation starts by considering how each artwork best communicates information to the reader. Like any two-dimensional art form, Potter's watercolors can only convey a single instant in a continuous narrative. The artist is thus compelled by the very nature of two-dimensional media to represent the scene most "pregnant" with meaning. For instance, certain choices over what to represent can induce anticipation in the reader, such as foreshadowing, or better yet, understanding what has previously taken place in the narrative. (Mackey refers to the same picture's foreshadowing but in the context of the artwork's technical and formal feature [9]. I draw a similar conclusion but one that is based on a humanistic and psychological reading of the text.) With regard to the former, Potter never misses a beat. On page 8, we read Peter's mother's admonishment to her children: "Now, my dears ... you may go into the fields or down the lane, but don't go into Mr. McGregor's garden."

A careless, uninspired rendering of the scene would have depicted Peter facing his mother and sandwiched among his siblings. But notice what Potter does on page 9. She represents Peter in the foreground, separated, with his back to his mother. By doing so, Potter induces in the reader a kind of psychological dissonance, a hint of Peter's future disobedience made explicit on page 19. This type of character-revealing art is the mark of an excellent illustrator, and no one does it better than Beatrix Potter. She knows the limits of her medium and, at the same time, uses those limits in inspired and creative ways to tell a story.

Among the six criteria, adherence to the third is the most profitable to art students. Up to now we have looked at the relationship of art to text, and how each influences the other. But the *integration* of art with text makes certain assumptions about both. The assumptions are critical to any aspiring artist turning to literature. One example has been discussed already. How an image can foreshadow events, or convey character, assumes certain limits and impositions on the medium itself. How does understanding these same limits direct the imagination to consider other visual possibilities that a simple prosaic illustrating of events might overlook? An integration of art with text addresses this question.

An example of the seamless integration between text and image is found on pages 10 and 11. Their combination could be interpreted as straightforward illustration. But Peter's mother's admonition to her children not to venture into Mr. McGregor's garden is more complex than it appears. On pages 10 and 11, Potter provides what is called in film language a "flashback" scene. Picture and text break narrative flow and transport us to another place and time. The fate of Peter's father, due to his reckless behavior, a trait Peter has evidently inherited, is euphemistically expressed in words such as "accident" or being "put" rather than "baked" "in a pie by Mrs. McGregor" (11). Potter deliberately softens the blow to the ears of young listeners and readers. But so that there is no equivocating on the matter, she juxtaposes the image of a hungry family and dog about to consume what's left of Peter's father. (According to the Publisher's Note in the 2002 edition of *The Tale of Peter Rabbit*, this picture was "sacrificed" in the 1903 edition to make room for illustrated endpapers. It has been wisely restored.) A good storybook has this factor always in mind, and I hope students are listening to this. Given the essential differences between art and text, how can they complement each other and tell a story sensitive to one's audience? Potter offers us this one, among many other very good examples.

A picture book's content can be so narratively arresting that we forget a book is a physical object occupying real space in time. The manipulation of its physical properties in a way that assists our getting "lost" in the story is therefore critical to its success as an artwork. The last three criteria address the perceptual aspects of a book and what the artist can do to enhance reading pleasure through their creative manipulation. They are openings and gutters, page turns, and overall design.

In perfecting a book's overall design, the artist must be sensitive to seemingly trivial matters. Openings, gutters, and page turns, as well as typeface, the spatial arrangement of images and text, and the ordering of printed line on the page, are all structured so as to produce a particular effect in the reader. Similar to the formal elements in a painting, their ordering psychologically impacts us below the level of conscious awareness. It is similarly the case in *The Tale of Peter Rabbit* (Mackey 10–12). The pre-planned ordering of visual elements contributes to the overall meaning of the text, and how this occurs and in what ways is most instructive to students.

One of the most difficult challenges confronting a teacher is convincing students of the power of the unconscious mind when experiencing art. Students mistakenly feel they are totally in control over their own thoughts and emotions before an artwork. But much more is at work at the level of the unconscious. For example, if one of the major themes of *The Tale of Peter Rabbit* is obedience to parental authority, where might we find visual elements that underscore this theme but occur at the level of the unconscious?

At each page "opening" the reader is confronted with alternating text and image. Regarding the images, Potter's tonal variations suggest something of the Impressionists. Most of her animal figures are created using predominately high-key pastels contained within well-defined lines, contours, and shapes. This relationship between line and color may seem trivial. But as art theorists and historians, such as Roger de Piles (168), have pointed out, color incites passion while line restricts it.

The debate over line versus color, and their respective roles in painting, is as old as the Renaissance. Anthony Blunt reviews the varying positions of Mannerist scholars on the topic in his text: *Artistic Theory in Italy, 1450–1600* (99–100; 141–43). During the seventeenth century the subject was hotly debated among French academics, e.g., Charles Le Brun and L.G. Blanchard, at the Royal Academy. For a sampling of the arguments refer to pages 177–92 of *Art in Theory: 1648–1815*.

In other words, line, as an intellectual feature of art, controls color and by implication the emotions it arouses. In *The Tale of Peter Rabbit*, Potter's animated world is filled with light and color, resulting in clearly recognizable delineated forms. But as whimsical and charming as Potter's little watercolors may seem, their psychological impact shapes moral character. While the narrative of *The Tale of Peter Rabbit* makes explicit the wise heeding of one's parents, the rationalizing effects of artistic form underscore this moral lesson at the level of perception. Within each image colors are clearly circumscribed within a strong sense of line. At the level of morality, however, Peter's impulsiveness contrasts sharply with the deliberate control of his artistic (linear) rendering. This contradiction seeks resolution in the story itself, so that by the end the reader hopes Peter has learned his lesson, and in the future will not cross any more "lines," so to speak.

Other aspects of symmetry, balance, and control are found in framing of text and image on the page. As Margaret Mackey points out, the amount of block text corresponds roughly in size to "the opposing water color vignettes" (10). Gutters partly situate text and image on the page. Balance and symmetry are not only present in the image and typeface but also accompany each opening in the equitable amount of gutter. These features as well contribute to the overall rationality of the book.

These observations on the ethical and psychological effects of art should cause the art student to think differently when it comes to illustrating narrative. Much more information is conveyed than simply a representation of interesting and charming characters. Reinforcing social norms, or digressing from those norms, can be powerfully conveyed through manipulating perceptual forms and color within and without the text and image.

In *The Tale of Peter Rabbit*, page turns for the most part function like film scenes. Each opening presents text and image, which signals both a termination in narrative flow and an expectation of what is to come. For example, pages 18–21 constitute a single scene: Peter's immediate disobedience as he rushes off to Mr. McGregor's garden. Termination of an opening builds anticipation, and where we find Potter using commas and semicolons at the end of a line suggests continued development on the next opening (19–20). Potter deploys each opening as a singular unit that creates a pattern and structure comparable to breaks in music, or chapters from a larger literary work. For instance, pages 26 and 27 come about as close to a "cliff hanger" as possible. Peter accidentally confronts Mr. McGregor, and, as the two stare each other down, anticipation builds and can only find resolution in the remaining page turns and openings.

Finally, design considers the whole package, that is, the story book as a complete perceptual phenomenon. Potter attends to design features and their relationship, such as the size of the book, choice of typeface, the arrangement of words and pictures on a page, and the arrangement of lines of print: gutters, openings, and page turns, etc. Much of this has been touched upon already. The final point I wish to stress to students is how all these elements come about, not by way of accident, but by deliberate calculation and planning, starting with the size of the book. Potter insisted the book be published at the right size for children, again, another example of the author considering her audience (Mackey 11), probably the most important factor in the success of any picture book.

Works Cited

Alberti, Leon Battista. *On Painting*. Trans. John R. Spencer. New Haven: Yale University Press, 1956.

Blunt, Anthony. *Artistic Theory in Italy: 1450–1600*. Oxford: Oxford University Press, 1963.

de Piles, Roger. "Remarks on De Arte Graphica." *Art in Theory: 1648–1815: An Anthology of Changing Ideas*. Oxford: Blackwell, 2000.

Harrison, Charles, Paul Wood, and Jason Gaiger. *Art in Theory: 1648–1815: An Anthology of Changing Ideas*. Oxford: Blackwell, 2000.

MacDonald, Ruth. *Beatrix Potter*. Boston: Twayne, 1986. Print.

Mackey, Margaret. *The Case of Peter Rabbit*. New York: Garland, 1998. Print.

Potter, Beatrix. *The Tale of Peter Rabbit*. London: Frederick Warne, 2002. Print.

For further information, see Taylor, Judy. *Beatrix Potter: Artist, Storyteller, and Countrywoman*. Harmondsworth, Middlesex: Frederick Warne-Penguin, 1986. Print.

Trees, Not Poles

Peter Macpherson

Often folk stories and myths exist with widely varying versions until a collector such as Hesiod, Snorri Sturluson, Charles Perrault, or the Brothers Grimm records a version which becomes the most "accepted" version. The original multi-branching story tree is pruned down to a single straight pole. This gives a basis for an academic exercise that I assigned. In this exercise, students learn to reverse the process and produce a multi-branching story from a familiar children's fairy tale. After selecting a suitable story, game development students were to implement it as an interactive game in which the player guides the hero. However, they were to take the sequential narrative and convert it to non-linear narrative, allowing the player to try alternative paths in completing the story.

The motivations of using a familiar story as a template are to force students to a starting point, cause them to consider alternatives, force them to predict how players will react, and allow them to produce a satisfying gaming experience for the player. In completing the exercises, students learn to identify plot branching points in the same way that Rossini's *La Cerentola* (a 19th-century opera) imagines the familiar Cinderella story but without a magic fairy godmother, glass slipper, or evil stepmother. Students often have difficulty in generating original story ideas; using an established story as a starting point eases the initial pain of creativity.

The Bachelor of Science in Game Development at Rogers State University is designed to enable graduates to implement games. The emphasis is on computer programming, with additional specialized courses in art, English, and physics. The students who participated in the fairy tale activity were seniors in the capstone class in the spring semester of 2014. At the time of the course, they had completed a sequence of seven programming classes and were seasoned programmers, having worked in Adobe ActionScript, C++, C#, and Java. In addition, all the students had completed ENGL 3033, Creative Writing for Game Design, in which they had studied story writing for games.

Background

The lawyer Edward Packard first wrote a "Choose Your Own Adventure" book in 1970, based on bedtime stories he spun to his two girls. In telling his story, he would pause and ask the girls what the hero, "Pete," should do next and branch the narrative from there. Seizing upon the idea of writing down the stories and mimicking the you-are-the hero approach, in 1979 he published *The Cave of Time* as the first of a very popular series of children's books. In his books, at regular intervals, the reader would be presented with a story element and then multiple choices to make (Kraft 6). For example, if you would like to taunt the troll Humongous the Invincible, turn to page 100; or, if you would like to run away, turn to page 120. The original series of 184 books, using "30 different writers," "sold 250 million copies worldwide" during the period of 1979–1999 ("History of CYOA"). Packard left the law and became a full-time author. One web analysis of the books found the average book has 117 pages, consisting of 47 "decision" pages, 40 "ending" pages, and 30 "story" pages (Swinehart). Mixing a writer narrative with reader decisions was forerunner to future computer text games.

In his seminal work *Screenplay*, Syd Field coined the term "plot point" to mean "any incident, episode, or event that hooks into the action and spins it around into another direction" (143). Although originally used to describe transitions into film's three act structure (setup, confrontation, resolution), I will use it in the more general sense of a decision by the player of the game which moves the story in another direction. The "Choose Your Own Adventure" (CYOA) concept, therefore, consists of many plot points which drive the story line to varying results. Mapping the book into a game requires reorganizing the page-turning/decision-making into a more computer-friendly format.

Data Structures for Stories

Data structures are the representations and arrangement of data within a computer program. Information needs to be organized in an appropriate manner for the algorithms to function correctly. There are many different data structures, such as sets, hashes, linked-list, vectors, heaps, lists, queues, stacks, and trees, all of which RSU Game Development students study in a specialized course, CS 3363, Data Structures. The two most appropriate for representing multi-branching stories are graphs and trees.

Graphs

In mathematics a *graph* consists of a set of vertices (nodes) and edges (links). They, respectively, could represent cities and roads, computers and networks, stereo equipment and cables, electrical components and wires, or many other objects connected in a one-to-one manner. Figure 1 shows an undirected (undirectional—two way roads), weighted (numeric values associated with links) graph.

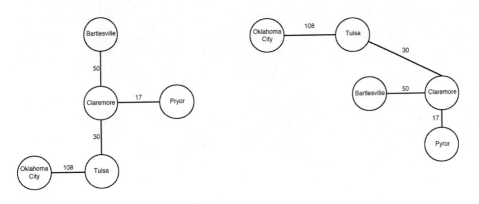

Figure 1. Two Equivalent Graphs

In the graphs, the vertices are shown as circles and the connecting edges as lines. Unlike a map, the positions and orientation of the vertices or scaling does not matter. The 108 miles between Tulsa and Oklahoma City is not drawn as a longer line than the line designating 17 miles from Claremore to Pryor. A directed graph indicates a one-way connection between the vertices and is indicated by arrowheads on the edges. So while an interstate system would be shown as an undirected graph, a city map of Florence would use a directed graph because of the many one-way streets.

The ability of graphs to abstract positioning and orientation makes the representation simple to store and manipulate in a computer program. In the board game Clue or Cluedo, players move from square to adjacent square, with the exception of secret passages which connect the non-adjacent rooms, such as the passage connecting the study to the kitchen and the one connecting the conservatory to the lounge. A graph easily allows for such irregular movements and is used widely to represent geographical locations and movement in games. Routing and AI pathfinding algorithms in games rely heavily upon graphs.

Trees

A tree is a standard data structure used widely in computer science. It can be considered a specialized form of a directed graph. It is hierarchical, in that a node (vertex) can only have one parent. A single node, termed a root, is at the top of the tree. Borrowing from genealogy, a *parent* node has one or more *child* nodes. If a node does not have any children, then it is termed a *leaf* node. When Packard was writing his CYOA stories, he would sketch the story outline as a tree. Dead ends or ending pages are leaves in the tree, with branching child nodes representing choices made by the reader. For example, Figure 2 represents the plot point given earlier. While the single parent rule is impor-

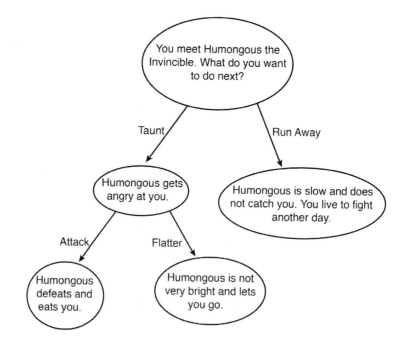

Figure 2. Simple Game Tree

tant in general, we relaxed this rule in the assignment to simplify redundant leaf nodes. So while two paths cannot lead to the same node in a strict tree, in this exercise, it was permitted. While a strict tree will terminate in a finite number of steps, allowing edges which loop back up the tree will not allow finite termination.

Implementing the Game Tree

The second half of the assignment was to implement a game based on the game tree. The students had the choice to implement a simple text-based game or a graphical click adventure. In previous courses, students had developed similar programs so they already possessed the necessary programming skills to complete the assignment.

If you're not a computer data person, you can skip the next section on game loops and go right to the section on Student Work (here we have a bit of "Choose Your Own Adventure"). The principal game loop consisted of the following:

1. If the current state is a terminal node, branch to step 7
2. Display the node state of the player including choices
3. Prompt the user for choice
4. Read and validate choice
5. Move the player to the next node based upon the choice
6. Jump to step 1
7. Display final state information and exit

The C++ implementation of the tree from Figure 2 would be as follows:

```cpp
#include <iostream>
using namespace std;
int main(int argc, char * argv[]) {
const int NSTATES=5;
const int MAX_CHOICES=2;
const int NO_TRANSITION=-1;
// Text description of the current state which is displayed to the user
char * stateDescriptions[]={"You encounter the troll Humongous the Invincible.\
\nDo you wish to 1) Taunt or 2) Run Away?",
"Humongous is angry at you. Do you wish to 1) Attack or 2) Flatter?",
"Humongous defeats and eats you.",
"Humongous is not very bright and lets you go.",
"Humongous is slow and does not catch you.\nYou live to fight another day.".
```

(continued)

```
};
// An adjacency matrix representation of a finite state machine
int stateTransitions[NSTATES][MAX_CHOICES]=
{{1,4},{2,3},{-1,-1},{-1,-1},{-1,-}};
int currentState=0;
int userChoice;
// Main game loop
while (stateTransitions[currentState][0]!=NO_TRANSITION) {
cout<<stateDescriptions[currentState]<<endl;
cin>userChoice;
if (userChoice<1 || userChoice>MAX_CHOICES)
cout<<"Invalid input. Please renter your choice."<<endl;
else
currentState=stateTransitions[currentState][userChoice-1];
}
cout<<stateDescriptions[currentState]<<"\nThe end.\n ";
}
```

Table 1: Sample run with user input shown in *italics*

You encounter the troll Humongous the Invincible.
Do you wish to 1) Taunt or 2) Run Away?
1
Humongous is angry at you. Do you wish to 1) Attack or 2) Flatter?
3
Invalid input. Please renter your choice.
Humongous is angry at you. Do you wish to 1) Attack or 2) Flatter?
2
Humongous is slow and does not catch you.
You live to fight another day.
The end.

Because C/C++ arrays are indexed starting at 0, the states are accordingly numbered in the same manner. The transitions are found by cross indexing the ***currentState*** with the ***userChoice*** in the ***stateTransition*** matrix. The state number of -1 is used as a flag to indicate that the node is a leaf. To expand the tree with a new node, it is only necessary to increment ***NSTATES***, add a line to ***stateDescriptions,*** and a new record to ***stateTransitions***. The above code is very brittle, using static allocation of the machine table and descriptions. A better solution would be to read that information from a formatted text file. Once that is done, the program becomes a general purpose solution to the problem and can be used for any number of adventures without modification by simply changing the text file. A simple format would be to use a colon as delimiter for the fields, as below:

> *description: state transition1: state transition2: ...*
> For example
> Humongous is angry at you. Do you wish to 1) Attack or 2) Flatter?:2:3
> Humongous defeats and eats you.:-1:-1

Student Work

The following are extracts from the game trees of three of the four students enrolled in the capstone course (used with their permission). Students were free to use their own notation in depicting the game tree, so the styles vary greatly. As a requirement of the project, there must be a height (maximum distance from the root to a leaf node) of 10. The assignment was split into three parts, each due after a week: (1) select a story, (2) draw the story tree, and (3) implement the game. Students generated and submitted a variety of graphical image files and .PDFs of their work. The assignment was given in the twelfth week of a sixteen-week traditional class.

Results

Although the concept was sound, it was a mistake to give this assignment to seniors in the capstone course late in the semester. They were busy working on completing their capstone projects; thus, the assignment was a distraction from their main focus. In addition, it was also too low-level a problem as they had been working on complex three-dimensional graphical programs for the past year. A text-based game simply did not engage their interest and, accordingly, their efforts. The game trees submitted were disappointing in their examination of alternative what-if scenarios and stayed rather narrowly within the confines of the original story. Because the three-part assignment proceeded sequentially without pause, the game trees were not reviewed before the students began work on the game. It would have been better to have made at least two passes at constructing the trees with more feedback from the instructor and their classmates prior to commencing the coding portion.

My current plan is to give a similar assignment to the freshman-level Introduction to Game Development class in the spring of 2015. As these stu-

Hansel and Gretel
The Game

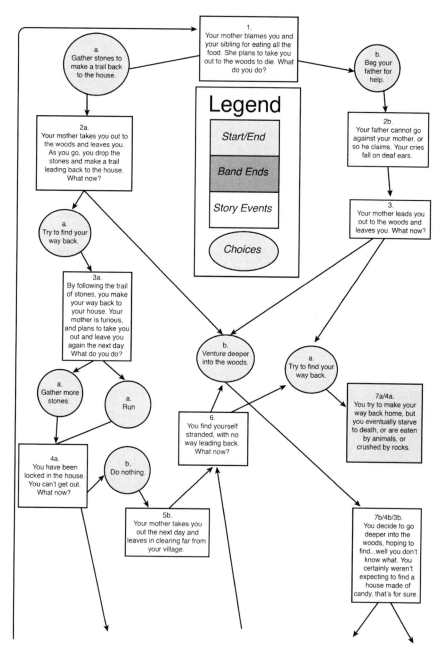

1.
Your mother blames you and your sibling for eating all the food. She plans to take you out to the woods to die. What do you do?

a.
Gather stones to make a trail back to the house.

b.
Beg your father for help.

Legend

Start/End

Band Ends

Story Events

Choices

2a.
Your mother takes you out to the woods and leaves you. As you go, you drop the stones and make a trail leading back to the house. What now?

2b.
Your father cannot go against your mother, or so he claims. Your cries fall on deaf ears.

a.
Try to find your way back.

3.
Your mother leads you out to the woods and leaves you. What now?

3a.
By following the trail of stones, you make your way back to your house. Your mother is furious, and plans to take you out and leave you again the next day. What do you do?

b.
Venture deeper into the woods.

a.
Try to find your way back.

a.
Gather more stones.

a.
Run

7a/4a.
You try to make your way back home, but you eventually starve to death, or are eaten by animals, or crushed by rocks.

6.
You find yourself stranded, with no way leading back. What now?

4a.
You have been locked in the house. You can't get out. What now?

b.
Do nothing.

5b.
Your mother takes you out the next day and leaves in clearing far from your village.

7b/4b/3b.
You decide to go deeper into the woods, hoping to find...well you don't know what. You certainly weren't expecting to find a house made of candy, that's for sure.

Figure 3. Patrick Hays, *Hansel and Gretel* extract

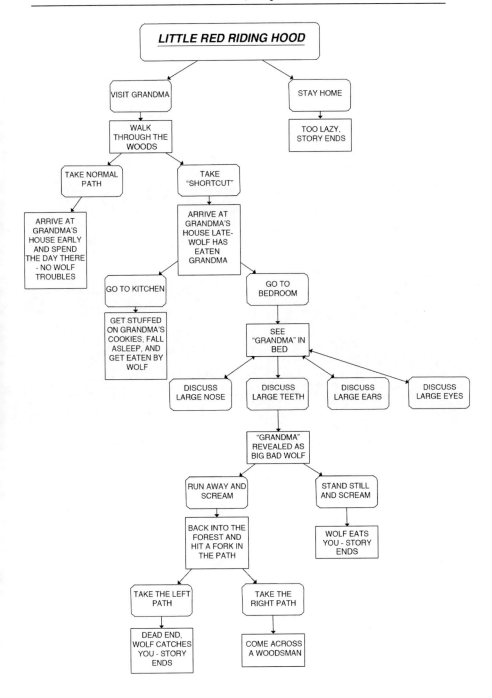

Figure 4. Alan Bible, *Little Red Riding Hood*

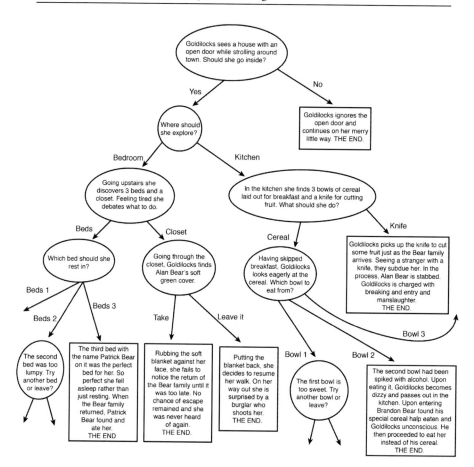

Figure 5. Austin Kreps, *Goldilocks* extract

dents will be lacking in coding skills, the instructor will create and provide a game engine to the students to read formatted text files to play their games. Removing the direct coding element will enable even non-coding students to complete game trees and still create a functioning game. A standard layout format and a stricter enforcement of the tree structure will be required. In addition, a single drawing application like Microsoft Visio or the online draw tool found at https://www.draw.io would make the student work more uniform and comprehensible to all. Peer review of their work would benefit from a common layout. In addition, testing their games with other players would allow an exploration of heat maps and data collection so vital in creating a satisfying game.

　　While the activity itself was not as successful as I desired, the soundness of the concept leads me to future assignments. Students completed the work on their own without additional help from the instructor. Targeting a lower-level class and removing the direct coding element should help to spur inventive game stories using a known story as their starting point. In other words, the assignment should be far more successful.

Works Cited

Field, Syd. *Screenplay: The Foundations of Screenwriting*, rev. ed. New York: Delta, 2005. Print.

"History of CYOA." *Choose Your Own Adventure*. 2014. Web. 4 May 2014.

Kraft, Scott. "He Chose His Own Adventure." *The Day* [New London] 10 Oct. 1981. Print.

Packard, Edward. *The Cave of Time*. New York: Bantam, 1982. Print. Choose Your Own Adventure Ser. 1.

Swinehart, Christian. "One Book, Many Readings." *Samizdat Drafting Co.* N.d. Web. 6 May 2014.

Freedom

Carolyn Taylor

"We all declare for liberty; but in using the same word we do not mean the same thing."—*Abraham Lincoln, 1864*

I teach an introductory American Government course in a regional university in the middle of America. The focus of my course is basic Constitutional principles. I find, however, that the moment students hear the word "politics" on the first day of class, many are inclined to disengage. One of my challenges is to overcome these unexamined reactions and to help students see that political theories have great practical value. To this end, I have refined a technique that enables students to get past their indifference and learn political ideas in a deeply meaningful and personal way. (College teachers in many disciplines may find this approach helpful.) The technique centers on using children's books to teach basic theories and ideas of democracy. Students develop positive attitudes toward political science and contemporary politics by linking new values and principles with familiar values and principles contained in children's literature.

It can be difficult in a political science classroom to elicit comments from students who may fear their own political naiveté. Children's literature can be used as a teaching tool in many ways. One approach uses children's literature to portray historical events; another utilizes the stories to debate specific issues; yet others use the stories as cultural narratives to explain and criticize political theories. Students are used to and are generally good at dealing with familiar and visual material; it would make sense to utilize the skills that they already have to help them in other areas. Most books and films touch people emotionally as they also reflect cultural values and historical meanings. They engage emotions, which contribute to the learning process. Finally, using children's books and films can actively contribute to reducing hierarchies in the class and encouraging discussion. By no means am I claiming that children's literature should replace the reading of primary literature and academic articles and books, but a combination of using children's material with the appropriate reading or topic for each class session does provide a fruitful addition to a traditional lesson.

In my earlier teaching years, I felt something was missing in my government classes and concluded it was the study of ideas. From the beginning of political history to today, men and women have fought and died over ideas, ideas like freedom, democracy, equality, power, and faith. I started to ask my students, "Who are we?" Our ideas tell us, and they tell the world. The United States government is built on ideas. Ideas affect the way Americans define their national ideals, their political goals, and their nation itself.

Political scientists, and many politicians, often describe the United States as a unique nation. Of course, every nation is distinctive in many ways. The United States is exceptional in large part because of at least seven key ideas that guide our politics. Most of them can be traced back to the Declaration of Independence. These seven big ideas are liberty, democracy, individualism, limited government, the American dream, equality, and faith. To begin with, all seven of these values I wrap together and introduce collectively as the concept of "freedom."

Freedom is a simple idea that is difficult to define. Freedom is essential to our political system but impossible to achieve. Do we even have the free will that is necessary to make political freedom a relevant concept? On the first day of the semester, I look at my students and say something like, "You think you are free, but look at yourself: You are sitting in a classroom with thirty other students reading from a silly syllabus from a silly professor in a course you are required to take to fulfill a silly requirement. You call that freedom? Are you free to stand up and tell the silly professor that you're already bored by her silly syllabus? If you were really free, you could do that. Go on, I dare you...." (Usually no one speaks and most look horrified.) I continue, "Don't worry. If freedom's 'just another word for nothing left to lose' (Kristofferson and Foster), and you're already enrolled for the course, why don't we dive deep in the concept of freedom and spend the next sixteen weeks trying to figure all of this out?" (Expressions of relief and interest now can be seen on their faces.) I tell them that in this course we are going to explore the complexity of freedom and liberty (using the terms interchangeably) with a focus on freedom in the political arena. A lively discussion of the following questions is the next step:

- What does it take for freedom to exist?
- What kinds of freedom are there: personal, economic, physical, intellectual, political, social, etc.?
- Who should enjoy freedom?
- Does personal freedom simply mean the right to be left alone, or something more, like freedom from want, from hunger, homelessness, illiteracy, unemployment, and illness?
- Does a society, in order to be free and flourish, need to suppress some freedoms?
- Does a "free" society abandon persons to "fend for" themselves?
- How has the concept of freedom changed?

"Everyone" agrees that freedom is a basic American value. But, in practice, Americans disagree about what it means—and what governments should do to ensure it. There are two different views: negative and positive liberty (or freedom). The more familiar view is negative liberty: freedom is the absence of constraints. Society's responsibility, from this perspective, is to make sure that others do not interfere with individuals pursuing individual goals. The government protects your right to believe what you wish, to say what you like, to profess any faith, all without constraints or fear of punishment. Negative liberty limits government action. Public officials violate your freedom when they collect taxes from you to feed the hungry or when they punish you for smoking marijuana. Negative freedom is the right to act as you want.

The alternative is positive liberty or the freedom to pursue goals. From this perspective, individuals cannot really be free if they lack the basic necessities of life. Protecting liberty means ensuring that every citizen has education, food, shelter, and health care. How can people truly be free if they are hungry or sick? This view justifies government action as a way to give all people an honest chance to achieve their desires and live the American dream.

I begin discussing these two views of freedom with my students and ask them if they believe in negative liberty or positive liberty, or do their beliefs fall somewhere in between? If they don't know yet, that's fine. Instead, let's think of a children's story that would be an example. Many times they come up with Cinderella as an example of negative liberty: freedom from constraints or the interference of others; and Hogwarts in the Harry Potter series as an example of positive liberty: freedom to pursue one's goals. Student comments include the following:

> There are many examples in young adult literature of freedom not always being the best thing. We see many examples of this in tales such as Harry Potter. Perhaps

total freedom is not such a good thing. Had Harry Potter been free to do as he pleased, then Voldemort would have probably killed him off a long time ago. Dumbledore knows what was best for Harry, so he made rules for Harry to follow, for his own safety. A balance must be achieved [Bryce Wilson].

Freedom is exhibited in the tale *The Little Mermaid*. As we are confined and limited by our government, Ariel is limited by her father. The government does not let us do certain things so that we are protected. Ariel's father only wants to protect her so he will not let her become human and get legs so she can go onto land and live a normal life [Garrett Hall].

Some people believe they are free *from* things, like persecution or having things stolen from them without punishments, while others believe they are free *to do* things, like write an article about their beliefs or to own a gun. The fact of the matter is that freedom is a mixture of both and can be illustrated in the famous story by Dr. Seuss, *The Cat in the Hat*.

Right from the beginning of the tale, the Cat demonstrates that the children are free to do as they wish. However, as the story goes on, the Cat begins to intrude on the life and wishes of the fish. Although these characters are simply made up, a connection can be made to real life people who interpret the term "freedom" too loosely. They forget that the people around them have the right to be free from the intrusion and infringement caused by their actions. One must beware of how one utilizes his or her freedom so that it does not harm others. This outright expression of freedom climaxed into full anarchy by the hands of the "Things" in *The Cat in the Hat*. This suggests that, paradoxically, freedom must be kept in order through control. However, can one be truly free if one is under the control of something?

When the Cat realizes the mistake that he made, he is able to pick up the pieces and correct what he had done; he was able to make himself better. That is also what freedom is about, having the opportunity of advancement, whether it be in education, in the workforce, or personally. Americans are able to change what they do not like about themselves, but also what they dislike about the community around them. This change can occur through peaceful assembly, protected by the First Amendment, but also through the underappreciated privilege of being able to vote. Americans can make changes and say what they dislike about something without being fearful of their government or of others infringing on their rights without punishment. Americans do not have to be fearful, bringing true peace of mind [Becka Pitts].

Now it's time for a beginning assignment. Early in the semester I ask them the following:

> Describe a situation in your life in which you faced a significant constraint on your freedom, either in one particular moment or over a longer period. What was the source of the constraint? How was the constraint imposed? What did the constraint prevent you from doing?
>
> Next, describe the institutional structure in which this constraint took place. How was power organized there, formally and informally? What roles did the peo-

ple involved play within that structure? How did all of this affect your ability to make meaningful choices?

Finally, with your case study in mind, construct your own definition of freedom in your own words. What is the core meaning of the term? What are the key components of a system that fosters freedom?

Much discussion and debate occurs after this assignment, and it's an easy segue to introducing political philosophers, such as John Locke, Thomas Hobbes, and Jacques Rousseau, and their respective theories regarding power and freedom. Thus, the semester is inaugurated.

Next we can begin to tie the discussion to today's government and political environment. Then we come to another assignment:

> Using a children's tale, or young adult literature, illustrate the meaning or concept of "freedom."

I now have a semester's worth of material from the student essays to use when we discuss all types of Constitutional issues as well as current events. Take *Cinderella*, for example:

> *Cinderella* is a good story that illustrates freedom because she was basically like a slave to her stepmother and stepsisters. Many, many Americans have felt like slaves at one point or another. A lot of us feel controlled by our jobs, or feel that society has too many rules that take away from our freedoms [Millie Wilson].

After reading quotes from these papers, we can more energetically talk about what freedom of speech or expression is. Why is it important? The creation and refinement of ideas—philosophical, political, artistic, and scientific—begin with thinking. If thought is limited, ideas also will be limited, and, eventually, expression will be inhibited.

Discussing a children's book in class provides a common reference point for participants in order to make their arguments, points, and views clear for the other members of the class. It can provide the "hook" with which to open a class discussion. At the same time, children's literature can make challenging abstract concepts, ideas, and theories more concrete. Works dramatize an event or idea by bringing a human face to even the seemingly more mundane issues in politics. A scene from a book, properly selected, can help students "step into the shoes" of a character acting in that scene; more importantly, they can be led to empathize, to consider the scope of options the characters may have available to them, and to reflect on the choices as well as on the normative implications at stake in complex circumstances. They might also learn that political reality, like drama, is essentially constructed.

This kind of dramatic confrontation with political (and sometimes violent) issues and theories dealing with questions of war and peace inevitably create a certain level of emotional engagement among students. These emotions evoke enthusiasm, encourage class participation, and, without a doubt, have the potential to provide the means for animated class debates and discussions. As students are familiar with children's tales and are used to talking openly about children's literature, the material can also work as a "leveling device" between the teacher and the students. The positive effect of familiarity with children's or teen stories is further underlined by the use of fantasy as metaphors for political events, issues, or theories. In contrast to clearly political adult literature where students may be more reserved about their comments, students seem to be more comfortable in participating in a discussion and hypothesizing about the meaning of a metaphorical story as there is no right or wrong interpretation. For example, according to Caleb Jones,

> One novel, *The Giver*, paints a vivid picture of what freedom is, what freedom is not, and why at a certain point, no matter how much it is called "freedom," we are not truly free. *The Giver* takes place in a place and time where all people are alike. Every day, citizens are given a drug to suppress senses that would make them otherwise unique. The concept of true freedom surfaces, though, when one boy decides to go against the law and refuse the drug and experience the world for what it truly is.
>
> Once the drug has worn off, a world of wonder and feeling opens up; he experiences true freedom. Instead of being an emotionless slave, he acquires a new sense of the world as he experiences emotions that exceed anybody's drug-induced state of disconnect. In addition, he now possesses one element that may very well be the backbone of freedom—free will. Free will is what makes freedom what it is. Free will lets us choose our own path and make decisions for ourselves. Free will is prevalent in several areas of our Constitution. For example, any of our "free of..." amendments are clear grants of free will. We have freedom of religion, freedom of the press, freedom of speech, freedom of assembly, and freedom of petition. All of these rights tell us that we have the absolute free will to choose what we believe, say, and so on. It was our craving of free will that fueled our Declaration of Independence from Great Britain. That is why this one aspect from *The Giver* illustrates well the concept of freedom.

One of the main strengths of using children's literature is that students are compelled to apply the theories to a much less self-evident object of study. Theories are scientific constructs, and, as such, they can be much better understood and their explanatory strengths and weaknesses can be much better uncovered if they are applied to a world which is as obviously artificially constructed as the theory itself, such as the world we encounter in a children's tale, movie, or even a video game. Sometimes by shifting the center of attention away from the "usual suspects" to an unfamiliar setting (a fictional world), students are encouraged to critically evaluate some basic ontological and epistemological assumptions and may gain a much better appreciation of closely-held (and otherwise unexamined) assumptions and theories. I have found this directs students away from stereotypes, labels, and personalities such as liberal/conservative, Obama/Romney, etc. That can lead to a deeper understanding of and more critical thinking about the theories' or subjects' potential and limits.

A good starting point is to identify in advance the respective theory's main assumptions in order to help students focus on the selection of a story which display the diverse bits and pieces of the theoretical approach. This serves to connect them to the material, and they feel invested in the subject. For example,

> In *Divergent* the government is broken down into factions. Each faction has a certain job and cannot do anything outside of that faction. One faction provides food, another protection, one law, another knowledge; and one governs the people. These factions dare not to step outside of their jurisdiction.
>
> *Divergent* is all about bridging the gaps in civil rights. A young girl risks her life and her families' to rebel against the factions. She breaks every law known and leaves the factions in hopes of finding freedom. Corruption has seeded itself deep within the government, as a single faction tries to take over. The story is one that inspires individuality and makes one happy to have the option to conform to choice of society [Cassandra Kibby].

After sharing this quote with the class from Cassandra Kibby on *Divergent*, we are set to have fruitful discussions regarding the branches of the U.S. government, the checks and balances, and the ever changing concept and application of federalism.

According to Pierce, there are four paths by which we as university or college professors can invite children (or our students) to experience the literature created for them:

1. The positive path of awe, wonder, mystery, and delight
2. The negative path of living through pain and suffering, daring the dark, and confronting our fears
3. The creative path of playfulness, imagination, and giving birth to new perspectives
4. The transformative path of justice and compassion, where pain is transformed into compassionate, just action [103].

I generally use the fourth path and examine the concept of "freedom" to hopefully create passionate lifelong readers, as well as informed and engaged citizens.

I ask students to think about the boundaries of freedom or who should enjoy freedom and what it takes for freedom to exist. Students have responded,

Alice in Wonderland (Carroll) exhibits what freedom looks like but, more importantly, exhibits that even when people thinks they're free, they still operate based on some type of governing. Alice thought getting away from the real world would be the key to her freedom but instead she just went into a little bit of a more chaotic world that still had its governing side showing through. Freedom doesn't come without some sort of limit. If there were no limit or boundary, then there would just be chaos and anything and everything would technically make sense. In all reality, however, that type of world could not function properly and would end up collapsing altogether. It is important to have a balance between the structure set in place and the freedom practiced within that, something Lewis Carrol showed in *Alice in Wonderland* [Nicki Saylor].

A specific children's tale called "Colourless Tiger" shows children the concept of freedom by using a black and white tiger trapped in a cage. An artist comes and frees the tiger from the cage while painting the tiger with color, causing the tiger to feel free: this shows children the concept of freedom in a fun story telling way. The story says being free is being happy and not being controlled by someone else. Even though in America people can't exactly do what they want, they have the right to speak, act, and think how they want. America has a lot of freedom, but we also have laws that are set to protect our country and the people. However, one main part of this freedom tale is that the tiger was set free where he was happy and never lost color again. It also shows children that the concept of meaning of freedom is to not be controlled by someone to a certain point, and also the freedom to express personality and feelings [Sierra Myers].

When *Frozen* is evaluated in an intellectual manner, it is easy to discover the relation to American freedom. Freedom is the ability to pursue goals, use talents, speak freely, take action, claim independence, and more. Since the characters in *Frozen* experience most of these privileges in some form, the movie provides a creative way to display some of the many variations of freedom [Kimberlee Nies].

Prompts and answers, such as these from *Frozen*, "The Colourless Tiger" (Sacristán) and *Alice in Wonderland*, provide a perfect introduction into a series of lectures and discussions regarding political philosophy, such as what happens when there is an absence of government, why governments are created, and where power should be, easily follow. We can even draw a connection from *Alice in Wonderland* (Carroll) to our political philosophers, such as Hobbes, Locke, Rousseau, and others.

We examine together the kind of people Americans have become from living in a free society. They are diverse, anxious, commercial, prosperous, hard-working, self-reliant, entrepreneurial, pragmatic, cooperative, proud, generous, idealistic, religious, convinced of their moral equality, jealous of their freedom, and committed to a national mission of extending that freedom to others. They are by no means perfect, however, as Britain's greatest Prime Minister Winston Churchill is alleged to have said, "Americans always do the right thing—after they've tried everything else." Mitchel Ortiz's essay on *Mulan* or Jessica Crowe's *Aladdin* gives a good introduction into class material dealing with civil rights and the history of struggles for suffrage past and present.

> The kinds of freedom that *Mulan* shows are equal rights, the pursuit of happiness, and the ability to break off from social norms. Mulan was destined to lead a submissive life in the beginning and in the end she was completely free. This type of freedom is the kind of freedom that is most associated with the American dream. The ability to overcome social class and past history in order to do what you were meant to is a fundamental liberty no better represented than in *Mulan*. This kind of freedom is exactly the kind of freedom that Thomas Jefferson had in mind when creating the Declaration of Independence, that man was born with the God-given right to life, liberty, and the pursuit of happiness. It is also the same ideal that Martin Luther King, Jr., spoke of when he said "I have a dream," that people from all over the world could escape the hauntings of their past and write a new destiny for themselves. This freedom allows for an individual to overcome what the statistics say and create a new course for the journey of life, freedom that works to give everyone an equal chance at happiness and to do what is necessary. The kind of freedom that *Mulan* depicts is the idea of the American dream today: to start on an equal playing field and then work to build the life that is wanted [Mitchel Ortiz].

> In Disney's *Aladdin*, Aladdin is faced with the struggle to get out of poverty and fulfill his dream to marry the princess, Jasmine. Jasmine is also battling for her own freedom to go beyond the palace walls and to marry whom she loves, not who her father chooses for her. These two characters both want freedom. This is where the extraordinary Genie comes into action. The Genie helps Aladdin fulfill his dreams by changing Aladdin's identity to Prince Abubu and equipping him to act the part of a prince suitable for Princess Jasmine. Genie symbolizes freedom, education, and endless possibility. Just as freedom and education can help people rise from poverty, the Genie helps Aladdin rise from poverty. Jasmine's situation can be looked at similarly. Genie helps Aladdin with the magic carpet to woo Jasmine and take her out to see the world, as she has always wanted to. This allows Jasmine to fall in love, and not with someone her father specifically picked for her to marry. Freedom allows people to do what they dream of, and marry whom they wish. Genie helped Aladdin and Jasmine do just this.

> *Aladdin* is just one of the many tales that can portray freedom as the authority to do what one desires. Many other tales may portray freedom as freedom from an oppressed government, freedom to be an individual, freedom from stereotypes, and more. Freedom can be taken on as many other meanings. Since freedom can be taken on by many other meanings, it can be hard to establish. In *Aladdin*, it took some

convincing for Jasmine's father to change the law to allow Aladdin to marry Jasmine, just as today's society struggles with allowing freedom but not too much freedom. Freedom is forever a changing concept, but with compromise and effort it can become a reality [Jessica Crowe].

Too often students are unenthusiastic or unengaged readers. It's never too late to change unenthusiastic, unengaged readers into enthusiastic, engaged, passionate readers and citizens. We are often shocked and disheartened when we encounter college students who are not readers themselves. It seems imperative for me to instill in them a sense that reading can and should be fun—and that it is okay to display an over-the-top love for books and, yes, politics too. This over-the-top love for books and politics is what I hope to demonstrate for my students and to instill in them some level of civic responsibility.

Many people can recall a children's book that turned them into a reader because they discovered that someone else had an imagination like theirs. One such person, Laura Miller, once observed, "It showed me how I could tumble through a hole in a world I know into another, better one, a world fresher, more brightly colored, more exhilarating, more fully felt than my own" (qtd. in Silvey). Many adult readers make these new discoveries of imagination for the first time in their college courses.

The political climate has resulted in a narrow, skills-based, standardized test-driven definition of reading founded on state and federally sanctioned and scripted instructional materials instead of a broader definition of literacy that suggests that literature provides multiple layers of meaning necessary for acquiring the strategies, stances, and ways of deep thinking that we should define as literacy. The results of this are often first experienced in college.

Instead of simply remembering specific dates or U.S. Supreme Court cases, young children and college students can be taught to read critically and to identify racism, sexism, and other prejudices that reproduce an unjust society and what the government can or should do about it.

Rather than discussing freedom in the abstract, I attempt to locate it in children's literature as a means of introduction and show how, at different periods in American history, different ideas of freedom have been conceived and implemented, and how the clash between dominant and dissenting views has constantly reshaped the idea's meaning. Freedom has always been a terrain of conflict, subject to multiple and competing interpretations, its meaning constantly created and recreated. Definitions of freedom relegated to the margins in one era have become dominant in the next, and long abandoned understandings have been resurrected when circumstances changed. The meaning of freedom has been constructed not only in Congressional debates and political discourse but on plantations and picket lines, in war zones and bedrooms. The story of American freedom has a rich and varied cast of characters, from Thomas Jefferson to Susan B. Anthony, to Franklin D. Roosevelt, to former slaves seeking to breathe meaning into emancipation during the Civil War, to gay rights activists seeking marriage equality. Examples from students on this point include the following:

> I choose *Mulan* to illustrate freedom because she believed that it was the right thing to disguise herself as a warrior to protect her father. Also, after being noticed as a woman, it did not stop her from going after her troops and saving the city. This movie can relate to the American history when women did not have any form of rights. Women did not have the right to vote, be treated equally or to join the army. However, Mulan went to the extent to defend her father knowing that he was not able to serve in the war and wanted to fight for what she thought was the right thing to do. She showed and proved to the city that bravery knows no gender [Arika Lee].

> The word pursuit defines the way freedom is accomplished. It was never given to us but it was won and it will always need to be defended. To me that is freedom, the ability to defend and fight for what I believe in even if it means standing alone. *A Bug's Life* represents this ideology better than any other story I can think of. The idea is that power should not come from fear but from the people [Abigail Peters].

> "It doesn't matter: *hakuna matata* ... sometimes bad things happen and there is nothing you can do about it. So why worry..." (*The Lion King*). Just when Simba was getting used to forgetting his past, his childhood best friend found him and reminded him of all the creatures he left behind that he was responsible for. Just as Simba, we often believe that when bad things happen, there is nothing we can do about it. But this statement is not true. Yes, bad things happen from both our own hand and the hands of others. Yes, we cannot change the past, but we can change the future. As an advisor of Simba put it, "the past can hurt, but we can either run from it or learn from it." As Simba lets this sink in, he finds his freedom. He returns to his people and lets the truth be told. He takes back the responsibility of being King. Freedom came drop by drop. It comes lesson by lesson. Every time we allow our past experiences to help us grow, we experience a little more freedom from our bondage to our past mistakes and our life circumstances. We learn how to be the boss of our futures.
>
> Simba's childhood, his isolation, and him taking responsibility for his kingdom, can show us patterns in the growth of freedom. The kingdom Simba will inherit in many ways is very similar to our own freedom. The way a king is able to make his own choices and not have anyone telling him what to do, is the way we see freedom. Yet we also see though a king that freedom *is* not without restrictions. Our choices and life circumstances can impair us from being completely free, but we can gain freedom by letting the past teach us so that we will be able to be the master of our future [Kristi Krumwiede].

The *Hunger Games* (Collins) books and movies have been a popular choice for students regarding this assignment.

> *The Hunger Games* is a novel about the "haves" and the "have nots"—that is, the people who have money and the people who don't. The Capitol has money and loads of it. This is personal freedom and also social freedom. The Capitol and the people in it have all the power, yet there is little power for the rest of the people. In order to achieve social and personal freedom, the districts rebel against the Capitol. Freedom is very limited in this society and the courage and determination by one woman shines all over the districts to bring that sweet freedom to everyone [Isaac Hollihan].

A fruitful discussion always then follows about how the *Hunger Games* is like American politics today, including how the game is played among elites, "it's a man's world," limited social mobility, jeopardizing the future with political paralysis, leaders ignoring real threats to their world, and race still mattering.

Good teaching is living your life honestly in front of students. From the framing of a course, to the choice of topics for inclusion on the syllabus, to the selection of readings, to the particular way we talk about ideas—teaching in the social sciences is political, through and through. Political, in this sense, does not mean partisan advocacy of a particular politician, party, or program, but rather recognizing the need to assess where real power lies, analyze how that power operates in any given society, and acknowledge the effect of that power on what counts as knowledge.

Every professor's "politics" in this sense has considerable influence on his/her teaching. The objective is not to strong arm students into agreement but to explain those choices and defend them. I tell students that the minute they think they have nailed down a definitive definition of freedom some new experience will force them to modify that. It is the struggle to understand the concept that matters, and I am just another person struggling as they are, albeit with the advantage of more extensive reading and life experience.

Students are initially amused or bemused to have a children's story used in a college class. With a dose of good humor, the themes of the books are initially applied to the day's lecture or activity. The class quickly gets into the spirit and lively discussion ensues as the lessons of the book are applied to daily reading and discussions.

Children's literature can be transformative for both children and adults, and I hope that the students who enter my classes will be moved to take action for social justice by the books we discuss.

The most important contribution of children's literature to the course is the communication climate it facilitates. Students understand that the instructor recognizes and legitimizes their fears and frustrations in the course. They come to understand the principles of politics arise naturally and need not be avoided.

The children's literature used in my course supports many learning objectives. It reduces student reticence, creates a positive communication climate, and provides common experiences that foster a creative learning environment. Children's literature makes a positive difference in teaching American government and politics.

The last several classes of the semester, we always focus on domestic and foreign policy.

I ask the students to talk about what kind of world we are living in today and how can it be made better. What hope is there for the future? Logan Hathcoat's comment on the *Grinch* is our introduction to this final topic.

> In *How the Grinch Stole Christmas*, one example of freedom is simple. It is simply the word "love." One could say that the Grinch is trapped in a hateful and lonely lifestyle. He doesn't experience true freedom at all, until he decides to turn his life completely around. He changes from someone who wants nothing good for anyone, to a man who just wants to help in any way possible. The book says, "His heart grew three sizes that day." There was a direct relation to the love he felt, and the sense of freedom that followed. A second representation of freedom in the *Grinch* is best described as a type of social freedom. The townspeople in the story are very much socially free. So what does it mean to have social freedom? It means a search for measures and possibilities to achieve the goals of social improvement. If you pay close attention to the small details of the story, you'll notice how all of the citizens work together to ensure the safety of the other citizens. They are free to do what needs to be done to improve society. This is true in today's world as well, when something is voted to be right or just, and the majorities agree, then the law will come into effect. So in a different way, we are still free to improve society to fit what we believe is right [Logan Hathcoat].

Works Cited

A Bug's Life. Disney-Pixar, 2003. DVD.
Carroll, Lewis. *Alice's Adventures in Wonderland and Through the Looking Glass.* New York: Bantam, 1984, Print.
"Cinderella." *Grimm Brothers' Home Page.* University of Pittsburgh, 2011. Web. 6 May 2014.
Collins, Suzanne. *The Hunger Games.* New York: Scholastic, 2010. Print.
Frozen. Disney, 2014. DVD.
Hobbes, Thomas. *Leviathan.* 1651. New York: Penguin, 1982. Print.

Kristofferson, Kris, and Fred Foster. "Me and Bobby McGee." 1969. *Kris Kristofferson: Me and Bobby McGee*. SMSP, 1990. CD.

Lincoln, Abraham. "Address at Sanitary Fair, Baltimore, Maryland." *University of Michigan Library Digital Collections*. University of Michigan, 2014. Web. 11 Oct. 2014.

The Little Mermaid. Walt Disney. 2013. DVD.

Locke, John. *Two Treatises of Civil Government*. 1690. New York: Everyman's Library, 1993. Print.

Lowry, Lois. *The Giver*. New York: HMH Books, 2014. Print.

Mulan. Disney, 2013. DVD.

Pierce, K. M. "Uses and Abuses of Children's Literature in the Classroom: Master Class for Teaching College Level Children's Literature Courses." *Journal of Children's Literature* 24.1 (1998): 103–05.

Roth, Veronica. *Divergent*. New York: Katherine Tegen, 2012. Print.

Rousseau, Jean Jacques. *The Social Contract*. 1762. New York: Penguin, 1968. Print.

Rowling, J.K. "Harry Potter" (series). *J.K. Rowling—Official Site*. 2012. Web. 6 June 2014.

Sacristán, Pedro Pablo. "The Colourless Tiger." *Free Stories for Kids*. Cuentopia Educativa SL, 2014. Web. 11 Oct. 2014.

Seuss, Dr. *The Cat in the Hat*. 1957. New York: Random, 1957. Print.

_____. *How the Grinch Stole Christmas*. New York: Random, 1957. Print.

Silvey, Anita. *Everything I Need to Know I Learned from a Children's Book*. New York: Roaring Brook, 2009. Print.

Thinking About
the Unthinkable

Paul B. Hatley

It is likely that if one teaches classes concerning twentieth-century United States history, some time will be devoted to various aspects of the Second World War. If a teacher wished to focus upon the Pacific Theater, she might tell students that, when the D-Day offensive against Adolf Hitler's "Fortress Europe" came on 6 June 1944, the U.S. Army, Navy, and Marine Corps had been battling the military forces of Imperial Japan since 7 December 1941 and were moving steadily in a two-pronged advance against the Japanese home islands. It might be useful also to mention the so-called top-secret Manhattan Project begun in 1939 to develop the world's first nuclear weapon.

The Trinity test, conducted in New Mexico at the Alamogordo Bombing and Gunnery Range on 16 July 1945, resulted in the first successful detonation of a nuclear device. With only two more remaining in the American arsenal, President Harry S Truman determined that the weapon's incredible destructive power would demonstrate to the Japanese leadership that ultimate victory was impossible. On 6 August 1945, the U.S. Army Air Corps B-29 *Enola Gay* dropped a 9,000-pound A-bomb nicknamed "Little Boy" over Hiroshima, Japan. Exploding at 1,800 feet above the city, the airburst killed at least 60,000 people instantly and leveled over four square miles. Two days later, the Soviet Union declared war on Japan and then proceeded to invade the southern half of Sakhalin Island, held by the Japanese since the end of the Russo-Japanese War in 1905, and Manchuria, renamed Manchukuo by its Japanese occupiers.

When the Japanese government responded to the nuclear attack with silence, Truman became convinced that a second bomb would have to be dropped. Thus on 9 August, another B-29, *Bockscar*, dropped "Fat Man" on

Nagasaki, incinerating perhaps as many as 40,000. After commanders within the army and navy launched an abortive coup d'état against him, Emperor Hirohito told his people by way of radio that they must "endure the unendurable" (qtd. in Fisher) and accept capitulation. Accordingly, on 15 August, Japan announced that it surrendered unconditionally, bringing the nearly four-year conflict to an end. To this day when historians discuss U.S. strategy in the Pacific against Japan, some argue that it was not nuclear blasts that led to surrender but fear of impending Soviet invasion. Others point out that it was the atomic bombs that played a critical role in achieving the American objective: they are correct, but why did some military planners believe that they were necessary and what about the human element? What was it like on the Japanese home front to experience and survive the blasts and what about the unintended and horrifying legacy of these wonder weapons that would continue to claim victims long after World War II had ended?

A non-fiction children's book that can provide a starting point for classroom discussion is Eleanor Coerr's *Sadako and the Thousand Paper Cranes* that appeared in 1977. Coerr draws her information largely from a work entitled *Kokeshi*, written by friends of a young Japanese girl named Sadako Sasaki. Coerr recounts that Sasaki, born in Hiroshima, was over two and a half years old when what some Japanese call the "Thunderbolt" struck her city. She also shows the reader that Sadako lived a normal life for several years after the war. Sadako loved to run. One day, however, she had some difficulty and doctors discovered she was affected by "the atom bomb disease," better known as leukemia.

The legend in Japan is that, if one can fold one thousand paper cranes, one can have a wish fulfilled. Sadako, hospitalized, folds cranes; her family folds cranes; her friends fold cranes. However, because medical science had no effective treatments at the time, she died on 25 October 1955.

But the story does not end there.

Coerr reports that a statue, the *Children's Peace Monument*, stands today in Hiroshima in Sadako's honor and that on Children's Day cranes folded by children around the world are heaped at its base.

Sadako's sad story has a preface and an afterword, but not in the book, *Sadako and the Thousand Paper Cranes*.

The preface is World War II.

Students typically will want to know and should be aware of how Western Powers and Japan came to conflict in the first place. The immediate causes of the Pacific War developed in 1940 after the French government signed an armistice (surrendered) with Nazi Germany in June. Well aware that the collaborationist Vichy government was too weak militarily to oppose its ambitions in French-Indochina (Vietnam), Japan believed it necessary to move troops into the north for strategic reasons. Behaving independently of governmental control from Tokyo, the Japanese Kwantung Army had occupied the Chinese province of Manchuria in 1931, renamed it Manchukuo, and continued to grab various Chinese towns until a Japanese invasion initiated the "China Incident" or the undeclared Second Sino-Japanese War in July 1937. Nationalist forces under Generalissimo Chiang Kai-shek continued to fight the enemy with economic and military aid supplied by Britain and the U.S. Accordingly, the Japanese occupied the port city of Haiphong on the Gulf of Tonkin and its rail lines in an effort to keep supplies from reaching Chiang. The Japanese also used other French landing strips, port cities, and rail lines.

January 1941 saw a Japan determined to go to war against the Western Powers as evidenced by the fact that its armed forces had already begun mobilization and the Imperial Navy expected to be ready for battle by 15 November. In July 1941, while Japanese aircraft pounded the new Chinese capital at Chungking with incendiary bombs, another indication of deteriorating relations surfaced when Japanese dive-bombers unintentionally dropped five bombs near the gunboat USS *Tutuila* anchored on the Yangtze River next to the U.S. embassy. A few days later, another bombing accident blew a hole in the ship's hull, but the crew managed to keep the gunboat afloat. The incidents were remarkably similar to another accidental attack in December 1937 that sank the clearly marked gunboat USS *Panay* on the Yangtze.

It was the Commander in Chief of the Japanese Combined Fleet, Admiral Isoruku Yamamoto, who designed the general operational plan for a surprise attack upon the U.S. Pacific Fleet anchored at Pearl Harbor on the Hawaiian island of Oahu. Historians often point out that Yamamoto's plan developed from his careful study of the successful British attack in November 1940 upon the Italian fleet at Taranto naval base, carried out solely by naval aviators from the aircraft carrier HMS *Illustrious*, operating in the Mediterranean Sea. Certainly this is true, but it should not be forgotten that the concept of a sneak attack upon a rival fleet was hardly new to Japanese naval planners; less than forty years earlier, without a declaration of war, Japan had begun the Russo-Japanese War in 1904 with a surprise torpedo-boat attack upon the Russian Asiatic Fleet at Port Arthur. In the following year, the fifty-three ships of the Russian Baltic Fleet had sailed around Europe, Africa, and Asia, only to be destroyed at Tsushima Strait by the Japanese Navy under Admiral Heihachiro Togo; the war's progression, its outcome, and legacy remained sources of great pride and continued to influence planning within the Imperial Navy.

On 7 January 1941, the Admiral presented his war plan, "Views on Preparations for War," to the Navy Ministry. By late April, Yamamoto's proposal had been evaluated favorably through a feasibility study and the specific aspects of the attack were hammered out over the following seven months. On 26 November, in keeping with the plan that became known as Operation AMO, the Kido Butai (Striking Force) of all six of the Empire's heavy aircraft carriers, *Akagi, Hiryu, Kaga, Shokaku, Soryu,* and *Zuikaku,* transporting the newly organized First Air Fleet, sallied from Hitokappu Bay in the Kuril Islands just north of Hokkaido Island to attack the U.S. Naval base on Oahu, over 6,000 miles to the southeast. Yamamoto maintained that if his naval aviators could deal the American fleet a devastating strike in the Hawaiian raid, Japan would have at least six months to a year to carry out unhindered Pacific operations.

Early on the morning of Sunday, 7 December 1941, without a declaration of war, "the unprovoked and dastardly attack," as Roosevelt put it, killed 2,403 Americans and wounded 1,178 more; among the capital ships present, four battleships sank while three others sustained significant damage. Ships were not the only targets. Aircraft sitting neatly on airfields at Ewa, Ford Island, Hickam, Kaneohe, and Wheeler were bombed and strafed to neutralize American airpower, though a few pilots did manage to get their planes airborne. The day following this "date which will live in infamy," Roosevelt spoke before the combined House and Senate; amid cheers and several standing ovations, Congress approved his request to go to war against the Empire of Japan.

Once the teacher has finished with the attack at Pearl Harbor, she can cover as many or few of the Pacific War battles as she wishes, but it is important that the student understands just how effectively the Japanese armed forces carried out their objectives in the Pacific offensive.

Among the depressing stories of one Japanese victory after another found in Western newspapers, there was, however, some positive news. In late December 1941, Roosevelt had instructed his service chiefs to devise a plan quickly to attack Japan itself. The top secret mission, conceived by a submariner, U.S. Navy Captain Francis S. "Frog" Low, was a task force under Admiral William F. "Bull" Halsey composed of the aircraft carriers *Enterprise* and *Hornet,* with sixteen B-25 Mitchells on each carrier's deck, and fourteen support ships, that sailed to within striking distance of Japan. On 18 April, the B-25s had done what few knew bombers could do—taken off from the deck of a carrier. Led by Lieutenant Colonel James H. "Jimmy" Doolittle, the planes with their five-man crews then headed toward Japan's main island, Honshu, where each bombed its predetermined military target successfully; incendiary bombs fell on Tokyo, Yokohama, Nagoya, Osaka, and Kobe.

Meanwhile, highly vulnerable to enemy air attack in the open ocean, Halsey's task force had turned around and sailed for Pearl Harbor. Short on fuel, Doolittle's raiders flew southwestward over the Sea of Japan, hoping to reach landing areas in China unoccupied by Japanese troops. All aircraft, except one whose pilot managed to land safely in the Soviet Union at Vladivostok, crashed and were beyond repair; seventy-one of eighty aviators survived. As Roosevelt had anticipated, news of the attack boosted American and Allied morale tremendously. In the midst of the largest defeats ever inflicted upon its armed forces, the United State had struck the heart of the Empire of the Rising Sun. The Japanese leadership was stunned by the raid that also left them clueless as to where the bombers had originated. Speaking to reporters and aware of the need for secrecy, Roosevelt claimed it was Shangri-La, referring to a fictional place somewhere in the Himalayan Mountains described in the popular James Hilton novel *Lost Horizon*.

The inter-war years saw the development of U.S. air power doctrine that placed primary importance on the bomber and its utilization in warfare. In the minds of prominent air power theorists, victory was to be achieved through high altitude precision daylight bombardment, carried out by unescorted bombers assaulting economic and industrial targets, which would erode an enemy's ability and desire to continue the conflict. Critical targets would be selected, targeted, and destroyed with minimal losses to attacking aircraft. The type of bombs to be dropped on Japan when the time came, however, was highly debated among airmen. As early as the 1920s, U.S. Brigadier General William "Billy" Mitchell noted that the highly flammable materials used in Japanese building construction, such as wood and paper, made the cities of the Sunrise People entirely vulnerable to incendiary ordnance dropped from aircraft.

With the weather's cooperation on 19 January 1945, the B-29s of XXI Bomber Command with their eleven-man crews made their way toward Kobe where they decimated a Kawasaki aircraft factory. Success, however, had come too late; the impatient Hap had already pulled LeMay from China to assume command. Initially, LeMay made no changes to the bombing techniques employed by former commander Hansell, but soon a series of disappointing raids made it obvious that a more radical approach was necessary. In the darkness of 9–10 March 1945, over three hundred B-29s appeared in Tokyo's skies. To negate the possibility of jet stream winds interfering with bomb trajectories, the aircraft flew at anywhere from 9,000 to 4,900 feet and rained at least 2,000 tons of napalm bombs on the capital city. Over 83,000 people were killed, 41,000 were injured, 250,000 buildings burned to the ground, and a million were left without homes. A bomb density of twenty-five tons per square mile had achieved staggering results. Bombings continued for the rest of the war, and Japan's Pacific Empire imploded as the Allies continued to drive the Japanese from islands such as the Philippines, Okinawa, and Saipan.

An American invasion of the Japanese home island of Kyushu was planned for 1 November. The War Department estimated that the Japanese archipelago had about 2,000,000 well-armed soldiers with plenty of ammunition, ready to defend it. Battles, such as the one for Okinawa, for example, were bloody demonstrations of how fierce Japanese resistance could be and likely foreshadowing what awaited the Americans in Japan. The U.S. had taken the island, but the cost was high. Ground forces lost 7,374 killed, with wounded numbering nearly 32,000; more than 4,900 U.S. Naval personnel operating in ships supporting the assault on Okinawa were killed, while 4,800 were wounded.

When President Truman received news of the successful atomic test on 16 July, whether or not to drop the bomb was never questioned; Truman believed that the weapon would hasten the end of the war and save thousands of lives. First, though, the Japanese were given the Potsdam Declaration that provided an opportunity to avoid the bombs. Sent via radio transmissions on 26 July, the Declaration called upon them to surrender unconditionally and explained how their nation was to be treated once the war ended. Four days later it was obvious that the Japanese leadership had ignored the Declaration, so Truman gave the order to "Release when ready...." The XX Air Force at Tinian was tasked with delivering the bomb to one of four cities not obscured by cloud cover: Hiroshima, Kokura, Nagasaki, and Niigata. The destruction of Hiroshima on 6 August was followed by another atomic blast at Nagasaki three days later and Japan's unconditional surrender on 15 August.

This is the point at which Sadako's story begins.

The war was over but life for the survivors in Hiroshima or Nagasaki would be quite different from other Japanese. In Japan, a person such as Sadako Sasaki is known as Hibakusha (exposed person). To some, the term means any survivor of an atomic blast; to others, it is someone who was within two kilometers (1.242 miles) of ground zero. Another Hibakusha is Toshiko Tanaka. Born in 1938, she was six years old when "Little Boy" devastated her hometown Hiroshima. Unlike Sadako, she never developed leukemia and today she travels the world explaining the legacy of the atomic bombs and what life has been like in Japan for the Hibakusha. On 2 December 2013, with an interpreter, Tanaka presented an informative and informal talk to a group of students and professors at Rogers State University in Claremore, Oklahoma.

She explained that from 1945 onward, the atomic blast survivors have faced considerable discrimination from the Japanese people. As a result, many Hibakusha have tried to hide their past, including Tanaka, who has only recently begun telling her story. Some shun them or will not employ them because they believe that the Hibakusha is contaminated with nuclear radiation that can be passed from person to person. Parents often forbid their children to marry Hibakusha because they believe that their babies will be born with severe birth defects. Tanaka noted that her own son, who is married and was born quite healthy over forty years ago, has long feared having children. In 2013, he and his wife agreed that it was time to start a family, but he remains anxious. Survivors also spend their lives wondering if their exposure to radiation will lead to various cancers. Accordingly, but without malice or recriminations, Tanaka made a case for banning nuclear weapons. At least 70,000 people died in Hiroshima when the bomb detonated, but another 70,000 were dead by the end of the year from severe tissue destruction and radiation poisoning. As years passed, those who were identified as Hibakusha endured discrimination from their fellow citizens; some developed cancers; others wondered if and when they might be diagnosed with cancer; still others worried that the bomb would deprive them of a normal family life.

Thus Tanaka opposes nuclear weapons not because of what occurred on the 6th and 9th of August 1945, but due to the legacy they left for the Hibakusha and the similar legacy which will remain if nuclear weapons are used again—a life that no one should have to experience.

These two stories will do for students what strict history lessons might not. From the facts, names, and dates, students will have the basic knowledge, intellectual knowledge to talk about the war—about the bombs, about the aftermath.

However, reading about Sadako and hearing about Tanaka will add emotional understanding of a perhaps necessary, but regrettable period in history.

Works Cited and Suggested Sources

Allen, Thomas B., and Norman Polmar. *Code Name Downfall: The Secret Plan to Invade Japan—And Why Truman Dropped the Bomb.* New York: Simon & Schuster, 1995. Print.

Arnold, Henry H. *Global Mission.* New York: Harper, 1949. Print.

Coerr, Eleanor. *Sadako and the Thousand Paper Cranes.* New York: Puffin Books. 2008. Print.

Cooling, Benjamin F., ed. *Case Studies in the Achievement of Air Superiority.* Washington, DC: Center for Air Force History, 1994. Print.

Donovan, Robert J. *Conflict and Crisis: The Presidency of Harry S. Truman, 1945–1948.* New York: W.W. Norton, 1977. Print.

Fisher, Max. "The Emperor's Speech: 67 Years Ago, Hirohito Transformed Japan Forever." *The Atlantic* 15 Aug. 2014. *The Atlantic.* Web. 5 Oct. 2015.

Frank, Richard B. *Downfall: The End of the Imperial Japanese Empire.* New York: Random House, 1999. Print.

Hilton, James. *Lost Horizon.* New York: W. Morrow, 1933. Print.

Hoyt, Edwin P. *How They Won the War in the Pacific: Nimitz and His Admirals.* New York: Weybright and Talley, 1970. Print.

Kreis, John F., ed. *Piercing the Fog: Intelligence and Army Air Forces Operations in World War II.* Washington, DC: Air Force History and Museums Program, 1996. Print.

Layton, Edwin T. *"And I was there": Pearl Harbor and Midway—Breaking the Secrets.* New York: W. Morrow, 1985. Print.

Nalty, Bernard C., ed. *Winged Shield, Winged Sword: A History of the United States Air Force, Vol. I, 1907–1950.* Washington, DC: Air Force History and Museums Program, 1997. Print.

Nimitz, Chester W., and E. B. Potter, eds. *The Great Sea War: The Story of Naval Action in World War II.* Englewood Cliffs, NJ: Prentice Hall, 1960. Print.

Prados, John. *Combined Fleet Decoded: The Secret History of American Intelligence and the Japanese Navy in World War II.* New York: Random House, 1995. Print.

Roosevelt, Franklin D. "Address to Congress Requesting a Declaration of War with Japan." *The American Presidency Project.* University of California Santa Barbara, 2014. Web. 5 Oct. 2014.

Schom, Alan. *The Eagle and the Rising Sun: The Japanese-American War, 1941–1943.* New York: W.W. Norton, 2004. Print.

Slackman, Michael. *Target: Pearl Harbor.* Honolulu: University of Hawaii Press, 1990. Print.

Truman, Harry. "Truman's Diary on the Atomic Bomb. Digital History ID 1186." *Digital History.* University of Houston, 2014. Web. 5 Oct. 2014.

Wainwright, Jonathan M. *General Wainwright's Story: The Account of Four Years of Humiliating Defeat, Surrender, and Captivity.* Garden City, NY: Doubleday, 1946. Print.

Weigley, Russel F. *The American Way of War: A History of United States Military Strategy and Policy.* New York: Macmillan, 1973. Print.

Biology Tales

D. Sue Katz Amburn

In my field, biology—specifically microbiology—I use stories as analogies to help students grasp new concepts and terminology. By introducing some terminology and concepts using stories, I hope to provide that "bridge" between common knowledge and field specific knowledge. It is only in the past few years that I have consciously developed the use of stories to illustrate some difficult concepts for my students.

Many biology and microbiology instructors use case studies to help students. Case studies illustrate concepts and assist the students' developing critical thinking skills. I do use case studies when I teach immunology. The immunology case studies I use include already-prepared and published cases and cases I create from the scientific literature. However, the majority of cases designed for microbiology are focused on disease and infectious agents, not illustrating the structure and function of microbes.

Microbiology studies microbes, especially Bacteria, Archaea, and viruses, which are very small. All living organisms can be divided into three groups. Those which contain their genetic information, DNA, in a nucleus are grouped as Eukaryotes, while Bacteria and Archaea are both groups of single-celled organisms which do not have nuclei and which have very different characteristics from each other. The last group, viruses, does not have many of the characteristics of living cells and consists only of nucleic acids wrapped in a protein coat. Microscopes can be used to see cells, but viruses are so small that they must be seen using the more highly magnifying electron microscopes or tracked by the damage caused in a host cell. The small size of these microbes offers one of the major challenges to student learning. Sure, you can culture Bacteria and Archaea—but only a small percentage of them. At the school at which I teach, all students who take the lecture portion of the course also take the laboratory. There, they get hands-on experience culturing and observing the organisms. (That is not the case at many schools.) As much fun as microbiology lab is, it is also an instructor-intensive and expensive course. Sometimes, microbiology courses have no lab or are taught online, and sometimes, the lab is a stand-alone course.

As a microbiologist, I am well supported by conferences and organizations. I have developed materials myself and provided peer review for other materials submitted to digital libraries, such as American Society for Microbiology's MicrobeLibrary.

A very important focus in my professional life is student learning and the acquisition and development of proper resources to help my students learn.

So, where did storytelling come into the picture for me as a teaching method different from case studies? In my second or third year teaching here, I thought of a story that would provide entertainment, a visual experience, *and* help students understand a concept. The class was an evening microbiology course. Most of my students in this class work hard all day and have a difficult balance of family, school, and work. This microbiology course is one that they *must* take to get into our nursing program, and they are usually not too enthusiastic when the course begins, preferring anatomy and physiology. Microbes seem more abstract than human anatomy, and understanding the material requires the student to be able to visualize what is being taught. This is one reason that I use many pictures and drawings during class—and animations when they are relevant. When I took my foundation courses for certification as a secondary educator, I learned about Piaget's stages of intellectual development. Although I have not tested my students to determine which stage they are in, I do believe that many of them are in the concrete operational stage (stage three of four), rather than formal operational stage (the fourth and final stage), limiting their ability—or perhaps their desire—to think in the abstract. But the abstract is what microbiology often seems to be.

I wanted to find a way to draw my students out of their "listen" mode. So, that first time, I brought a bag of about 500 test tube caps to class. These are small plastic caps that pop onto the top of the culture tubes we use in lab. They are about an inch wide and an inch-and-a-half long. I had reached the section of the course where I begin describing how cells grow–something with remarkably practical aspects. For instance, when prescribed antibiotics for an infection, who among us has dutifully taken *all* the prescribed antibiotics? Many individuals take them until they feel better, and a lot of people will admit to stockpiling the pills "for later use." That is a really bad practice, and this concept of cell growth tells why—once you grasp it, that is.

In order to introduce the concept, I tell students a fractured fairy tale (apologies to *Rocky and Bullwinkle*), combining two different stories. It goes something like this: Long ago, in faraway Persia, there lived a great king. His wife did him wrong, and being king, he took his revenge by killing her. But he grew lonely and decided that he needed female companionship, but that he would never trust a woman again. So he held searches throughout his land to find the most beautiful women. Each day, he would marry a beautiful woman and spend the wedding night with her. Each morning, she would be killed, and he would marry again. In that manner, he never invested his heart and could not be hurt. Scheherazade was beautiful, and she caught his eye one day. He forced her (he was king, after all) to marry him. That night, in the bed-chamber, she entertained him by telling him a story, but she had not concluded the story by the time the king fell asleep. In the morning, the king allowed her to live another day so that she could finish the story. So Scheherazade did finish the story that night, but she quickly started another story. She continued doing this for ... 1001 nights. At that point, the king decided that his faith in women was restored and that he loved her and she him. Pretty standard telling of the story to this point. Interestingly enough, my younger students don't know it. Still, everyone in the class gets a little antsy—this fairytale doesn't seem to have any relevance. But the relevant part is coming up.

The king tells her that he loves her and she has restored his faith in wom-ankind. In return he owes her, up to half his kingdom. She thinks it over and tells him she doesn't want much, just a little rice. Now for the microbiology part. That game that people play, chess? There are, what, 64 squares on the board? How about just a little rice—one grain on the first square (the first student gets one test tube cap), doubling the number for each square. Well, the king thinks he has a bargain. The second student (square) gets two test tube caps, the third gets 4 (the whole class is now calculating and counting), the fourth gets 8, the fifth gets 16, the sixth gets 32, the seventh 64, eighth 128, ninth 256 (let's round to 250).

By the fifth student, I can stop counting out the caps. But it shortly becomes very clear that by doing this, Scheherazade has outwitted the king, her husband. There is not enough rice in the kingdom to pay her off. She now owns the kingdom and we all cheer for woman's lib, since there are typically many women in the class. Then we turn to the more serious course material. *Now* the relevance to microbiology becomes obvious to students. Cells can multiply from very small numbers into gigantic numbers in short periods of time. When you redo the numbers (1 cell becomes 2 in one division; two cell divisions make 4 cells; three become 8 cells; four become 16 cells; five—32;

six—64 ... (keep at it for a little while), and add in time required for each cell division (for *Escherichia coli*, 20 minutes, for instance), you can see that organisms can regrow from very small numbers into very large numbers in a short span of hours. So, to complete the lesson, I have them revisit their concept of taking an antibiotic "just until you feel better." When you do that, you select for the organisms which are a little more resistant to the antibiotic, and by leaving them alive, they can regrow quickly. By taking a course of antibiotics the full length of time, you should be clearing them all out of your body. The story makes the point more obvious.

I use a shorter vignette when trying to push students into comprehending the differences between structure and function of two cell components: cell membranes and cell walls. All living organisms (not viruses: they don't count as cells) have a cell membrane. Cell membranes control movement of materials into and out of the cell; they provide the boundary between the inside (cytoplasm or cytosol) of the cell and the outside environment. They have lots of other functions too, which aren't relevant here. But cell membranes must be flexible so that temperature doesn't affect the permeability. On the other hand, some organisms have cell walls (not us, we are animals). Plants, fungi, bacteria, and Achaea do have cell walls, although the cell wall compositions are different. Cell walls provide a rigid support on the outside of the membrane, an exoskeleton for the cell. They give the cell its shape, and they protect the cell by preventing it from blowing up through absorption of water when in a low salt concentration. Two different structures. Two entirely different functions. Students have a devil of a time telling the difference and conveying that they understand the difference on a test. To be fair, I have seen some published papers, texts, and non-scientific articles totally confuse the two as well. But *not in my class*!

Enter Big Bad Wolf and the three little piggies. If you were the three little pigs, would you rather be in a tent while the Wolf huffed and puffed to blow it down to get to you? Or would you rather be in a brick building while he huffed and puffed? Tents (flexible cell membranes) don't protect. Bricks (making a rigid cell wall) do.

There are a couple of other stories I tell with concepts. Goldilocks is one I have just begun to use in the past two years. We refer to the Goldilocks temperatures. All organisms have an optimal temperature at which they can function. There is also a minimal and a maximal temperature at which they can function. Each organism is made of one or more cells. Each cell, whether a single celled organism or a multi-celled organism also has optimal, maximal, and minimal temperatures. A final layer of detail is that each cell contains many proteins that help it organize properly and function. Each different protein, because of its unique construction (sequence of amino acids) has its own optimal, minimal, and maximal temperature. These three temperature points are the cardinal temperatures.

We can easily determine the cardinal temperatures for cells in the lab by incubating at different temperatures. The cardinal temperatures of an organism are used to classify it as a member of a particular temperature group. But the cardinal temperature concept and terminology seem to be difficult for my students—not just for those who hope to enter the nursing A.S. program, but also those who are taking the upper level biology majors microbiology course. One day, I apparently did not get the point across (students had a hard time on the test; they confused the cardinal temperatures with the temperature *groups* that are determined by the cardinal temperatures). When I started to reteach, I found myself telling the story of Goldilocks. When I got to "It was toooo hot," all the students started chorusing with me. We all chanted "toooo cold" and then, "just right," and you could see the light click on. So now, the cardinal temperatures are the Goldilocks temperatures. We have extended the analogy to salt and pH concentrations as well.

The last story I commonly tell in my microbiology courses is to illustrate feedback inhibition. This process is encountered when we study metabolism. Feedback inhibition is a process used to block a metabolic reaction as long as there is too much product present. Because there is a cost to a cell to do each metabolic reaction, it benefits cells to prevent unnecessary metabolic reactions from occurring. In my story, I speak of a bakery whose only product is chocolate cakes. In this story, to avoid waste, the owner has decreed that the store cannot have more than two chocolate cakes at any one time. Once a cake has sold, the three men in the back can warm the oven, measure and mix the materials for one cake, put it in the oven and bake it, then remove it and decorate it before they send it up to the front of the store to be displayed and sold by the worker in front. As long as two cakes are up front, the three men in back sit and play poker, only working when one cake has sold and they collaborate to make a new cake.

My use of these stories doesn't involve students in a deep analysis of the meaning of the stories. But they make learning microbiology more enjoyable, creating a break from the normal lecture, and, in the process, the concepts become more transparent. For me, the stories serve several functions. They help the invisible world be more approachable, showing students that these little cells have similar components and are affected by the same things that affect us bigger organisms. Because students come from a wide variety of backgrounds, my stories are unusual enough to provide a "hook" for many students to link new knowledge into. And when needed, they provide a framework for students to correct information that they learned partially or incorrectly, allowing them to succeed academically. And, after all, that's what we teachers really desire.

Biblical Studies through Yertle, Aslan and Little Red Riding Hood

GREGORY STEVENSON

Teaching Biblical studies courses at a Christian liberal arts college is a privilege, but one that is often challenging. In a typical freshman course on biblical literature, I normally have students representing various denominational and non-denominational perspectives. Some are fundamentalist Evangelical Christians who read the Bible as the literal, inspired Word of God, and others are secular atheists who view the Bible as just a "fairytale." If I were a historian teaching an introductory class on ancient Egyptian history, I could walk in on day one relatively confident that my students know as much about Egyptian history as they do quantum mechanics. Instead, I walk into a class full of students who bring with them years' worth of hardened preconceptions and who are conditioned to read the Bible through a very specific lens—and often only that lens.

Consequently, when introducing academic concepts into such a diverse minefield, I seek out common ground. Though students may debate the historical witness of the Bible or how it functions as a sacred text, what they all agree on is that the Bible is *literature*. When I can first get students to think about how great literature functions, the task of getting them to apply those same concepts to the Bible becomes much easier. Children's literature, in particular, serves this purpose well. It provides a neutral starting point that is comfortable, familiar, and non-threatening. A student intimidated by meeting an advanced, critical concept in an academic classroom is charmed when meeting that same concept in *Where the Wild Things Are*. By tapping into the universal qualities of literature as represented in children's stories, students recognize patterns and features that, when applied to academic concepts, make those concepts more accessible. So I introduce the creation story of Genesis 1–2 by way of *Yertle the Turtle*, the apocalyptic symbolism of Revelation by way of the Chronicles of Narnia, and the literary function of the Gospels by way of "Little Red Riding Hood."

Yertle the Turtle *and Worldview Formation*

Dr. Seuss (aka Theodor Geisel) once said that the reason he communicates so well to children is that he doesn't try to communicate to children, but instead treats them as equals (Nel 4–5). This sort of adult-oriented perspective combined with the imagination and wonder of childhood allows his works to build a bridge between the complex and the simple. His writings are thus perfectly suited for stripping away the often-confusing veneer of academia and leaving a truth behind that is powerful in its simplicity.

The creation account of Genesis 1–2 is one of the more controversial sections of the Bible due to its prominent role in debates over evolution versus creationism. One group treats the biblical account as a pre-scientific record of superstition, while the other treats it as a science textbook. My goal in class is to change the nature of the debate by getting students to appreciate how Genesis 1–2 was designed to function as a *story*. One valuable function of stories (whether non-fiction or fiction) lies in the way they challenge existing worldviews and aid in the construction of new ones. The rise of Hitler, the threat of Nazism, and the atrocities of World War II presented an all-too-common narrative of how arrogance, ambition, and prejudice combine to create totalitarian regimes and oppressive ideologies. The stories that we tell of that time are not simply neutral accounts of historical events but are also stories designed to highlight the failure of such ideologies and point to a better way.

The worldview put forth by Nazism had a profound effect on Dr. Seuss, who once confessed that he had possessed no real social consciousness until the rise of Hitler (Nel 46–47). Thereafter, Seuss recognized the need to counter the worldview proposed by Nazism with a better one. One such attempt was "Yertle the Turtle."

If my students are puzzled when I begin my introduction to Genesis by reading *Yertle the Turtle*, they don't protest too loudly—or, in fact, at all— because most of them would rather read "Yertle" than Genesis. *Yertle the Turtle* is a story about an ambitious turtle who is the king of a pond, but not content to be so. His ambition drives him to build a throne higher than all he can see, thus expanding his kingdom to everything within his view. He announces, "I'm Yertle the Turtle! Oh, marvelous me! For I am the ruler of all that I see" (Seuss 166). Yertle builds his throne literally on the backs of the regular turtles who live in his pond, forcing them to stack themselves one upon the other with him seated at the top. As Yertle's ambition propels him to build his throne ever higher, eventually one small turtle at the very bottom of the stack, a simple turtle named Mack, decides he's had enough. He burps, and his burp dislodges Yertle from this throne, causing him to plummet and sink deep in the mud. As the great and marvelous Yertle plummets from his throne to become nothing more than "King of the Mud," *Yertle the Turtle* concludes with the line:

> And the turtles, of course ... all the turtles are free
> As turtles and, maybe, all creatures should be [Seuss 179].

Once my students become aware of the fact that, as Dr. Seuss himself has stated, the character of Yertle was deliberately modeled on Adolf Hitler (Cott 29), they immediately begin to see the story as more than just a tale of turtle politics. It becomes instead a story about how human ambition can lead to oppression of others and about the nobility of the common person who dares to defy tyranny. It offers them a different worldview than that proposed in Nazi Germany.

When we turn our attention towards Genesis, I inform my students that Genesis 1–2 was not the only creation story in antiquity. About the time when Genesis was written, another creation story was the dominant one in the culture of the Mesopotamian world. This Babylonian account of creation, called *Enuma Elish*, envisioned creation as the result of divine ambition and conflict. Set in a time when many deities were jockeying with each other for position, the god Tiamat challenged Marduk's sovereignty. Marduk defeated Tiamat in a violent and bloody war and then split Tiamat's carcass in two, forming the earth with one piece and the sky with the other. Finally, Marduk killed another deity aligned with Tiamat and used his blood to create human beings for the purpose of feeding and serving the gods.

Any creation story is not only about the world's origin but also about proposing a particular interpretation of the world. I ask my students, "Assuming that the creation account of *Enuma Elish* is an accurate description of how the world came into being, how does this story make you feel about the world and about yourself?" The responses are very predictable. They say it makes them see the world as a place of chaos with no discernible purpose for its existence and provides them with a devalued sense of self-worth since the sole purpose of humanity is enslavement to the gods.

Then I read them excerpts from Genesis 1 in which God creates the world in a deliberate and orderly fashion, creating human beings in his own image and granting them responsibility to care for his creation, and, as his creation unfolds, he seven times declares it to be "good," with a final declaration that all he has made is "very good" (*New Revised Standard Version*, Gen. 1:31). When I then ask students how this account of creation makes them feel about the world and about themselves, I receive very different responses. The point I emphasize is that Genesis 1–2 is not a science textbook designed to give detailed answers as to *how* the world was created; rather, it is a theological story telling us *who* created the world and *what* kind of world he created. A purpose of the Genesis account was to provide an alternative narrative to the dominant creation story of that time. In a world that viewed creation as resulting from a chaotic war of ambition between rival deities in which humanity was an afterthought, Genesis 1 asserts that creation was not an act of divine ambition but of divine love, with humanity formed in the very image of God.

Once students realize how Genesis 1–2 functions as a story, they then recognize how it continues to function in the same way today. Just as the ancient Mesopotamian world had a dominant creation story (*Enuma Elish*) that Genesis 1–2 countered, so also we today have a dominant creation story (The Big Bang and attendant evolutionary theories) that Genesis 1–2 counters. Arguably, the similarities between *Enuma Elish* and the Big Bang Theory are noteworthy. Both represent creation as an act of violence and disorder (war vs. random gases igniting in an explosion); both represent the world as a place with no higher purpose; and both present a low view of humanity (humans as slaves vs. humans as descendants from lower life forms). In this context Genesis 1–2 functions today much as it did in its original context by offering an alternative understanding of the world and of humanity.

Trying to get students to move past the typical debates regarding which creation story (Big Bang vs. Genesis) is more scientifically accurate and instead getting them to think in terms of how each of these creation stories shapes our worldview differently is a difficult task, but one made much easier by Dr. Seuss whose tale of a plain old turtle named Mack and his ambitious overlord demonstrates how stories shape the way we see the world.

Narnia and Apocalyptic Symbolism

One of the most intimidating books in the New Testament is the book of Revelation. It is the only book in the Bible of which I hear students claim to be frightened. Part of that fear stems from the book's content, with its visions of widespread devastation and eternal judgment. Yet, ultimately, what most intimidates people is the book's seeming incomprehensibility. Revelation belongs to an ancient literary genre known as apocalyptic literature; one of the hallmarks of this genre is the heavy use of symbolism, which can easily promote confusion. What I envision as my primary task in classes on Revelation is to lessen that fear and intimidation by helping students better understand how symbolism is designed to function within apocalyptic literature.

One common misconception among many of my students is that the symbolism of Revelation functions as a code designed to obscure the book's real message from everyone except the Christians who possess the key to breaking that code. The problem with this viewpoint is that it treats the symbolism of Revelation as a problem to be solved, essentially something that needs to be removed in order to find the message behind it. What I stress, instead, is that the symbols *are* the message. Reading Revelation does not require decoding the symbols but embracing the symbols by learning how symbols reveal truth.

Because Revelation is such a highly charged book, students find this concept much easier to accept when they first meet it in another, less intimidating form. Whenever I tell students that reading Revelation often feels like reading a fantasy novel, I see multiple heads nodding in assent. With its description of fantastical journeys, demonic creatures, cataclysmic battles, dragons, and multi-headed beasts within a story about good versus evil, the book of Revelation reads more like *The Lord of the Rings* than what one normally expects from a Biblical text. As a genre, fantasy employs symbolism as a means of communicating truth, providing a valuable framework for thinking about apocalyptic symbolism as well.

C. S. Lewis's classic work *The Lion, the Witch and the Wardrobe* tells the story of the four Pevensie children who travel through a magic wardrobe into the land of Narnia, a land populated by fauns, centaurs, talking animals, the evil White Witch, and a lion named Aslan. When Aslan willingly offers himself to the White Witch in place of the traitor Edmund and is then killed on the stone table only to be resurrected shortly thereafter, informed readers understand that they have just witnessed a very familiar story: the death and resurrection of Christ. The question I pose to my students, however, is, why would Lewis choose to relate the story of Christ using a lion, a witch, and a stone table?

Lewis strongly resisted any description of his work as an "allegory," instead arguing that he had created "fairy tales." He claimed that "the Fairy

Tale seemed the ideal Form for the stuff I had to say" (Lewis 37). What made it ideal is that fairy tales employ symbolism as a way of presenting the familiar in an unfamiliar form. Lewis felt that the Christ story had become domesticated and robbed of its emotional force through too much familiarity. Christians hear the story regularly in church and are told that they should feel emotional about it. Lewis believed that this sense of obligation to be moved by the story actually worked against the achievement of any genuine emotion. Yet, by recasting the all-too-familiar story of Christ in a new, nearly unrecognizable form, Lewis believed that the story could regain its emotional power. In his essay "Sometimes Fairy Stories May Say Best What's to Be Said," Lewis states, "But supposing that by casting all these things into an imaginary world, stripping them of their stained-glass and Sunday school associations, one could make them for the first time appear in their real potency? Could one not thus steal past those watchful dragons? I thought one could" (37).

The symbolism in *The Lion, the Witch and the Wardrobe* makes us see a familiar story from a new angle and, thus, see it afresh. Apocalyptic symbolism functions in much the same way. When John (the author of Revelation) wants to talk about how Christian victory comes not through displays of power or physical resistance to the ruling authorities but rather through peaceful, sacrificial witness, he does so by presenting Jesus initially as a lion who suddenly transforms into a slaughtered lamb (Rev. 5:5–6). When John wants to define Christian existence as a time of spiritual warfare, he does so with the story of a gigantic, seven-headed red dragon who seeks to devour a pregnant woman (Rev. 12:1–17). When John wants to demonstrate that Roman Imperial society is not as benevolent as some members of his churches suppose, he presents it in the form of demonic beasts that deceive the whole world with trickery and lies (Rev. 13:1–17). The symbolism of Revelation steals past the watchful dragons of familiarity and self-deception and compels its readers to look at themselves, their story, and the world around them in new ways. Lewis's "fairy tale" helps students grasp this concept in a way that no academic treatise or college lecture could.

"Little Red-Riding Hood" and the Gospels

One of the unique features of the New Testament is that it contains four versions of the same story. These four versions—known as the Gospels of Matthew, Mark, Luke, and John—all narrate the story of Jesus's ministry, death, and resurrection. They do so in ways that are sometimes remarkably similar (even word-for-word identical) but at other times notably different, a reality that has led academics to label the literary relationship between the gospels a "problem" ("The Synoptic Problem"). Rather than viewing four gospels as a problem to be solved, however, I encourage my students to appreciate the value of having four gospels by inspiring them to think about why people might tell the same story with variations. To explore that, we examine the case of "Little Red Riding Hood." Now, lest my students think I am comparing the life of Jesus to a fairy tale, I emphasize that although the Gospels are accounts of a historical person, they do not relate as much detail as an historical biography. After all, they only share about three to five years of Jesus's life. Rather, the Gospels present their historical account in the form of a story. Consequently, paying attention to why and how different versions of a story develop helps to bring the Gospels into sharper focus.

"Little Red Riding Hood" is one of the most famous and often-told fairy tales, with a rich textual history going back centuries. The story first existed in oral form where it circulated among peasant communities. Some notable differences in these early versions, particularly those from Europe in the 16th and 17th centuries, include heightened sexual innuendo, cannibalism (the wolf tricks the girl into cannibalizing her grandmother), and an identification of the "wolf" as a werewolf. Set against a time period in which trials of purported witches and werewolves were reaching epidemic proportions, one function of this story was to serve as a cautionary tale (Zipes 19; Orenstein 85–106). Making bad choices (choosing the wrong path to grandmother's house, as it were) can lead young women into a life of sexual promiscuity, "witchcraft," or victimization (Chase and Teasley 774–776).

The earliest known written version of "Little Red Riding Hood" comes from Charles Perrault in 1697. Perrault's version introduces Red Riding Hood as "the prettiest creature who was ever seen" (Ashliman). When she encounters the wolf on the way to grandmother's house, she speaks with him because she "did not know that it was dangerous to stay and talk to a wolf." When she arrives at grandmother's house, the wolf, who has already eaten the grandmother, asks Red to climb into bed with him. She takes off her clothes and does so, and then the wolf eats her up. The story thus concludes with no happy ending.

Perrault wrote his version for an upper-class French audience at a time when the witch hunts and werewolf trials across Europe had receded. By emphasizing the attractiveness of Little Red Riding Hood, having her climb naked into bed with the wolf, and then presenting being eaten by the wolf in consequence, Perrault turned the tale into a warning against talking to strangers who might prey on little girls. Particularly noteworthy is the absence of any significant male figure in Perrault's version of the story, an absence that suggests women in 17th-century French society would meet a bad end without male guidance and protection. In fact, the only time any male figures are referenced in Perrault's version is when the wolf dares not eat Red in the forest because woodcutters are nearby.

The most well-known version of "Little Red Riding Hood" is the 1812 tale from the Brothers Grimm. The Grimms retain many of the elements from Perrault's version but alter the tale slightly in line with "the ethics of the emerging bourgeoisie in the 19th century" (Zipes 37). Most significantly, they add the character of the huntsman who provides the story with a happy ending as he cuts open the wolf's belly, allowing Red and her grandmother to emerge unharmed. That a male figure is necessary for the achievement of a happy ending also echoes the need for male protection suggested in Perrault's version—this variation therefore reinforces gender norms and gender expectations of its time.

After taking the students through a quick survey of these versions of "Little Red Riding Hood," I introduce them to an episode of the ABC television series *Once Upon a Time*. In the series, the evil Queen has cast a curse on all inhabitants of the Enchanted Forest, banishing them to a small town in our world called Storybrooke. As part of the curse, these fairy tale characters have no memory of who they were in the Enchanted Forest but are instead granted new identities and memories. In a typical episode, the show cuts back and forth, showing a particular character's life in both of the two worlds.

The episode titled "Red-Handed" (season 1, episode 15) features the story of Little Red Riding Hood, known simply as "Red" in the Enchanted Forest but called "Ruby" in Storybrooke. When we meet Ruby, she is a put-upon waitress in a local diner who is riddled by insecurities and self-doubt. Perhaps to compensate for those insecurities, she dresses in provocative clothing, though always with a nice dash of red in the ensemble, and flirts with customers. The episode alternates scenes of her life in Storybrooke with those of her former existence as "Red" in the Enchanted Forest where she lived with her grandmother and had a boyfriend named Peter. The townspeople had formed a hunting party in hopes of killing a local wolf that was attacking sheep and villagers. The story takes an interesting turn when Red discovers that herself is the werewolf (in a return to the oral tradition) who has been terrorizing the village—a fact unfortunately learned only *after* she has eaten her boyfriend, a nod to the cannibalistic undertones in earlier versions of the story.

Once Upon a Time's version of "Little Red Riding Hood" addresses a different age with different societal values than those of Perrault and Grimm. Whereas their versions implied the importance of male protection and guidance for young women in European society, *Once Upon a Time*'s version becomes a tale of female empowerment. This Red is not the prey, but the predator. Not only that but she happens to eat the only significant male figure in the story. Red is certainly no victim, but neither is Granny a pushover, either. She commands the respect of those around her, compels the male hunters to bow to her forceful will, and wields a mean crossbow ("Red-Handed").

Whereas the wolf (or werewolf) is always a figure of evil or danger in prior versions of "Little Red Riding Hood," here it becomes a positive metaphor of inner strength, a fact made clear through the show's alternating scenes in the Enchanted Forest and Storybrooke. As the Enchanted Forest's Red learns of her identity as a werewolf, we witness Storybrooke's Ruby similarly discover unexpected strength and confidence within herself, even leading to a change in her attire to more mature and appropriate clothing—though still rocking some nice touches of red.

These various versions of "Little Red Riding Hood" illustrate how changes in time periods and social situations change *how* a story is told. The same story of "Little Red Riding Hood" communicates a different message based on the social situations it is addressing. This feature helps my students to recognize that the early Christian church canonized four different versions of the same story because each version was tailored to different communities at different times, and so each Gospel spoke to the unique needs and concerns of those communities.

Conclusion

The author of Hebrews describes the Word of God as "living and active" (Heb. 4:13). That's a fairly apt description of all great literature. The best stories live on because they are capable of adapting to the spirit of each age. The same stories that charmed me as a child inform me as an adult. The reason why some "children's literature" is so valuable in higher education is not just because these stories communicate concepts with simplicity, but because these stories are just great literature. They come alive in each retelling and challenge us to see the wonder and imagination in the world around us. These stories engage us both as children and adults because they cut through all of the nonsense and take us to the heart of the matter. After all, that is what the best stories do.

Works Cited

Ashliman, D. L., trans. and ed. *Little Red Riding Hood and Other Tales of Aarne-Thompson-Uther Type 333.* 15 Oct. 2013. *Folklore and Mythology Electronic Texts.* Web. 22 Apr. 2014.

Chase, Richard, Jr., and David Teasley. "Little Red Riding Hood: Werewolf and Prostitute." *The Historian* 57.4 (Summer 1995): 769–76. Print.

Cott, Jonathan. *Pipers at the Gates of Dawn: The Wisdom of Children's Literature.* New York: McGraw Hill, 1985. Print.

Lewis, C. S. *The Lion, the Witch, and the Wardrobe.* New York: Harper, 2009. Print.

_____. "Sometimes Fairy Stories May Say Best What's to Be Said." In *Of Other Worlds: Essays and Stories.* Ed. Walter Hooper. New York: Harcourt Brace Jovanovich, 1965, 35–38. Print.

Nel, Philip. *Dr. Seuss: American Icon.* New York: Continuum, 2005. Print.

Orenstein, Catherine. *Little Red Riding Hood Uncloaked: Sex, Morality, and the Evolution of a Fairy Tale.* New York: Basic Books, 2002. Print.

"Red-Handed." *Once Upon a Time.* ABC. 11 March 2012. Television.

Seuss, Dr. *Six by Seuss: A Treasury of Dr. Seuss Classics.* New York: Random House, 1991. Print.

Tolkien, J. R. R. *The Lord of the Rings,* 2d ed. 1965. Boston: Houghton-Mifflin, 1993. Print.

Zipes, Jack, ed. *The Trials and Tribulations of Little Red Riding Hood,* 2d ed. New York: Routledge, 1993. Print.

Timber!!!

Francis A. Grabowski III

Philosophers have a knack for making mountains out of molehills. At least that seems to be the opinion of most undergrads. Can you blame them? Who but a philosopher would question the existence of the material world, or puzzle over whether the sun will rise tomorrow, or suggest that we might be nothing but brains in vats or the playthings of a malicious demon? Who but a philosopher would entertain such fanciful—some might even say foolish—thoughts? This is not to say that philosophy is unappealing—far from it. Who does not like to have his mind opened to unconsidered possibilities or her reason pushed to its limits? Zeno's Paradoxes, the Prisoner's Dilemma, the Ship of Theseus—these are fun problems, no doubt about it. But fun does not put food on the table; it does not clothe the naked, heal the sick, or bring about world peace. Philosophy might be loads of fun, but of what use is it? Given how abstract and impractical philosophical questions tend to be, what difference does it make if we answer them or not? What does all of this mountain-making get us, anyway?

It does no good to insist that philosophers are not mountain-makers. Let's face it—they are. What's more, most philosophers would gladly cop to the appellation. Like anyone else, a philosopher has his priorities. Giving attention to workaday concerns, however, is usually not among them. Some people ask questions owing to a practical need. A philosopher asks them out of an instinctive desire. He is like a curious child who queries, "Why is the sky blue?" There is no money in it for the child, no career advancement, no fame, no glory; there is only an intellectual hunger fueled by wonder. Most students share this child-like impulse to wonder—an impulse that can be impeded or even deactivated by a student's practical drive to pass tests, fulfill program requirements, and become certified. An instructor should be at pains to reactivate this impulse in students, to help them to rediscover their inner child, to encourage them to ask the fun and fanciful questions that philosophers ask, and to exhort them to make mountains of their own. For there is an underappreciated joy and beauty to mountain-making, whether those mountains are formed through the violent collision of interpersonal debate or the volcanic eruption from a solitary mind. They rise above narrow, quotidian concerns, allowing one to survey life freely and openly from their lofty peaks. But what could convince students to become mountain-makers themselves? There is, evidently, magic in the stories that we read and had read to us as children. After all, they first ignited and fueled our impulse to wonder. Perhaps the magic in these stories can reignite this impulse in us as adults.

No attempt will be made here to enter the debate over what qualifies as children's literature. Although this might be an issue of scholarly interest, it is not one of relevance to the present discussion. Of considerable importance, however, is the selection of children's books, for it seems that not all are suitable for philosophical study. Books for toddlers and preschoolers, for instance, designed primarily to develop basic communication skills, are not likely to be grist for the philosopher's mill. *The Very Hungry Caterpillar* (Carle) and *Goodnight Moon* (Brown) are charming and wonderfully illustrated stories, but they are short on most kinds of philosophical significance. The same cannot be said about books for teens and young adults, which often do address, explicitly or implicitly, grave moral concerns: homicide in *The Wizard of Oz* (Baum), slavery in *Charlie and the Chocolate Factory* (Dahl), and the limits of personal devotion in *Charlotte's Web* (White), to mention but a few examples. On the positive side, these are books replete with philosophical grist. The downside is their length and narrative complexity. A sixteen-week semester provides barely enough time to cover the basics of philosophy. "Sacrificing" a week or two analyzing *Charlotte's Web* as a work of literature is an added cost that few instructors would be willing to pay. What is needed, therefore, is a children's book targeted ideally at grade-schoolers. It should be short enough to fit into an already-congested lesson plan yet weighty enough for philosophical discussion, and it should have a narrative sufficiently complex to keep student interest yet not so complex that its philosophical content appears faint alongside its literary features. What is needed, in other words, is a book like Shel Silverstein's *The Giving Tree*.

Silverstein's story features only two characters: a boy and a tree. We do not know how they first meet, yet from the beginning we are made aware of their loving relationship—a carefree, unpretentious relationship based on adolescent fun-and-games. The boy as a youngster visits the tree every day, plays games with her, eats her apples, and sleeps beside her. Each is the other's world entire. The boy loves the tree, and the tree loves the boy. Nothing else seems to matter. But over time, the boy becomes an adult, and as he changes, so too does their relationship. For one thing, the boy spends less time with the tree, more time with a special lady friend, and begins having grown-up urges and aspirations. After long absences, he returns to the tree, asking her for money and other things of material value. The tree, unable to give them directly, gives parts of herself instead: first, her apples so that the boy can obtain money; next, her branches so that he can build a house for his family; and finally, her trunk so that he can build a boat to travel. By the end of the story, there is nothing left of the tree but a stump. She has nothing left to give. Or does she? The boy, now an elderly man, visits the tree one last time. Old and weak, he no longer has the energy for fun-and-games. He has also lost his ambition for wealth, the desire to start a family, and the longing for adventure. He is tired, and the regal tree, deprived of her crown and trunk, gives him the only thing she can—a place to rest. The story ends with an image of the two together once again. Visible at the stump's base is the uneffaced carving that the boy made as a child: "M.E. & T." Life has come full circle.

The narrative is easy enough to follow. Interpreting it, however, takes a fair amount of effort. Some may consider *The Giving Tree* to be a cautionary tale urging parents against spoiling their children. If you shower them with gifts while they are young, so the reading goes, they will never learn to provide for themselves and become codependents as adults. Others could discern a pro-environmentalist message: just as Mother Nature bestows her gifts on us with no special demands or limits, so too must we treat her with unconditional kindness and respect, not as an object from which to profit but as someone to love, lest she become like the story's arboreal protagonist—barren and lifeless. Still others might think that the story is making a religious point: no matter how selfish and unthankful we are, God will always treat us, as long as we are faithful and contrite, with a generosity far more than we deserve. Interpretations like these are natural and fit the text fairly well. In the context of classroom discussion, however, because of their moralistic and religious undertones, they are more likely to incite stubborn disputation than fruitful discussion. They are also liable to distract students from the broader philosophical concerns of the story, most notably the nature of friendship and the contribution that friendship makes to human happiness.

Before assigning the story, instructors should have students first give thoughtful consideration to what friendship is. The aim here is to prime the philosophical pump and to get them to see friendship as a complex and greatly disputed concept—a mountain, not a molehill. In order to keep their minds neutral and objective, no philosophical readings should be assigned yet. Reading Aristotle on friendship too early could potentially sway their thinking from the start. All students have friends of some sort and will therefore have pre-philosophical intuitions about what makes somebody a friend. The instructor can tap into these intuitions by asking a series of questions:

- What is friendship?
- Are all friendships the same?
- How are friendships made?
- What is friendship for?

Some students will treat these as mere "opinion questions" having no right or wrong answer. This is a natural response that should not be lightly dismissed, but it should also not meet with uncontested approval. For instance, take the first question: "What is friendship?" One may insist that there is no answer—at least not a single answer that would apply to everyone. After all, some people have very high standards for friendship, whereas others set the bar much lower. Does this mean that a person is a friend as long as he is considered as such? Is friendship just a matter of personal preference? Some students will say "yes," but to this one should respond: if simply regarding someone as a friend were enough to make him a friend, then mistakes about friendship would never happen. But we know that mistakes do happen, for just about everyone has said at one time or another, "I thought that you were my friend, but I was wrong." Moreover, if friendships were subjective and simply a matter of personal preference, we could never justifiably criticize someone for the friends she keeps. Consider someone struggling with alcoholism. He wants to stay sober, but surrounds himself with people who contribute to his addiction. He may regard them as friends—they are the people with whom he elects to fraternize—but are they truly friends? If they were not good for him, if they contributed to his physical or moral corruption, then there would be reason to say that he is wrong to call them "friends." Would we not say that they are not true friends at all, but rather false friends? And does not the very idea of a false friend—someone who is a friend not in fact, but in name only—suggest that there is more to friendship than mere subjective personal preference? By struggling with these questions, students will learn that there are no easy answers, that friendship deserves a deeper, more systematic study, and that they should prepare themselves for some mountain-making—or at the very least some fairly steep mountain climbing.

Once students have their minds focused on friendship as a subject of philosophical scrutiny, they can turn their attentions to *The Giving Tree.* They should be cautioned from the start not to cast the book aside as another jejune children's story in the vein of *Dick and Jane: Go, Go, Go* or *Curious George Flies a Kite* (Rey). It will take more than a cursory reading to feel the story's philosophical weight and sense its narrative depth. Students should pay particular attention to Silverstein's calculated choice of words. Consider, for instance, how he always refers to his male protagonist as "the boy." Even as a geriatric, he is still a boy. Yet this makes little sense: how can an old man be a boy? One suggestion is that "boy" refers not to the character's physical age, but rather to his level of maturity. Growing older does not necessarily mean becoming more mature. Some will insist that this is definitely true of the boy: although physically an adult, emotionally he remains a little child. But this is not the only possible interpretation. Maybe Silverstein's point instead is to draw attention to the age disparity between the two protagonists. Compared to a venerable old tree, even an elderly man would be no more than a boy. Besides, the tree herself refers to him as "boy" throughout the story. Is this the tree's way of calling him "immature," or is it simply a case of the tree addressing him as she always has—like the parent who still calls her grown-up son "Junior"? Something else to note is the emotional state of the characters. On four separate occasions, the tree is described as "happy," but the boy not once. Some will suggest that Silverstein is sending a moralistic message: happiness lies in acts of giving, not in acts of receiving. In other words, getting a bunch of stuff—money, houses, boats, and so on—is not going to make you happy, but being generous and selfless will. The trouble, however, is that giving does not always result in the tree's happiness, for there is a point in the story where, after she gives the boy her trunk, the reader is told, "And the tree was happy ... but not really." Students should be invited to reflect upon these difficult passages, not in the hopes of settling on a definitive reading of the text, but rather to make them aware of its narrative depth and openness to interpretation. A children's book it might be, but childish it is not.

Having come to appreciate *The Giving Tree* as a piece of serious literature, students can begin to examine it through a philosophical lens. Of special interest is the relationship between the boy and the tree. Is it appropriate to call them friends? If one person gives and gives and the other takes and takes, does this constitute a friendship? Can friendships be one-sided like the relationship between the boy and the tree? But is this even a fair question? Is their relationship one-sided? The first thing to note is that the boy never takes anything that the tree herself does not offer. The boy is not a Lockean laying claim to the tree as his natural right, and he is no thief. He always asks for the things that he wants, and the tree obliges as she can. One may accuse the boy of getting more than he deserves, but it is not as though he takes anything from the tree by force: what he receives are gifts, pure and simple, and who is to decide when and to whom gifts are deserved? At this point, one could argue that, indeed, the tree gives willingly and unconditionally, but insofar as the boy does not intend to reciprocate, he is exploiting the tree's kindness and generosity. Friendships, it seems, should be based on mutual trust and reciprocity, and, evidently, the boy lacks either the willingness or the moral awareness to reciprocate. But should one really say this about the boy? Since the tree never asks for anything, there is nothing to suggest that the boy is unwilling to return her favors. Furthermore, there is no reason to think that the boy is unaware of the tree's needs. What are her needs, anyway? How would he know unless she made them known? Besides, one could just as easily accuse the tree of misunderstanding the nature of their friendship. Not all friendships are the same: some are based on pleasure, others on utility; some are long lasting, others relatively brief; some involve equal amounts of giving and receiving, others are not so egalitarian.

A careful reading of *The Giving Tree*, therefore, reveals a complicated dynamic behind the friendship between the boy and the tree. In fact, one can discern three stages in their relationship. The story opens with stage one. The boy, as a young child, spends his time playing games. But the tree is no different. She is not some disinterested chaperone; she participates. Their friendship at this stage is one of insouciance and youthful exuberance. Boys and girls play games like baseball and hopscotch, oblivious to the worldly concerns troubling their teachers and parents. Life for a child, ideally, is undemanding and pleasant. With time, however, comes change. Our focus shifts from the here-and-now to the there-and-then. The boy in the story experiences this shift, marking stage two of the relationship. During this stage, their friendship is one of convenience. Adults need to get from one place to another. They need to get things done. Our schoolyard friends have become business associates: instead of pitching baseballs, they pitch sales; instead of trading jokes, they trade stocks. These are practical friendships. They might not always be as pleasant as the friendships of youth, but as adults we could not live without them. So much of what the boy has—his personal possessions and accomplishments—he owes to the tree. But acquisition and travel can satisfy us only so much and for so long. If we are always on the go, we are in a state of perpetual movement and constant transition, neither here nor there. The boy realizes this as he ages. Or perhaps his age catches up with him. Whatever the case, the boy has grown tired; his only desire is a place to rest, and perhaps a companion with whom to share time. The tree provides both. With this, their friendship enters its third and final stage. We do not know what they do after the story ends—if they talk about the weather, reminisce, or just sit silently together. One thing, however, seems certain: they no longer need games or commerce to sustain their friendship: they only have need of each other.

The Giving Tree does not present anything like a comprehensive or systematic philosophy of friendship, but from the story does emerge a series of insights that align closely with the systematic thoughts on the nature and value of friendship found in Aristotle's Nicomachean Ethics (NE). Consider, for instance, the insight from The Giving Tree that there are different kinds of friendship. The boy and the tree remain friends throughout the story, but the basis for their friendship changes. What begins first as a friendship of pleasure becomes later a friendship of convenience and then finally a friendship of fellowship. Aristotle, interestingly enough, draws a similar distinction. There are, he says, three objects of human love—the pleasant, the useful, and the good—that serve as the basis for three kinds of friendship (NE viii. 2–4). The young, owing to their passionate nature, commonly strike up friendships of pleasure. These friendships, depending as they do on emotional vicissitudes, are temporary, lasting for only as long as one's tastes and feelings stay the same. Friendships of utility are different. They tend to be found mainly among adults. These friendships are marked by a sense of need—one person seeks out another for purposes of mutual benefit. In the business world, this is called "networking." Thus, there is a sort of friendship that exists, for instance, between a barber and his client. They do not spend time together outside of work like friends of pleasure do; however, their relationship is still important because each friend provides some good for one another—the client gets his hair cut (which the barber makes possible) and the barber gets paid (which his client makes possible). Different from friendships of pleasure and utility are those that aim at the good. These, according to Aristotle, are "complete friendships," which hold between people who are good and alike in virtue. Friends of pleasure or utility are loved not for their own sake, but rather for the sake of the pleasure or utility derived from one's association with them. In a complete friendship, by contrast, each person wishes the good for the other insofar as both are good. These friendships are rare but stable and dissolve only with great difficulty. Although there are other kinds of friendship, friends who together aim at the good are, according to Aristotle, friends most of all.

There is an obvious connection between friendship as depicted in The Giving Tree and friendship as conceived by Aristotle, but students will undoubtedly have questions. For starters, that the young boy and the tree share a friendship of pleasure is indisputable. That they share a friendship of utility, however, is a harder claim to make. In friendships of utility, each person seeks out that which is useful for himself or herself. Certainly, the boy is after things useful to realizing his aspirations, but is this true for the tree? How is it useful for the tree to make sacrifices and get nothing in return? What is the tree after? Her goal is not to receive money or some other kind of material compensation. She merely seeks the boy's happiness. Perhaps, then, insofar as his happiness contributes to her own, she does come away with something. But on second thought, maybe their friendship at the second stage is not a pure friendship of utility after all. Aristotle, at one point in his discussion, refers to hybrid friendships, which involve mixtures across kinds (*NE* ix. 1). Thus, whereas in a pure friendship of utility individuals have the useful as their goal, in a hybrid friendship one person might aim at the useful while the other aims at pleasure. Perhaps the boy and the tree, during the second stage, have a hybrid friendship, where the boy loves the tree for her usefulness and the tree loves the boy for the pleasure that he brings. There are a host of other issues relevant to *The Giving Tree* addressed by Aristotle. The class might consider the following:

Giving and Receiving (*NE* viii. 8, 12 and ix. 1–2, 7): Are the ethics of giving the same as the ethics of receiving? Should there be equal love shown between those giving favors and those receiving them? How does this apply to *The Giving Tree*? Does the boy love the tree as much as the tree loves the boy? Should he show her as much love as she shows him?

Friendship and Separation (*NE* viii. 5): Can living apart from one another have a deleterious impact on a friendship? Can one enjoy a friendship of pleasure or a complete friendship while not in regular physical contact with one's friend? This prompts one to wonder: is separation a principal cause of change in the friendship between the boy and the tree?

Friendship and Happiness (*NE* ix. 9, 11): How does friendship contribute to human happiness? Although the boy and the tree remain friends throughout the story, why is only the tree described as happy? Is it something about how the boy conceives their relationship that deprives him of the sort of happiness that the tree feels?

It would be unwise to insist on a set of definitive answers to these questions or a definitive interpretation of *The Giving Tree*. Like so many great works of literature, the story invites open and ambitious minds to swim in its vast sea of literary tropes and philosophical ideas. When first confronted with Silverstein's story, some students may raise a skeptical eyebrow, thinking it out of place in a college classroom setting. But when drawn together with a works from the philosophical canon such as the *Nicomachean Ethics*, those students will more readily come to appreciate *The Giving Tree* as a story that can touch our hearts and teach us not only about the friendships that we have, but also about those that we passionately desire.

Introducing philosophy through children's literature, therefore, provides instructors with an innovative way to disarm students. They tend to see philosophy as a pointless endeavor. Who cares what friendship is? What will knowing the essence of friendship get us? For the practical-minded student, friendship is something to be enjoyed, not dissected. Aristotle, for one, would not disagree. Moral philosophy, he says, is not a theoretical science: it aims not at knowledge alone, but at practice (*NE* ii. 2). It does no good, for instance, to know what virtue is and then not be virtuous. Likewise, it does no good to know what friendship is, but not have friends. Yet if the goal is to disarm students, to dispossess them of the tendency to view philosophy as so much pointless mountain-making, then instructors ought to consider the benefits of incorporating children's stories. Philosophical works are long and complicated. They speak to students in a foreign tongue. Children's stories are shorter and more accessible. They speak with the unassuming voice of a child—a voice that invites students to surrender themselves to a game of make-believe. So a boy befriends a tree and they spend their time together having fun—what a sweet and pleasant image. To some, the story is sad; to others, it is joyous. But by engaging the story, students raise questions and form opinions about the nature of friendship. Little do they know that these questions and opinions are like layers of limestone built upon each other. With each layer, their ideas bulge and swell into a mountain, atop which they can survey and assess friendships like the one in *The Giving Tree*, not to mention their own. Children's literature is not the only means of getting students to make mountains, but it is a creative and effective way of instilling the habit. As the twig is bent, so the tree is inclined.

Works Cited

Aristotle. *Nicomachean Ethics*. Trans. Joe Sachs. Newburyport, MA: Focus Publishing, 2002. Print.

Baum, L. Frank. *The Wonderful Wizard of Oz*. Mineola, NY: Dover, 1996. Print.

Brown, Margaret Wise. *Goodnight Moon*. Illus. Clement Hurd. New York: Harper, 2007. Print.

Carle, Eric. *The Very Hungry Caterpillar*. New York: Philomel, 1994. Print.

Dahl, Roald. *Charlie and the Chocolate Factory.* New York: Penguin, 2007. Print.

Dick and Jane: Go, Go, Go. New York: Penguin, 2003. Print.

Rey, H.A. *Curious George Flies a Kite.* New York: HMH, 2009. Print.

Silverstein, Shel. *The Giving Tree.* New York: Harper and Row, 1964. Print.

White, E.B. *Charlotte's Web.* Illus. Garth Williams. New York: HarperCollins, 2012. Print.

Growling Bears

Weldon Lee Williams *and*
David Blakely

Weldon Lee Williams: We're going to talk about using children's literature to teach "voice." First, let's tell our backgrounds. I come at vocal performance from a career in broadcast journalism, mostly TV, both as a reporter/
anchor and as a news director who sometimes coached talent. David is a theatre
professional, an actor, writer, and director. In addition to our professional work,
we both teach. And we both utilize children's literature in our classes. These
stories are already ingrained in students' brains and hearts. They already know
what word should be stressed. They know the joy, fear, sadness, discovery, and
wonder. The goal is to get them to transfer the same awareness to adult stories.

David Blakely: The lovely thing about children's stories is that they have
all these emotions. I usually give students a range, you know. What is the intensity of this particular emotion? You're going from "I'm irritated with you" to
"really, leave me alone: I don't want to see your face ever again." And it's the
range and intensity that gets you from point *A* to point *Z*, consciously and
continuously stepping it up.

WLW: Yes, we used *Goldilocks and the Three Bears*. As my student read
it, I thought, "This is perfect. Goldilocks walks through the house and she
experiences, 'this is too soft—hard, hot—cold,' matter-of-factly, but stepping
up a bit each time."

Then, it steps up a lot when the bears come in with alarm because of an
intruder. Students have to learn how to pace themselves through all these
developments. Then, there is interpretation: You hear from baby bear who's
in awe, a view from momma bear who is more concerned for her family, and
then the papa bear readying for war. So, students try on all these different
characters and emotions.

DB: Exactly. And you are telling the story or broadcasting the story from your point of view. You're reporting, "This is what happened the other night in the forest to a young lady named Goldilocks," as a news event, as opposed to what I'm doing in theatre, presenting the story dramatically. But still telling the same story, trying to get the same meaning out of it.

WLW: And, still using the same tools, mostly. News people look serious; but, if you really listen to their voices, they're using a lot of expression, controlling volume, stressing the right words, and phrasing the right parts of a sentence together. Many of the best newscasters are singers, and they know how to milk the meaning out of sentences and words. It may not look like they are in a high state of interpretation, but, if you are ever standing beside an anchor or field reporter, many are coming up out of their shoes, literally their heels are coming up to get the kind of volume, projection, power, variety, and expression they want.

DB: Yes, I think that's true. I have recently been in contact with three different news reporters on three separate occasions in the last three days and have been amazed about how animated they are, especially when they are not on camera. They know they need to boost their vocal qualities.

WLW: True. Many reporters don't know why they can't make it to the anchor chair, and that's often the reason. They don't know how to interpret the words and express them with emotion. So, children's stories really help when I try to teach journalists how to be conduits for meaning.

I asked students to share with us how children's stories helped them learn to interpret copy and deliver words with power and variety, whether prose, poetry, news, or stage plays. One remarked,

> I would say that children's stories already have expressiveness built into them by nature. I think you go into the child's mindset, too. You kind of get this innocence in the way that you interpret the story and you think, "OK, what if I'm a seven year old now?" [Laranda Wieden].

DB: Right, absolutely. One other thing that I would point out about children's literature is that it is often done in context. For example, some of the stories that I am talking about are pieces that are intended to free the voice and explore language. And that's one of the things that as adults we have a tendency to ignore: having fun with language. And then there are other pieces; I'm going to give the example of Margaret Wise Brown's *Goodnight Moon* which is intended to be a bedtime story, and so its intonation and its meaning and its purpose is completely different from what Dr. Seuss's *Green Eggs and Ham*. As one student says about *Moon*,

I think it helps with duration and stressing the correct words. I know in my book the words they wanted you to stress were italicized. So that helped me to read it and to really punch that certain word [Hannah Barnoski].

WLW: I love *Goodnight Moon*; I've read that book to my daughters somewhere between five-hundred and a thousand times. And since you said you were going to use it as an example, I jumped online and listened to Susan Sarandon reading it. Near the end, as the bunny is saying goodbye to everything in his/her room, he looks out the window into the night sky and says, "Goodnight stars, goodnight air, goodnight noises everywhere," stretching the *ahhhhhhhhhrrrrsss* in stars and the *aiiirrrrrr* in air. And that open mouth expresses the open sky, awe, and wonder. Every time I read it, I feel myself leaving waking reality for the boundless universe of sleep and dreams.

DB: *Goodnight Moon* is a book that is intended for children who don't yet know how to read. It's intended to be read out loud. Margaret Wise Brown did a beautiful job in taking the plosives out, the *P*'s, *B*'s, *T*'s, sounds that interrupt the air flow. In contrast, in those final words you have stars, you have the *S*'s, and you have "air," and you have "noises," and you have "everywhere."

WLW: And by that time my daughter was out!

And now for something completely different. Let's use *The Three Little Pigs* to talk about pitch, volume, duration, and also emphasis or phrasing—holding meaning together for series of words or thought grouping. Students know *The Three Little Pigs* so well, they will automatically get louder and louder, "I'll huff, and *I'll puff*, and *I'll blow your house down*." Almost anyone would interpret that by raising the pitch and volume on each successive phrase, and then really sending it up at the end. "I'll huff," my pitch is up, and "I'll *puff*," "still holding my pitch up, and, big volume here, "*I'll blow your house down*." There are also anger and threat, emotions to interpret. So it allows, one, for students to instantly understand what to do; two, to feel licensed to express it; and, three, to prepare to deal with more complex sentences, whether it's news, prose, poetry or drama. Margo Blue commented,

> It can bring more animation into our daily conversation because, when else do we speak so exaggerated, dramatic? So, we go there, then, we go back to our regular life and may go up a notch just because of the behaviors we've learned.

DB: As a teaching tool, children's literature uses repetition to create intensity. "I'll huff, and I'll puff, and I'll blow your house down!" is repeated three times in the story, each time with more threat. It appears as a group of three clauses, and each part increases the intensity of the group. The threat is increased incrementally either through increased emphasis (or volume, etc.). Or a decreased emphasis (or volume, etc.). Or some variation of that.

WLW: Yes, it is a great example of building intensity and delivering the climax. So many students are unaware that all great stories are begging them to stress the right words and amp up volume and pitch.

DB: There is a poem that I use by Shel Silverstein called "Always Sprinkle Pepper." It starts with "Always sprinkle pepper in your hair" (1). If you do sprinkle pepper, it will help to keep the bad guys away. The last three lines state that you will be safe "If you always, always, always, / Always, always, always, always, / Always, always sprinkle pepper in your hair" (13–15). Having to say "always" nine times is similar to the wolf saying, "I'm going to huff, puff, and blow." Only this time the speaker is not going to use three different words that will differentiate his actions ("huff," "puff," and "blow"), he is using the same words nine times. How do you deliver that in a way that increases intensity and keeps interest? You will need to use all of those expressive tools that we've been talking about—elongating some of them, using volume (starting in low, then starting to grow), attaching emotional intensity to "always, always, always, always, always." You are conveying meaning with one word repeated nine times, using the same techniques you used on the wolf's line. It is exaggerated. And, again, it's children's literature that allows you to work that.

WLW: As you say *always, always*, you might punch the pitch way up or way down, or you might hold the pitch at the same level to connect several words. It certainly pushes students to use every tool in their "voice toolbox."

DB: You can experiment with pitch, and you can vary that so that your pitch is going up, so that it reaches its apex about seven *always* in, and then you drop your pitch for the last two words, and yet your volume is going from 1 to 9. All those techniques create meaning, and the poem itself allows you the opportunity to use the language as you wish. There's a muscularity to the language. By muscularity I mean the varying lengths of phrases and contrasts between vowels and consonants that create texture in the language—and using that muscularity to create context and meaning.

WLW: I think students come to understand that they can make any word have an incredible range of meanings, even opposite meaning, by how they say it. For example, you might go down in pitch where you would normally go up, and you might get quiet where you would normally be loud. Sometimes actors get very scary by talking low and slow:

One thing I was focusing on was characterization, trying to raise my voice or lower it, like high voice for baby bear. When you have Poppa Bear, there's that deep angry voice. I mean it all comes down to how you want to use your voice to get that character moving. There are certain parts in the book where they were mad because someone broke their chair, someone messed up their bed, or ate their soup. When you're reading, are they upset, are they happy? You *think* how you want to use your voice [Cody Carroll].

WLW: Recently, I have come to realize, more than ever, the importance of duration. Duration means stretching the vowel sound or stretching the word. Actor Morgan Freeman is the master of duration. He will really stretch the words. Like in *March of the Penguins*, he talks about "coooooolld" and the "faaaarrrthest place on earth." When he talks about cold he really stretches the "O" sound, so you almost feel it in your bones, and most students don't think of that at all. Also, he often uses slight pauses before and after the most important words, which are usually verbs, words of important action. Some students, even news anchors, will stress unimportant words. I've even heard anchors and reporters stress *the* and *a*, and, I say, "No, no, stress the verbs." These anchors don't get far, and they don't know why.

I try to get my students to understand how to infuse words and phrases with meaning. A lot of them are good, crisp readers, but there is no emotion in the words. They might say in short choppy words, "I feared the night." I'll make them try again and stretch the word *feeeeaaared* and stretch the word *niiiiight*. They get a much deeper and more powerful meaning.

DB: And I think that happens all the time, when they get to have fun with the children's stories we're talking about. Stories like *The Three Little Pigs* and *Goldilocks, Goodnight Moon*, or *Green Eggs and Ham*. I actually use Seuss's other one, *If I Ran the Circus*, in which he makes up words. That muscularity of language allows them to do what you're suggesting. Students need to learn how to deliver such phrases as the "dark of night."

WLW: Yes, that's a good one. "The dark of night" is spooky, at least, the way you say it.

DB: They seem innocuous on the page, but once the students are rolling the words around in their mouths, words come to life.

WLW: Yes, when they vibrate their own mouths, throats, and noses (their resonators) with these sounds, it helps them feel and understand what they are talking about. Roxana Ninkovich, a native Spanish speaker, notes,

> Learning how to read children's books has helped me with the language. When I first moved to this country, I remember the first book that they wanted me to read was called *Into the Wild* by Krakauer, and, for me, that was a super hard book. I finally know how to learn a children's book, and it's just everything has been so easy now. Before, it was just kind of like ... they're talking, but I'm not sure what they are saying.

DB: Let's move on to rate, the speed at which one talks. I often bring in a children's book by Charlotte Pomerantz called *The Piggy in the Puddle*. Using this book allows the students to work on how fast they can go. The book starts simply and quickly. It is a great book to practice speed. You can start off slow, and just increase tempo, and the words run the gamut from some that go together quickly (like *piggy in the puddle*) to ones you cannot say quickly (words like *squishy squashy* and *mooshy squooshy* and *oofy poufy*). It also allows students to work on correct pronunciation. We often substitute the *D* sound for the *T* sound, especially as we talk faster. Here, the correct pronunciation is *muDDy liTTle puddle*. But when the going gets fast, that will turn into *muDDy liDDle puddle*. So the trick is to get students to say these words and pronounce these words in an articulate way and still have them make sense as they increase their rate:

> The way the books are written, it forces you to be more expressive with the way you say things. I think it helps with your volume also. It helps you push those limits because these books have a lot of emotion [Hannah Barnoski].

DB: Intonation, you can say it ironically. For example, "There's nothing I like better than being in a room with Lee Williams," can be said earnestly or ironically.

WLW: Or sarcastically, which is most often the case. Here's another example: "They laughed themselves to death." With that comment, you can express great joy, or you can be snide and sarcastic.

DB: Children's literature is packed; it's really packed solid with opportunity. Opportunity to use your diaphragm, use your range, use your volume, to use all these tools we have. Children's literature begs for the reader (in our case, our students) to discover the emotions and figure out the meaning.

WLW: Helping students learn how to interpret and build to *discovery* and *revelation* is an advanced skill.

DB: I use the tongue twister, "Peter Piper picked a peck of pickled peppers." I add in Peter Piper's vocation, "the pickled pepper picker." Every time we say Peter Piper's name we add his vocation to it. "Peter Piper, the pickled pepper picker, picked a peck of pickled peppers."

WLW: So, it wasn't hard enough to begin with?

DB: It adds an extra pack—into the mix. Then we can add more: there are four lines to that tongue twister. I ask them then to say it using one breath per line. Then using two breaths breaking after the second line. Then two breaths again, breaking after the third line. Finally, all four lines in one breath.

WLW: They have to work on breath support. They have to figure out how to use their diaphragm to load up on air, and then control air through their vocal cords.

DB: Exactly. And so we practice that:

> A children's story is so simple that you really have to learn how to breathe correctly, or it's really not going to make sense. I have really learned how to slow down and work on my breathing [Adrienne Munoz].

WLW: I have a lot of students who don't keep an open throat. They will bend their head down and close off the air that flows up from the lungs, vibrating through their vocal cords, throat, and mouth and out through their lips and nose. Restricting the airflow through the throat is a major malady. We work on that a lot. I'll often have them pick up their scripts instead of looking down on the desk. I make them stand up, and hold their scripts in front of their faces, and keep their shoulders and necks back and open. You'll hear this flow, increased volume, and improved tone.

DB: That's why children's literature is so helpful here. They already know it.

WLW: I agree. It's in their heads already. As an example, let me read a little bit of *Goldilocks and the Three Bears*. It really helps students to *stress* the right words. I'll tell it, highlighting the important words: "The three bears all decided to *look around* some *more*; when they all got *upstairs* to the big *bedroom*, Papa Bear *growled*." So, which of these words is important? *Growled*—children's stories make expression easy to understand. Usually we make the main word pop with volume, but there are other great tools, such as stretching the word, and dropping pitch very low, and making a *grrrrrr* sound, or all four: Grrrrrrrrrrrrooowwwwwellllllld!

And then, "Goldilocks woke up..."—now we have a huge change in pitch and also *rate* when we get to the most important part of the sentence—"and *screamed*." Students understand they have to read this fast. "She *jumped* up and *ran*," the verbs—action.

DB: I think you gave a great example of a strategy that children's literature uses to convey meaning: onomatopoetic words, words that sound like their meaning. The word *growl* sounds like a growl, just as the word *buzz* sounds like what it means, or *meow* or *moo*. Children's literature abounds with words that allow them to emphasize growling in a way growling needs to be emphasized (We should add a picture of a bear growling to this article. Just for emphasis.):

> The way children's stories are written. It's like four or five lines per page, and you can interpret it very easily. Also for me it helps, when I can see the colors and the pictures, I can kind of get the whole image in my head of how I want to focus on it [Dalton Brunson].

WLW: I used to have a news person who stressed the article *A*. She wouldn't change the long sound *a* to the short sound *uh*. Unfortunately, by doing this, she made the articles—little words—really stand out. Not only did it obscure meaning, it was irritating. She said, "*AY* man drove *the* car." This is a bad case of stressing the wrong word. I was a reporter for six years before I sought out a speech and drama professor at a local university. The professor helped me tremendously to learn to stress the right words and make meaning clear and powerful. That's what we do now!

> You get that variety and vast of expressiveness, and you have to force your pitch up or down to show that expression [Gavin Rose].

DB: And the most important words are usually what you suggested: the action of the sentence, the verb. Or the agent of that action, usually the subject.

WLW: I think we've hit most of the things. Is there anything else you want to address? Both of us like to get in the last word? We'll have to battle for last word. So, here's my last word, and then you can supply one; we'll take a vote just between the two of us. My last thought is, "We all knew children's stories are magic. Now we know they are magic for another reason—which is to teach voice and articulation."

DB: I got nothing! You get the last word.

WLW: That can't be true.

DB: Okay. We're just going to leave it with that.

Works Cited

Brown, Margaret Wise. *Goodnight Moon*. Ill. Clement Hurd. New York: Harper, 2007. Print.

Freeman, Morgan, narrator. *March of the Penguins*. 2005. Warner, 2005. DVD.

Goldilocks and the Three Bears. Ill. F. Rojankovsky. New York: Golden Books, 2012. Print.

Krakauer, Jon. *Into the Wild*. New York: Random House, 2009. Print.

Pomerantz, Charlotte. *The Piggy in the Puddle*. Ill. James Marshall. New York: Aladdin, 1989.

Seuss, Dr. *Green Eggs and Ham*. New York: Random House, 2013. Print.

_____. *If I Ran the Circus*. New York: Random House, 2013. Print.

Silverstein, Shel. "Always Sprinkle Pepper." *A Light in the Attic*. New York: HarperCollins, 2005. Print.

The Three Little Pigs. Sacred Texts. N.d. Web. 11 May 2014.

Girls and Boys Stay
In with Media

JULIET EVUSA

When I teach the Women and Minorities in the Mass Media undergraduate course, I always begin the class by asking students whether they usually make judgments about individuals or groups of people on the basis of their gender, ethnicity, class, sexual orientation, or race. Most admit judging others on those bases. When I challenge them to put on their critical thinking hats so as to examine the presence of stereotypes in media, beginning the discussion with children's media (then continuing that discussion with adult media), most are surprised that some of the children's entertainment media that has shaped their judgments contained latent stereotypes that initially escaped them because they were too tuned into the plot, animation, and music to notice.

My approach to teaching students enrolled in my Women and Minorities in the Media course is to offer insightful analyses of the popular culture that they are consuming or may have consumed by helping them reflect on aspects of life that they may take for granted. My role as a college instructor and media studies scholar is to arm students with the ability to step out of their familiar environment by critically examining how popular culture shapes their existence and, in doing so, to help them become conscious of the stereotypes they might have encountered and even embraced as true. Sut Jhally, founder of the Media Education Foundation, described this approach as "getting the fish to think about water" (3). Since students taking this class hope to pursue careers in various media entities, my hope is that they will become proactive in contesting these stereotypes in a manner that will make them unsustainable.

Themes Emerging from Student Responses

After going through the process of analyzing two years of students' responses to questions addressed at the end of each chapter and findings from their final research papers, I narrowed my focus to five main themes related to children's entertainment media: presence of inauthentic ethnic accents, the "beauty and the beast" syndrome, the male-gaze concept, Disney ideology mirrored in other texts, and the social construction of femininity in Disney texts.

Presence of Inauthentic Ethnic Accents

When I observed students' reactions to the reason Hollywood-created "Indian talk" existed for decades, I came across two different reactions. While some students acknowledged Hollywood's deliberate use of what they referred to as "broken" or "clipped" language, others stressed that the language was authentic because they believed that many Native Americans could not speak English during the period that these films were produced. Those who recognized Hollywood's deliberate use of inauthentic Native American language indicated that children find the thought of Indians running around, stomping, and singing "pretty cool," "interesting," and "funny." This group of students also recounted their own childhood experiences mimicking the "false" Native American accent while playing the "Cowboy and Indians" game that was influenced by movies like *Pocahontas* and *Peter Pan*. It did not come as a surprise to me when I encountered responses that reiterated what psychologists refer to as cognitive structures, also known as *schemata,* that allow us to make judgments about people from different social groups based on, as Gorham says, "the limited information that we have stored in the category that we have for that group" (qtd. in Lind 17). Since stereotypes are so prevalent in the media, viewers internalize them to the extent that, when they encounter someone of a particular group, "the stereotype for that group is primed and automatically activated and influences subsequent cognitive processing" (qtd. in Lind 18). This cognitive process was very well articulated in some of the responses behind the persistence of "Indian talk":

> Children like to play a role ("Cowboys and Indians") other than what they traditionally are. Many children like the action that comes with this game [L.W.].

> Because of the reinforcement of the issue over the years, children's movies like *Pocahontas* and *Peter Pan* portray Native Americans speaking in broken language. Chil-

dren mimic what they see on television. There is so much content about Native Americans that young children see that unfortunately only portrays Native Americans as either "noble" or "savage" with no real human depth [M.Y.].

Stereotypes remain unchanged because it makes it easier to identify with a people we don't understand [B.W.].

However, the few who did not believe that Hollywood deliberately used inauthentic Native American language argued that Caucasian actors hired to play Native American roles spoke in a "clipped" manner in an attempt to portray what occurred during the time frame that these movies were produced. One student elaborated on this point at length by stating that producers had no intentions of portraying Indians as "dumb" or uncivilized because many Native Americans hardly spoke English during the era these movies were produced. The student added,

The Cherokee language, for example, is full of syllables and words that often times sounds like a strange assortment of grunts, which may be why the film industry had added this into the speaking roles of Native Americans. While I agree that they should get the historical facts correct, it does not stand to reason that showing that the Native Americans did not know how to speak English very well is offensive because it is a historical fact [B.G.M.].

Most students tended to frame the problem as being larger and more significant in current children's entertainment media. These students cited the most current examples of Disney Channel sitcoms featuring characters with accents, including *Jessie's* Ravi (portrayed by Karan Brar), who plays a smart animal-loving boy with a fake Indian accent and *Shake It Up's* Gunter and Tinka Hessenheffer (portrayed by Kenton Duty and Caroline Sunshine) portraying the "funny foreigners" roles stereotypical about students from a small mountainous country in Europe. Other students cited Disney movies featuring protagonists with thick accents like the *Cars* franchise in which Mater (Daniel Lawrence Whitney's voice over) is depicted with a distinctively thick southern accent that can be construed to serve the function of emphasizing his country mannerisms. This group of students attributed the endurance of "Indian talk" to the central role that children's entertainment media has assumed in reinforcing these stereotypes over the years.

I noticed that most responses did recognize the effects that this trend could have on children's perception of people from ethnic groups, thus validating social learning theory's proponents like Baran and Davis who contend that the media becomes an "early window" that allows children to see the world well before they are capable of competently interacting with it (193). These concerns have been reiterated by academic linguistics like Rosina Lippi-Green who claims that some animated features teach children to "ethnocentrically discriminate" by portraying bad characters with foreign accents (qtd. in Wenke par. 19). A few responses expressed confidence in parents' ability to teach their children that the stereotypes prevalent in children's entertainment media are not a true depiction of their peers from different ethnicities. These group of students felt that Hollywood's use of inauthentic accents will fade with time if parents take the initiative to teach their children that the use of ethnic accents is often not only inaccurate but also insensitive. One student's response averred that the only way to confront these stereotypes is to produce more movies that strive to paint an accurate picture of Native Americans—and those from other cultures as well. Some responses took this point even further by drawing parallels that exist between the portrayals of Indians in key western and Disney movies with that of other ethnicities in contemporary media. For example, three students mentioned that

> this is really no different from the way movies portray those cowboys from the Wild West. This is the way consumers relate and generalize other races and cultures [D.P.].
>
> "Indian talk" as we know it will continue to occur with children just like "Chinese talk" will [B.G.M.].
>
> hearing people use the Hollywood "Indian talk" continues to this day as a result of Indian stereotypes portrayed in so many movies, television programs, and cartoons such as *South Park* and *Looney Tunes* [E.U.].

While most students admitted that Hollywood's use of inauthentic media was present in today's children's entertainment and also acknowledged being captivated by these portrayals while growing up, there was one student's response that stood out:

> If children do use "Indian Talk" it's probably because of what they learn in school every year around Thanksgiving. Children also mimic the sounds of different languages, Chinese, Spanish, French, etc. Even adults do it; I think it is human nature [L.W.].

This student believed that the school system, where children spend the majority of their time, plays a significant role in socializing them to stereotypical depictions of Native Americans, especially around the Thanksgiving holiday.

The majority of these students' observations are supported by findings from research conducted on the effect of Hollywood's portrayal of ethnic accents on the general public, especially children. Examples include Eric Wenke's critical analysis of *Oliver & Company* in which Cheech Marin's voice is utilized for the character of Tito—enforcing a negative stereotype associated with Hispanics living in New York (par. 15); in addition, Naomi Rockler's textual analysis of Disney's *The Lion King's* claims that the portrayals of hyenas acting "comically inarticulate and insipid" while conversing in Ebonics (African American vernacular) echoes offensive stereotypes of African Americans living in the ghettos (Rockler 170). Other scholars studying how regional linguistic competence affects the evaluations of a character's personality reveal that the more ethnocentric an individual listener's orientation is, the more favorably children would react to speech of standard accent, and consequently the less favorably they would react to speeches of a regional or foreign accent (Lambert qtd. in Wenke par. 17). These conclusions suggest that children who spend a significant amount of their time viewing negative portrayals of characters, enhanced by accents, will not only be entertained by such portrayals, but come to adopt negative attitudes towards those who possess the characteristics portrayed.

"Beauty and the Beast" Syndrome

There is no question that the "beauty and the beast" syndrome, a major theme in Disney's popular film *Beauty and the Beast*, has also made its way to contemporary genres of entertainment media. Several cultural scholars, mainly feminists, have been critical of this syndrome, more specifically in terms of the role it plays in normalizing patriarchy and downplaying sexism and, by doing so, limiting the capability of young girls to step out of their prescribed gender roles. Not only is this syndrome detrimental to female viewers, there has also been a trend in contemporary media, especially situation comedies targeting preteens and teens, as well as adult audiences, to portray male protagonists as the "bumbling buffoon" who plays an inferior yet dominant role (Luther et al. 179). The tendency to stereotype some males in this light, most would argue, stands to limit their potential and sends out the message that incompetency is a trait to strive for. For these reasons, I find it necessary to include responses that tie this Disney syndrome to contemporary media and, by doing so, to showcase the effects this syndrome may have on viewers who grew up watching children's entertainment that might have alluded to the "Beauty and the Beast" trope.

The end of chapter question addressing this syndrome solicited very stimulating responses. When asked to draw parallels between "the gender role representations in films and sitcoms portraying the 'beast' as inferior yet dominant male characters and superior yet submissive female characters" (Luther et al. 180), all students admitted that they had noticed what they referred to as the "modern day beauty and the beast" syndrome carried out in various genres of entertainment TV. The responses cited a couple of Disney Channel's sitcoms like *Dog with a Blog, Good Luck Charlie,* and *Liv and Maddie.* While some found it normal and humorous for adult situation comedies, like *According to Jim, The King of Queens, Everybody Loves Raymond,* and films, like *The Hangover, Knocked Up, Tommy Boy, Hall Pass, Wedding Crashers,* and *The Proposal,* to depict this ideal, others seem bothered by this portrayal. What was common among these responses was the concern that women were always relegated to traditional gender roles—no matter how strong, intelligent, and independent they were, while males, on the other hand, always played a superior gender role despite being sexist, underachieving, and dominating. Several student responses mentioned examples of "Beauty and the Beast" tropes in contemporary media:

> I have seen the television show *According To Jim,* and it has always bothered me that the wife puts up with all of her husband's words and actions; he never treats her well unless he has something to gain from it. The movie *The Hangover* portrays this same ideal; the woman is left to submissively deal with the fact that her husband-to-be shows up late and sunburnt to their wedding after a night of mischief with his friends in Las Vegas. All of these "beauty and the beast" shows, while humorous, are reinforcing this thought that, no matter how strong and intelligent women become, they will always be controlled in some way by a man [B.G.M.].

> There are several films that come to mind that are also part of this genre. Some examples are *Hall Pass, Wedding Crashers, Tangled, Paul Blart Mall Cop,* and any movie featuring Kevin James for that matter [V.W.].

While a majority of respondents stated that they were disturbed with the images of women portrayed as inferior and the existence of "I cannot help being a man" mentality, a few responses seemed to embrace the notion that entertainment media offers a realistic depiction of reality. For example, one response claimed,

> I don't think the "beauty and the beast" syndrome is a product of television and film. I see it as an accurate representation of real life relationships. We all know at least one couple like Doug and Carrie (*King of Queens*) or Ray and Debra (*Everybody Loves Raymond*) [J.W.].

On the other hand, those that were bothered by these portrayals completely disagreed. For example one student response stressed the need for a more realistic portrayal of relationships in the ideal world:

Movies and films should portray a man and a woman of equal attractiveness, compatible in earning potential, and, when they fight, it isn't always the woman caving into the man for being unruly or disobedient [A.M.].

One response that caught my attention expressed some concern regarding the tendency for contemporary media shows to send conflicting messages to women, especially those striving to find a balance between working in the corporate world, in which they must embrace strong and independent female ideals, and the need to fulfill traditional gender roles of a wife and family woman. The student's observation is supported by findings from a study conducted by Towbin and her associates involving a qualitative analysis of 26 Disney feature-length animated films (35). The study revealed instances of mixed messages directed towards female viewers in Disney films, including *Beauty and the Beast*'s female protagonist's non-traditional gender behaviors (her love for reading and adventure and her lack of attraction to her suitor Gaston, who also happens to be good-looking) contrasted with traditional gender behavior, such as her need to be rescued and falling in love and marrying the beast, despite his abusive behavior; *The Little Mermaid*'s leading character who is initially portrayed as an independent character who disobeys her overbearing father but later ends up sacrificing her voice to win a relationship; *Pocahontas*'s leading character initially decides to disobey her father by falling in love with an outsider, yet ends up making the ultimate choice to stay with her family and community (37–40). The morals behind most of these Disney films, as well as other contemporary shows, is well summarized by Luther and her colleagues who argue that "in the resolution of the struggle between patriarchy and feminism, it remains the task of the female protagonists to acquiesce to the 'natural' force of patriarchy" (168). Contemporary media's propensity to send mixed messages to female audiences was well captured by a student response:

> While society has become more accepting of strong and independent women in society as well, as in several TV roles, these frequent stereotypical roles of the trophy wife and mediocre husband or love interest could lead to lower expectations for women and the outcome of their lives [A.R.].

In other words, these students are not only familiar with Disney's *Beauty and the Beast* storylines in contemporary media, they are also able to recognize the trope's detrimental effects on both genders.

The Male Gaze Concept

Students were initially not familiar with the concept of the "male gaze." It was only after they gained an understanding of the required text's definition of the concept, that male gaze occurs when "the image of a woman is created from the perspective of an implied male observer," that they were able to identify plenty of examples of this concept at work (Luther et al. 200). When asked why this concept is prevalent in advertising and other forms of media, the responses were divided along gender lines (Luther et al. 204). Responses from some male students indicated that "males have been viewed and continue to be viewed as the dominant sex for centuries" and that "some women accept and even embrace the practice." This response suggests that female teenagers are not the only ones who internalize the higher level of importance placed on being beautiful, sexy, and desirable, and that the "male gaze" concept sends messages to male teenagers that women are mere objects that enjoy their gazes.

Not only is objectification a recurring theme in a variety of advertisements and other forms of entertainment media, studies have also shown its prevalence in some children's entertainment media. Student responses provided examples of Disney female characters taking shape through male gaze, particularly within the norms of attractiveness and body composition. What was common among these responses was the tendency by some Disney films to portray female characters overly sexually with unnaturally small waists, large breasts, and huge, wide eyes with long, fluttering eyelashes. One student response even noted that almost all Disney female bodies appear disproportionate no matter how diverse the characters are. Examples provided by this student observation included Jasmine, Mulan, and Tiana (*The Princess and the Frog*). A recent example of the so-called gender dimorphism in animated films is the movie *Frozen* in which Anna's eyeballs are actually wider, as reported in Kothari's article, than her wrist. Cultural critics argue that it is damaging to depict women with exaggerated features due to the concern that some young girls might be led to believe that there is only one ideal—one of an unrealistic body type that rarely exists in a broader cultural context. More on this later.

What was of particular interest was the decision by some students to use this concept as the central focus of their final research papers. One student's research paper, "'Super' Stereotype: Sexism in Comic Books," surveyed the amount of sexism in comic books and the impact this has on their target audience—mainly pre-teens. The student noted,

> The attire of female characters tended to be skimpy with their chests exaggerated and usually exposed, with small pieces of cloth covering them. The strength, skill, and autonomy of these characters rarely existed without the grossly obvious sexual portrayal of the female body. Wonder Woman is seen in a gold corset that barely covers her breasts and does not cover her back at all. Everything about her is supposed to be playing to the male fantasy [N.F.P.].

Another student who also chose to analyze the presence of the "male gaze" concept in comic books targeting pre-teens admitted that she, for a long time, has been infatuated with and idolized superheroes depicted in DC and Marvel comic books, namely *Batman*, *The X-Men*, and *Mighty Morphin Power Rangers*, as well cartoon series shown on television and movies. Since she considered herself media literate as a result of taking this class, she expressed concern regarding the so-called "male gaze" lens used to depict women that are currently relayed to adolescent children and called for the need to confront this concept.

"Through the Eyes of the Gaming Industry: Gender Stereotypes in Video Games" is a research paper that set out to analyze the presence of the "male gaze" concept in *Grand Theft Auto V*, *The Elder Scrolls: Skyrim*, and *Final Fantasy*. The paper's author, a self-proclaimed gamer, counted the frequency of sexual content within a game, the gender of the character initiating sexual acts, the number of women wearing suggestive clothing, the number of times women were shown domesticated, and the number of times males were portrayed as muscular. Not only did his results confirm that video games depicted women in a sexual or domesticated way so as to appeal to male gamers, he also found that male protagonists wielded more power.

Disney's Ideology Mirrored in Other Media Texts

Henry Giroux is well known for his criticisms about the influence of the so-called "Disney's ideology" on children. Giroux argues that the Walt Disney Company possesses the power to not only produce animated films that attract children's attentions but also shape their values and, by doing so, is "controlling the fields of social meanings through which children negotiate the world" (par. 13). This argument was articulated in a student's response:

> I have seen the film *Aladdin* a couple times. When I was a child, I just knew some of the characters as "the bad guys." That exact thought is why this film should be looked at as portraying Arab people the wrong way; for instance, the peddlers and villains are given thick accents, dark complexions, and stereotypical Arab features [B.G.M.].

While the above student acknowledged "buying into" the negative representations of the film *Aladdin* despite evidence of inaccuracies within the storyline, another student's research paper, "Historical Analysis of the Accuracy of Disney's *Mulan* and the Real Life Mulan," shared a different perspective. Her historical analysis of *Mulan* revealed consistencies in the film's depiction of cultural background as far as the historical dates, beliefs, dress, language, type of weapons used during wars, and the original legend that the story is based on. The only major inaccuracy the student found relates to the intelligent horse and small red dragon depicted in the Disney version of the story. The student also noted that the real Mulan fought for twelve years and was offered twelve ranks as a reward for her skills in battle. The student's paper concluded that *Mulan* does play a role in teaching children bravery and self-confidence.

When asked to identify the existence of Disney's ideological lessons relating to race, hierarchy, and segregation (Lind 172) in new forms of media consumed by pre-teens and teens, a few students observed that it is not uncommon for children exposed to negative depictions of the Arab and Arab-Americans in Disney productions, such as *Mickey in Arabia*, *Aladdin*, and *Hidalgo*, to also play video games vilifying these characters, as well as African-Americans. Hollywood critics like Jack Shaheen, author of "Real Bad Arabs: How Hollywood Vilifies a People," argues that these portrayals serve to encourage young players to accept these stereotypes as natural (28). To investigate this, one student's paper, "Destructive Cultural Warfare: Stereotyping Culture in Video Games," analyzed three popular videogames, *Call of Duty: Modern Warfare*, *Resident Evil*, and *Grand Theft Auto V*, for instances of Middle Eastern and African-American stereotypes, as well as any presence of discrimination against those and other groups. The student solicited the help of five coders, who also happen to be avid players, to count frequencies of violent acts, stereotypical behavior, criminal activity, and opposition to the U.S. government. The study found a high frequency of minorities depicted as violent and criminal; a great number of Middle-Eastern characters portrayed as barbaric and torturing U.S. soldiers; and an overwhelming tendency to portray other countries, mainly Middle-Eastern, in a negative manner. The students provided examples, such as racial slurs and depiction of African-Americans as savage, rampant in series as well, specifically pointing at a scene in *Grand Theft Auto V* showing a Caucasian person frightened by African Americans robbing houses and one character shouting, "Help, he's Black!" This, according to the student, shocked some of the coders, mainly because they had played the game before and thought nothing of this scene prior to participating in the study. The students did confirm the Social Learning Theory notion that video games popular with pre-teens and teenagers *could* play a role in helping provide a new means for young players to shape their constructs about other cultures.

When I asked students to identify a social group that has been ignored in children's entertainment media, it did not come as a surprise to me when they cited the lesbian, gay, bisexual, and transgender (LGBT) community. What surprised me was that most felt that lack of LGBT characters in children's entertainment media, especially Disney movies and television, perpetuates an ideology that reinforces male hegemony and by doing so symbolically annihilates or ignores individuals who are not straight. Some argued that having a gay or lesbian character would shatter Disney's ideology that perpetuates the notion that princesses or princes must be heterosexual. As a matter of fact, a couple believed that the inclusion of LGBT characters would introduce children to the idea in a family-friendly way before they overhear inappropriate and hateful remarks from their peers or guardians. When asked whether they have witnessed "instances in which gay characters are featured on primetime entertainment programming" (Luther et al. 230) targeting children and teens, the majority of the responses cited an episode on Disney's *Good Luck Charlie* 2014 finale episode that featured a lesbian couple who were parents of the character Taylor. Only one response cited *Glee*. Although a few students' responses did not support Disney's decision, the majority seemed comfortable with Disney's inclusion of a lesbian couple (Luther et al. 230):

> Showing average everyday LGBT characters in television, especially directed to a younger demographic, helps promote public tolerance and knowledge of the LGBT community. There was a time, before the 80's, where gay people were virtually invisible on television [L.W.].

> The lesbian moms in *Good Luck Charlie* appeared on screen briefly because of Disney's conservative ideology and fans. Introducing younger audiences to gay characters helps them to believe that gay people are just as normal as straight people. It helps to create a more tolerant future generation [E.U.].

> Take the show *Glee* for instance; its target demographic is middle to high school children. The common theme throughout the whole series is tolerance and self-acceptance. By having multiple gay characters it promotes a connection for gay youth, as well as teaching children to be more accepting. It shows the issues that all kids face and sets an example [B.W.].

The majority of responses mentioned that the subtle way Disney chose to introduce Taylor's lesbian mothers in a non-stereotypical manner, not only "promotes tolerance and acceptance" of the LGBT community, but also elevates Disney as a pioneer in including LGBT characters in children's entertainment media. However, not everyone was thrilled by Disney's decision. This 2014 finale episode was met by a protest by One Million Moms, a right-wing anti-gay group who vow to stop what they considered as the exploitation of children by entertainment media ("Purpose of One Million Moms" par. 3).

This so-called Disney ideology is not only confined to the U.S.'s domestic audience; it has also extended its reach to overseas markets. The company has also started new trends that made it possible for some of their popular movies, including and not limited to *Iron Man 3*, *The Avengers*, and *The Amazing Spider Man 2* to debut abroad, inspiring the charge that "Disneyfication" has led to the homogenization and, ultimately, Americanization of many foreign cultures which partake in entertainment products produced in the United States.

Disney's move to expand its audiences abroad was well articulated in a student's research paper titled "Comic Books' Role in Shaping World Views" in which he informed his readers about the merger between a popular comic market, Marvel Comics, with the Walt Disney Company, enabling the capitalizing of overseas markets.

This phenomenon is well captured by another student's research paper titled "The Disney Effect: A Study on Cultural Globalization and Its Effect on Children Living Abroad." The student stated,

> Using the Ecological Systems Theory along with the Socio-Culture Theory, I was able to identify influences, such as teachers, parents, peers, as well as their environment, that rely on Disney to provide wholesome entertainment. This enables Disney to promote the "American Way." I was able to provide evidence that Disney can provide some negative as well as some positive influences into other cultures [M.Y.].

In addition to responses about the ubiquity of American (Disney) culture, some responses alluded to the amount of adult language that occurs in Disney films, despite the fact that most children would not be able to comprehend it. Although adult humor is meant to be discreet, some student responses cautioned that such humor may have a negative effect on young viewers. Besides, these students argued, as children get older, inappropriate jokes in children's media become more and more apparent. A few responses noted that this kind of language "finds it way in all forms of children's entertainment including Disney's sitcoms *Jessie*, *Good Luck Charlie*, and *Shake It Up*." This concern was well articulated in a student's research paper "More Than a Movie: A Content Analysis of Adult Content in Six Popular Computer Generated Films Produced by Pixar and DreamWorks" that set out to determine the frequency of adult content, as well as visual occurrences of violence, nudity, and sex and auditory occurrences of offensive language, verbal aggression, sexual innuendo or reference, and drug use references in *Shrek the Third*, *Ratatouille*, *Over the Hedge*, *Cars*, *Shark Tale*, and *The Incredibles*. Results from the student's research study concluded that while all movies used adult language/content, violence, and aggression, *Shrek the Third* had the highest incidence of adult content/language.

The Social Construction of Stereotypical Femininity

An excerpt from one student's research paper titled "Social Construction of Reality and Endangerment in Disney and Disney Pixar films" captured examples of stereotypical femininity portrayed as natural, normal, and universal. The student's quest to critically analyze the portrayal of feminist depiction of *Snow White and the Seven Dwarfs, Cinderella, Alice in Wonderland, Sleeping Beauty, The Little Mermaid, Beauty and the Beast, Pocahontas*, and *Mulan* suggests that feminine protagonists in Disney animated films appeared to be at the mercy of the monarchical or patriarchal society groups in which they reside in.

The above excerpt captured sentiments echoed by feminist scholars who are concerned that Disney films present a skewed portrayal of femininity and masculinity that may lead children who are developing cognitively to organize their views on gender into schemas driven by these limited representations. Also conveyed in this excerpt are concerns regarding the presence of the "Damsel in Distress" narratives in Disney films that place female protagonists in subservient roles in relation to males, and hence supporting male hegemony. What I found particularly interesting about the student's findings was Disney's tendency to place the needs of female protagonists' communities before their own personal desires, a narrative, according to Dundes (353), normally reserved for Disney's male protagonists.

The social construction of femininity was well captured by a student's research paper titled "Disney's Enchanted Mirror: An Analysis of the True Reflection of Disney's Global Women." The central thesis of this paper revolved around the tendency by some Disney films to construct their princesses' physical attributes using standard traits consistent with European standards of beauty—an ideal standard that casts females in terms of body type with long legs, tiny waists, delicate and feminine facial features, long hair, and flawless skin. According to the student's research paper, Disney's attempt to create ethnic princesses (as depicted in the films *Mulan, Pocahontas, Aladdin*, and *The Princess and the Frog*) through the lens of European stereotypical femininity unraveled inaccurate cultural depictions. The student added that

Disney Princesses are frequently redesigned, and with each remodel they tend to become more Americanized and lose color. Although there is a lot of negative reaction to these films, many countries do not have the financial means to rebuke the system, and others simply ban the items before ever entering their country [B.G.M.].

However, this skewed portrayal of femininity and masculinity in Disney films takes a different form in media targeting teenagers. When asked to draw parallels between the portrayal of stereotypical femininity present in Disney with those present in contemporary teen films (Luther et al. 180), students alluded to "post-feminist" characters preoccupied with their own personal desires usually involving falling in love, obsessing with their own appearance, and indulging in dramatic "cat fights" between female protagonists. These sentiments were captured by one student response:

> The main female characters in all of these movies are examples of post-feminist characters. In *Clueless*, the high school girls all keep a sense of femininity throughout the film. The same scenario occurs in *Legally Blonde* as well, just with a college student instead of high school girls. The textbook goes on to say that a child watching these films may learn that being beautiful or thin is an intrinsic and desired part of being a female (Luther et al. 162) [M.B.].

Although most students reported that they witnessed stereotypical portrayal of femininity written in Disney scripts, and that not much has changed with recent films, they reported that this trend has found its way in contemporary entertainment media targeting teens, the main difference being the portrayal of modern feminist characters preoccupied with personal desires, a trait associated with Disney's male protagonists.

Conclusion

My analysis of students' responses and final research papers' evaluation of entertainment media targeting children revealed that there are distorted views of femininity, race, and ethnicities embedded in children's entertainment media, especially Disney films and shows featured on the Disney Channel. What the responses had in common was student recognition of the tendency in entertainment media, namely sitcoms, video games, and films, to include contemporary versions of inauthentic ethnic accents, the "beauty and the beast" syndrome, the "male-gaze" concept, Disney's ideology, and the social construction of femininity. These analyses illustrate that, although most students admitted having internalized a lot of assumptions about representations of race, gender, and sexuality, they are capable of critical analysis that disrupts limited representations they have been offered in mainstream popular culture and media and, most especially, Disney films and sitcoms featured on the Disney Channel.

After this start, dealing with material with which students are comfortable and familiar, we can begin our examination of other media. We have begun our journey.

Works Cited

According to Jim. Writs. Tracy Newman and Jonathan Stark. ABC, 2001–2009. Television.

Aladdin. Dirs. John Musker and Ron Clements. 1992. Walt Disney Video, 2005. DVD.

Alice in Wonderland. Dirs. Clyde Geronimi, Wilfred Jaxon, and Hamilton Luske. 1951. Walt Disney Studios Home Entertainment, 2010. DVD.

The Avengers. Dir. Joss Whedon. 2012. Walt Disney Video, 2012. DVD.

Baran, Stanley, and Dennis Davis. *Mass Communication Theory: Foundations, Ferment and Future*. Boston: Wadsworth Cengage Learning, 2008. Print.

Batman. Creators Bill Finger and Bob Kane. DC Comics. Origin. 1972. Print.

Beauty and the Beast. Dirs. Gary Trousdale and Kirk Wise. 1991. Walt Disney Video, 2002. DVD.

Cars. Dir. John Lasseter. 2006. Disney-Pixar, 2006. DVD.

Catwoman. Creators Bill Finger and Bob Kane. DC Comics. Origin. 1975 (appears in 1537 issues). Print.

Cinderella. Dir. Clyde Geronimi. 1950. Disney, 2012. DVD.

Clueless. Dir. Amy Heckerling. 1995. Warner Bros., 2005. DVD.

Dog with a Blog. Writs. Michael B. Kaplan and Philip Stark. Disney, 2012–present. Television.

Dundes, Lauren. "Disney's Modern Heroine Pocahontas: Revealing Age-old Gender Stereotypes and Role Discontinuity Under a Façade of Liberation." *The Social Science Journal* 38.3 (2001): 353–65. Web. 8 July 2014.

The Elder Scrolls V: Skyrim. Xbox 360 vers. Rockville, MD: Bethesda, 2011. DVD-ROM.

England, Dawn E., Lara Descartes, and Melissa A. Collier-Meek. "Gender Role Portrayal and the Disney Princess." *Sex Roles* 64 (2011): 555–67. Web. 14 July 2014.

Everybody Loves Raymond. Writs. Ray Romano and Philip Rosenthal. CBS, 1996–2005. Television.

Fantastic Four. Dir. Tim Story. 2005. Fox Searchlight, 2005. DVD.

The Fantastic 4. Creators Stan Lee and Jack Kirby. Marvel Comics. Origin. 1961. Print.

Final Fantasy. Playstation vers. Redmond: Squaresoft, 2003. DVD-ROM.

Frozen. Dirs. Chris Buck and Jennifer Lee. 2013. Walt Disney Studios Home Entertainment, 2014. DVD.

Giroux, Henry A. "Animating Youth: The Disnification of Children's Culture." *Socialist Review* 24:3 (1995): 23–55. Web. 14 July 2014.

Glee. Writs. Ian Brennan, Brad Falchuk, and Ryan Murphy. Fox, 2009–present. Television.

Good Luck Charlie. Writs. Phil Baker and Drew Vaupen. Disney Channel, 2010–2014. Television.

Grand Theft Auto V. Xbox 360 vers. New York: Rockstar Games, 2013. DVD-ROM.

Hall Pass. Dirs. Bobby Farrelly and Peter Farrelly. 2011. Warner Bros. Pictures, 2011. DVD.

The Hangover. Dir. Todd Phillips. 2009. Warner Home Video, 2009. DVD.

Hidalgo. Dir. Joe Johnson. 2004. Touchstone Pictures, 2004. DVD.

The Honeymooners. Dir. Frank Satenstein. CBS, 1955–1956. Television.

The Incredibles. Dir. Brad Bird. 2004. Walt Disney Home Entertainment, 2005. DVD.

Jessie. Writ. Pamela Evans. Disney Channel, 2011–present. Television.

Jhally, Sut. *Dir. Stuart Hall: Representation and the Media*. Northampton, MA: Media Education Foundation. 1997. Web. 14 July 2014.

The King of Queens. Writs. David Litt and Michael J. Weithorn. CBS, 1998–2007. Television.

Knocked Up. Dir. Judd Apatow. 2007. Universal Studios, 2007. DVD.

Kothari, Monika. "Why Is Disney Still Making Female Characters with Such Cartoonish Bodies?" *Huffington Post.* N.p., 11 March 2014. Web. 14 July 2014.

Legally Blonde. Dir. Robert Luketic. 2001. Fox Searchlight, 2001. DVD.

Lind, Rebecca A., ed. *Race, Gender, Media: Considering Diversity Across Audiences, Content and Producers,* 2d ed. Boston: Pearson, 2010. Print.

The Lion King. Dirs. Rob Minkoff and Roger Allers. 1994. Walt Disney Video, 2003. DVD.

The Little Mermaid. Dirs. John Musker and Ron Clements. 1989. Walt Disney Studios Home Entertainment, 2013. DVD.

Liv and Maddie. Writs. John D. Beck and Ron Hart. Disney Channel, 2013–present. Television.

Looney Tunes Bugs Bunny/Yosemite Sam Series. Dirs. Friz Freleng. Warner Bros Picture, 1960. Cartoon Series.

Luther, Catherine A., Carolyn R. Lepre, and Naeemah Clark. *Diversity in U.S. Mass Media.* Malden: Wiley-Blackwell, 2012. Print.

Mickey in Arabia. Dir. Wilfred Jackson. Columbia Pictures, 1932. Film.

Moffitt, Kimberly, and Heather Harris. "Of Negation, Princesses, Beauty, and Work: Black Mothers Reflect on Disney's *The Princess and the Frog.*" *The Howard Journal of Communications* 25 (1995): 56–76. Web. 14 July 2014.

Mulan. Dirs. Barry Cook and Tony Bancroft. 1998. Walt Disney Video, 2004. DVD.

Oliver and Company. Dirs. Dan Hansen and George Scribner. 1988. Walt Disney Studios Home Entertainment, 2009. DVD.

Over the Hedge. Dirs. Karey Kirkpatrick and Tim Johnson. DreamWorks, 2006. DVD.

Paul Blart: Mall Cop. Dir. Steve Carr. 2009. Sony Pictures, 2009. DVD.

Peter Pan. Dirs. Clyde Geronimi, Wilfred Jackson, and Hamilton Luske. 1953. Walt Disney Studios Home Entertainment, 2013. DVD.

Pocahontas. Dirs. Eric Goldberg and Mike Gabriel. 1995. Walt Disney Home Entertainment, 2005. DVD.

Power Rangers. Creators Haim Saban and Shuki Levy. Mighty Morphin Power Rangers Comics. Origin. 1993. Print. Television.

The Princess and the Frog. Dirs. John Musker and Ron Clements. 2009. Walt Disney Studios Home Entertainment, 2010. DVD.

The Proposal. Dir. Anne Fletcher. 2009. Touchstone Home Entertainment, 2009. DVD.

"Purpose of One Million Moms." *One Million Moms.* N.p., 2001–2006. Web. 20 August 2014.

Ratatouille. Dirs. Brad Bird and Jan Pinkava. 2007. Disney-Pixar, 2007. DVD.

Resident Evil. Nintendo GameCube vers. San Mateo: Capcom, 2006. DVD-ROM.

Rockler-Gladen, Naomi. "Race, Hierarchy, and Hyenaphobia in 'The Lion King.'" *Race/Gender/Media: Considering Diversity Across Audiences, Content, and Producers.* Ed. Rebecca Ann Lind. Boston: Pearson, 2010, Print.

Shaheen, Jack G. "In Its New 'Family Film,' Disney Clobbers Arabs—Again!" *Washington Report on Middle East Affairs* 23 (4), 66–69. Web. 14 July 2014.

_____. *Reel Bad Arabs: How Hollywood Vilifies a People.* New York: Olive Branch Press, 2001. Print.

Shake It Up! Writ. Chris Thompson. Disney Channel, 2010–2013. Television.

Shark Tale. Dirs. Bibo Bergeron, Rob Letterman, and Vicky Jenson. 2004. DreamWorks Animated, 2005. DVD.

Shrek the Third. Dirs. Chris Miller and Raman Hui. 2007. Paramount Home Video/ DreamWorks, 2007. DVD.

The Simpsons. Writ. James L. Brooks. Fox, 1989–present. Television.

Sleeping Beauty. Dir. Clyde Geronimi. 1959. Walt Disney Studios Home Entertainment, 2008. DVD.

Smith, Stacey L., and Crystal A. Cook. "Gender Stereotypes: An Analysis of Popular Films and TV." thegeenadavisinstitute.org. The Geena Davis Institute on Gender in Media, 2008. Web. 14 July 2014.

Smith, Stacey L., Catherine Pieper, Amy Grandos, and Mark Choueitik. "Assessing Gender-Related Portrays in Top-Grossing G-Rated Films." *Sex Roles* 62 (2010): 774–786.

Snow White and the Seven Dwarfs. Dirs. Dick Richard and Dorothy Ann Blank. 1937. Walt Disney Video, 2001. DVD.

South Park. Writs. Trey Parker and Matt Stone. Dir. Trey Parker. Comedy Central, 1997– present. Television.

Spiderman. Creators John Romita, Jr., et al. Marvel Comics. Origin. 1962 (appears in 10460 issues). Print.

Spiderman. Creators Stan Lee and Steve Dikto. Marvel Comics. Origin. 1962. Print.

Tangled. Dirs. Nathan Greno and Byron Howard. 2010. Walt Disney Pictures, 2011. DVD.

Tommy Boy. Dir. Peter Segal. 1995. Warner Bros., 2005. DVD.

Towbin, Mia. A., Shelly A. Haddock, Toni S. Zimmerman, Lori K. Lund, and Litsa R. Tanner. "Images of Gender, Race, Age, and Sexual Orientation in Disney Feature-Length Animated Films." *Journal of Feminist Therapy* 15.4 (2003): 19–44. Web. 14 July 2014.

The Walt Disney Company. *The Walt Disney Company Reports Fourth Quarter and Full Year Earnings for Fiscal Year 2013.* N.p., 7 Nov. 2013. Web. 14 July 2014.

Wedding Crashers. Dir. David Dobkin. 2005. New Line Home Video, 2006. DVD.

Wenke, Eric. "Accents in Children's Animated Features as a Device for Teaching Children to Ethnocentrically Discriminate." Paper submitted to conference on *Language and Popular Culture*, 2008. Web. 14 July 2014.

Wong, Curtis M. "Disney's 'Frozen' Slammed by Mormon Grandmother for 'Gay Agenda to Normalize Homosexuality.'" *Huffington Post.* N.p., 18 Feb. 2014. Web. 14 July 2014.

X-Men. Creators Stan Lee and Jack Kirby. Marvel Comics. Origin. 1963. Print.

The Whole Picture

ERIKA CARTER

My initial encounter with children's literature in college is one I will likely remember for many years to come. While literature for children and young adults is expected in some college courses (such as Young Adult Literature), I was surprised to find that one of my professors used a children's book to help demonstrate the principles of literary analysis in Composition II. Sitting in class one day I was completely shocked as the professor pulled a brightly colored hardback book from her bag. I was even more astonished as she read *Martina the Beautiful Cockroach: A Cuban Folktale* aloud to the class. Although I was interested to see how the book fit in with the material we had been covering in class previously, I was also certain there would be some sort of unforeseen twist to this lesson, because obviously being read to—and certainly from an illustrated children's book—seemed too good to be true. I found the experience of listening to the audible expression in the professor's voice and the simplicity of the story enjoyable, but I had no idea the impact this seemingly elementary lesson would have on my future.

After finishing the story, the professor asked the members of the class to outline the plot of the story. We then discussed the setting in which the story takes place. As we began to discuss the characterization of Martina, the main character, the professor asked us to refer to specific instances from the book which influenced and supported our ideas. The professor then encouraged us to think about the deeper meaning of the story and the themes the author conveys to the audience through the story and characters. After we had finished discussing *Martina the Beautiful Cockroach: A Cuban Folktale*, the professor reminded us that the same techniques and thought processes we had used to discuss this children's book are the ones we should apply when analyzing more complex works of literature. She used this as a way of demonstrating various literary devices she expected us to be able to discuss about each of the selections we would be required to read for the class. Not only was this experience enjoyable, but it also allowed us to have a class discussion about the foundational principles and approaches that can, and should be, utilized when approaching more complicated and sophisticated texts. Making the process seem simple and less intimidating allowed me to develop a more complete understanding of what literary analysis entails.

Despite the fact that I have enjoyed reading from the time I was a little girl, I have always found formal literary analysis and discussion intimidating. I typically kept my thoughts to myself during group discussions, as I have always found discussions to be uncomfortable, and I worried I did not have enough knowledge about a given literary genre to discuss it effectively. Reading the children's story in class helped me more fully understand the methods used in literary analysis, making the whole task seem less intimidating to me than it had in the past. I had just proven I had the ability to dissect the components of this simple children's story, so why couldn't I do the same with a more complex piece of literature?

I was inspired to draw on these same basic approaches to literary texts we had been assigned as a class, rather than being intimidated by the task of breaking down a complex literary work. As I began to think of the connections and similarities that exist among different forms of literature, I began to gain confidence in my own ability to ponder the deeper meanings and ideas conveyed through an author's words. This formal conversation about a simple children's story enabled me to realize that similarities exist among all types of literature, regardless of the author's purpose, the intended audience, the genre classification, or even the length of the work. I even decided to focus my education on studying English in hopes of assisting others in coming to the same realization and love of reading and literary analysis I now possess.

An additional way to study and analyze literature written for both children and young adults lies in my newfound awareness of the vital role of the illustrations that often accompany the text. I have always enjoyed experiencing the artistic expression included in certain pieces of literature, especially when I was much younger, but since studying works of children's literature in an academic setting, I am able to approach literary artwork from an intellectual perspective, rather than solely one of personal enjoyment.

Reading and discussing Neil Gaiman's book *The Wolves in the Walls*, also assigned in the composition class, encouraged me to think about the function of the illustrations. I began to contemplate the ways the reader is affected by the visual images accompanying the text. I had not previously thought about the ways visuals in children's books contribute to the story as a whole, primarily because I had not read them since I was young. Pictures not only assist children in understanding stories but also help keep their attention. Children are able to comprehend visual images long before they are able to decipher words on a page. As Mabel Segun states in *Illustrating for Children*, "the pictorial code is a more direct means of communication than the verbal code. Such children will look at the pictures and tell the story in their own words. This helps to develop their imagination" (25).

Illustrations are generally appealing to children and also help to convey messages and/or tone that may be absent from the text itself. For example, well-chosen pictures and colors can make a seemingly scary story seem less fraught to child readers. Many stories intended for children take advantage of this very technique. For example, many Disney movies that are geared toward young children have very dark, frightening themes that are magically minimized by the animation. Despite the fact that it may seem the pictures are present in children's literature just for looks, they actually play an important part in children's reading experiences.

As I focused on the ways these different visual elements affect the story as well as the reader's response to it, I began to see the incredible storytelling quality the images hold all on their own. I found myself paying close attention to the visual details the illustrator, Dave McKean, includes in the pictures present in *The Wolves in the Walls*. The simple inclusion of a picture not only enhances the experience of a reader but can also completely change one's perception of the words that accompany it. Pictures can cause a story to bounce off of a page and even come to life, which is the way McKean's illustrations function for me in this particular piece. Although I have always had an appreciation for artistic expression, it was not until studying this children's book that I became fully aware of the ways visual images serve as yet another form of communication.

The illustrations in *The Wolves in the Walls* help set the tone of the story. McKean's portrayal of Lucy and her family contribute to the eerie tone of the story. The family looks as if they are carved from wood, and their circular, sunken eyes make them appear less alive. The lines of their faces are also very rigid, rather than curved, which would usually be more in line with reality. This not only adds to their less than human appearance but also to the unsettling feeling given to the reader. Color is another element that effectively sets the tone in the illustrations. For example, the red coloring of the jam found on the wolves' mouths and paws, which is also the color of blood, implies the danger of the wolves. The tone of this work is somewhat determined by the text's diction and syntax, of course, but the illustrations play a prominent role in it as well.

Dave McKean combines multiple graphic elements in his illustrations for *The Wolves in the Walls*. His unique style is certainly not the usual technique one would expect in a children's book. Charles DeLint describes McKean's style as being "a bit confrontational, rather than typical picture book pretty" (27). He uses sketches, photographs, and computer-generated pictures throughout the book. This adds visual interest while also affecting the tone of the work. Some of the images are realistic, such as the sandwich at the end of the story, while others, such as the illustrator's depiction of the wolves, are unrealistic and clearly drawings. The colors McKean employs to depict the wolves visually are green, yellow, and primarily black—contributing to the eerie feelings the drawing evokes in the viewer. Studying the illustrations in this book suggests that visual images can contribute to, and alter, the reader's experience. The cartoon-like images and the unrealistic aspects of some of the pictures help remind the viewer of the fictitious nature of the events being relayed. Stories are able to come to life with the simple inclusion of an illustration, helping readers "see" into the story even further than the actual words allow. Illustrations are a captivating element of children's literature that should never be ignored.

Analyzing the impact of the illustrations present in *The Wolves in the Walls* encouraged me to see beyond the mere images present and focus my attention upon the personality in art and the artistic interpretation foundational to other types of artistic expression. Art is no longer simply a visual experience for me as a viewer, as I once believed it to be; I am now able to truly experience it in a way I was previously unaware of. I view each piece as an artist's expression or interpretation of the world in the way he or she views it. Art is an expression of the artist's perspective, rather than simply a representation of whatever the subject may be. Art allows an artist to communicate ideas and feelings to an audience, and, while I do not claim to fully comprehend the artistic process because I myself am not driven in this manner, I do understand the desire people have to express and communicate their ideas and feelings and, ultimately, themselves as individuals. As someone who is interested in the English language and the ways in which people communicate with one another, it is fascinating to me to learn about the beautiful, and universal, "language" of artistic expression people are able to achieve through visual images. Although people may experience or even view a piece of art differently, there are no language or cultural barriers or limitations in terms of what an artist can communicate.

Recognizing the value of the visual images present in many works written for children opened my eyes to the ways in which artistic expression is a form of communication, while also leading me to develop an interest in a form of literature that I was unfamiliar with at the time—the graphic novel. As I was researching *The Wolves in the Walls*, I came across a statement by LuAnn Toth that sparked yet another thought. Toth says, "This rather lengthy picture book displays the striking characteristics of a graphic novel: numerous four-panel pages" (178). Several pages in the book do resemble graphic novel pages, containing a series of panels which serve to tell a specific aspect of the story. Thus, many scholars have identified McKean's work as serving as a transitional piece between picture books and graphic novels. Although I had previously only read one graphic novel, I immediately became interested in the ways in which graphic novels are both similar to and different from the illustrated works I was familiar with, which primarily included children's literature.

I became captivated with the ways authors and illustrators are able to use images to portray elements of plot, theme, and even emotion and personal perspective to the reader. Marjane Satrapi's graphic novel *Persepolis: The Story of a Childhood* documents the author's struggle to free herself from the societal expectations forced upon her as a young girl. Satrapi explores her thoughts concerning religion, family, society, and politics as a girl growing up in Iran during the Islamic revolution. She recalls wishing she were allowed to voice her own thoughts and opinions concerning the expectations of society, yet she was forced to remain silent, at least for a time, due to her parents' concern for her safety. Eventually, Satrapi is able to emerge as a more confident, self-aware individual who possesses her own identity and ideals. Much of the emotion of the graphic novel *Persepolis* is depicted through the black and white visual images she presents in the panels. One example of the way Satrapi uses images to portray emotion is demonstrated as she describes the day her neighborhood was bombed. Satrapi recalls being out on a rare shopping trip for new clothes when she suddenly hears the explosion (138). She remembers being allowed to enter her street only after explaining that she lived there, as government officials had already blocked off the area by the time she arrived (139). After finding her mother, Satrapi recalls hearing the news that the bomb had hit her friend's house. She sees her friend's bracelet amidst the rubble surrounding her, and she realizes it is still on her friend's arm. In order to convey the overwhelming emotion this created in her, Satrapi displays an image of herself covering her mouth. The next panel depicts her young self with her hands over her eyes, and the final panel of the chapter is solid black with a caption reading, "No scream in the world could have relieved my suffering and anger" (142). Satrapi is able to convey her pain, sorrow, and anger by using a mixture of simple but striking visual images and text. The combination of Satrapi's words and images is an effective method of conveying her emotions to the reader.

At the beginning of *The Wolves in the Walls*, there are images on the walls of patterns and drawings which resemble those seen elsewhere in the book. *Blankets*, a graphic novel by Craig Thompson, also uses visual images and illustrations in order to reference events or help the reader understand what a character is thinking or remembering at a given point in the story, without actually referencing a different portion of the story textually. For example, Thompson uses the blanket Raina makes for Craig as a recurring image throughout the story. Thompson also uses recurring patterns and drawings in order to visually link certain aspects of the story together. For example, the patterns on the quilt Raina makes for Craig appear throughout the story. When she gives the blanket to Craig she tells him that each of the patterns she used to make it remind her of him (Thompson 183). The punishment young Craig and his brother received as children is also referenced later on as Craig associates an experience he is undergoing with the guilt and fear he felt as a young child being abused by a babysitter. Craig recalls the horrible events, recognizing that the fear and shame he associates with himself is because of the detachment he developed toward his body in order to deal with the abuse he dealt with during his childhood (291–94). Some of the panels in *Blankets* (as well as some in *The Wolves in the Walls*) help visually link events, situations, and even memories and emotions visually in order to help the reader understand some of the background and motivations of the characters.

Children's literature has profoundly shaped the path of my college education in ways I definitely would not have expected. From children's literature, I have learned the basic techniques of literary analysis and the ways in which these foundational approaches can be used to think critically about a variety of texts. Children's literature also helped introduce me to the graphic novel, which has ultimately led me to a greater understanding of artistic expression and its capacity to convey not only the talent of its artist, but also messages and ideas the artist seeks to communicate to viewers.

Works Cited

DeLint, Charles. "The Wolves in the Walls (Book)." *Fantasy and Science Fiction* 105.6 (Dec. 2003): 26–27. *Academic Search Complete.* EBSCO. Web. 24 Mar. 2011.

Gaiman, Neil. *The Wolves in the Walls*. Illus. Dave McKean. New York: HarperCollins, 2003. Print.

Satrapi, Marjane. *Persepolis*. New York: Pantheon, 2003. Print.

Segun, Mabel. "The Importance of Illustrations in Children's Books." *Illustrating for Children*. Ed. Mabel Segun. Ibadan: CLAN, 1988. 25–27. *Academic Search Complete*. EBSCO. Web. 31 Mar. 2011.

Thompson, Craig. *Blankets*. Marietta, GA: Top Shelf, 2003. Print.

Toth, Luann, et al. "The Wolves in the Walls (Book)." *School Library Journal* 49.9 (Sept. 2003): 178. *Academic Search Complete*. EBSCO. Web. 24 Mar. 2011.

Sources of Morality
Kimberly Qualls

In her children's novel *The House of the Scorpion*, Nancy Farmer offers an interesting perspective into what it means to be human through her protagonist: a clone child. As the genetic duplicate of a 140-year-old drug lord nicknamed El Patrón, Matteo Alacrán struggles to be a normal boy. He daily faces the propaganda that "clones aren't people," as Emilia, one of the children who frequent the Alacrán opium farm, venomously informs five-year-old Matt (26). Additionally, Matt is resented by the rest of the Alacrán family for the favoritism El Patrón shows him. This partiality, however, means nothing in the end, considering how El Patrón wants to harvest Matt's organs to prolong El Patron's own life.

Farmer's novel illustrates the problematic nature of defining humanity in narrow terms. Her protagonist makes choices that distinguish him from his malevolent but technically identical counterpart. By illustrating morality through a child protagonist in a way that young readers can comprehend, Farmer effectively illustrates the foundations of what it means to be human. In *The House of the Scorpion* the complexity of ethics is concentrated, and morality, for Matt, comes down to making compassionate choices. This simplification of morality's sources constitutes the relevance of the novel in a college setting. While ethical gray areas do exist within the novel (e.g., Tam Lin commits suicide, Matt uses violence to save his friend Fidelito from a severe beating, etc.), Farmer makes it clear that a character's choices are directly related to whether he or she is considered good or bad. This obvious relationship helps establish a characteristic of humanity, conscious decision-making, that serves as a basis for philosophical discussion. While there is certainly more to a complete definition of humanity than the ability to make choices, *The House of the Scorpion* exemplifies the difficulties of attempting to define our species, making straightforward connections between a character's actions and his or her status as a human or, more accurately, as humane.

The House of the Scorpion is relevant to college curriculum in the way that Matt represents real human struggles. The novel's related themes of morality as a choice and of defining humanity coincide with literature courses that focus on the nature of humanity. Though fictional, the novel provides an intriguing look into the human mind, making it applicable to psychological and philosophical discussions. Farmer's novel, premised on the science of the future, meshes ideas of morality and technology in a way that represents both the positive and negative potential of a person. For this reason, Farmer's work would be an effective text in seminar classes involving discussions about happiness, ethics, and innate human nature.

Since Matt is a clone and, therefore, is not accepted by most of the people around him, his position as an outsider is painfully clear. Only three characters consider Matt a person: Celia, the woman assigned with the task of raising him; María, a girl Matt's age who cares nothing about social conventions; and Tam Lin, Matt's personal bodyguard. Through learning the meaning of friendship and love from Celia, María, and Tam Lin, Matt's fate diverges from the clones who preceded him. Perhaps more than anything, Matt wants others to see him as a real boy. He puts great effort into his schoolwork for this reason: "He was in a rage to learn. He would excel, and then everyone would love him and forget he was a clone" (Farmer 91).

Less obvious than the protagonist's struggles to be accepted are the ways Matt's forced isolation reflects reality. Discrimination against clones in *The House of the Scorpion* relates to both historical and current instances in which individuals and peoples were and are oppressed for being different. Before Matt is allowed to live in the Alacrán mansion, he spends his days in Celia's house. While watching television alone, he has an epiphany that relates to his plight: "*It's not real,* Matt thought with sudden terror. *It's like the [stuffed] animals.* He could talk and talk and talk, but the people couldn't hear him. Matt was swept with such an intense feeling of desolation, he thought he would die" (9). Five-year-old Matt's disheartening realization that he cannot communicate with the people on the television foreshadows the loneliness he feels throughout his young life, rejected by society because of his origin. Matt tries to understand how he is unlike other children, but he can find no fundamental dissimilarities. "Matt looked at the mirror in Celia's bathroom. He couldn't see much difference between himself and Tom, but perhaps he was different inside," the narrator explains (71), illustrating Matt's attempts to comprehend why others consider him nonhuman.

Within the society of the novel, the law requires clones to be injected with a drug that destroys their minds. El Patrón, however, has the power to break the law and allows his clones to grow up as "real" boys might (125). Even though Matt's brain is still intact, he is considered a disgusting animal. Farmer's establishment of a great chasm between normal humans and clones in a futuristic society helps to illuminate discrimination that may be less evident in contemporary times. The science fiction setting in which human clones exist reminds readers that the society in the novel is perhaps more realistic than one might expect, regardless of whether or not humans will ever be cloned.

The connection between fiction and reality is a relationship worthy of exploration at a college level, and Farmer's novel offers ethical criticism of discrimination that can be applied to ongoing biases related to race, origin, gender, and personal philosophy. In a moment thematically related to social stagnation within the novel, Matt discovers that poisonous chemicals leak from the farm's holding tanks, killing anyone who happens upon them. He asks why no one cleans the tanks, and a Farm Patrol worker replies, "It's how we've always done things" (174). This attitude of maintaining routine and normalcy, regardless of need, applies to the treatment of "others" within the novel. The question "Is normal actually good?" hovers over Farmer's representation of her protagonist, who is neither a normal boy nor a normal clone. This duality, this oddity eventually enables Matt to return to the Alacrán estate with the mission of ending enslavement.

While society expects Matt to act like an animal, three characters help him to understand the power of friendship and love: Celia, María, and Tam Lin. The text implies that Celia has raised El Patrón's other clones, all of whom were sacrificed to prolong the drug lord's life. Although she has experienced the atrocity of raising children with the knowledge that they will be killed, she has not detached herself from Matt's fate. Protecting herself from emotional pain is not Celia's goal. The woman often tells Matt that she loves him, calling him "mi vida," which translates literally to "my life" (12). Celia does not tell Matt about El Patrón's intentions, but she protects him in the best way she can. She covertly feeds Matt small doses of arsenic to make his heart too unstable to transplant (234), which ultimately saves his life. This act of treachery against El Patrón is highly dangerous, but Celia cares more about Matt than about the probable punishment of being turned into an "eejit" (i.e., a brain-dead slave). While Celia scolds Matt when he forgets that she is not his mother, saying "Don't call me 'Mamá'" (Farmer 11), she treats the boy as her own.

María is Matt's age, but her wisdom and compassion far surpass that of the grown-up Alacráns. She calls Matt "Brother Wolf," basing her humane treatment of him on Saint Francis' teachings. Initially, María believes that Matt lacks a soul, maintaining the idea that he is like an animal (159). María is problematic in the way she treats Matt with kindness but not as an equal. For most of the novel, Matt is equivalent to María's dog, Furball, deserving compassion and pity but incapable of morality. Eventually, the girl changes her mind, arguing that Matt is "much, much more" than a dog (217). María believes that loving a clone is sinful, but she does not seem to mind the risk that she will "probably go to hell for it" (222). Although María is contradictory in many ways, she has a profound impact on Matt's perception of compassion. Matt's love for her motivates him to excel beyond others' negative expectations.

The most influential figure in Matt's life, however, is Tam Lin, the hulking Scottish bodyguard who teaches Matt about the beauty of nature and instructs him in survival techniques. Because of the man, Matt is able to escape the farm after El Patrón dies and the Alacráns "no longer have a use" for him (238). In addition, Tam Lin instills in Matt the importance of choice. While the boy is still enamored of El Patrón and all his authority, Tam Lin illustrates the sort of person the old man is through a memorable metaphor: "When [El Patrón] was young, he made a choice, like a tree does when it decides to grow one way or the other. He grew large and green until he shadowed over the whole forest, but most of his branches are twisted.... What I mean to say is this: When you're small, you can choose which way to grow. If you're kind and decent, you grow into a kind and decent man" (70). The reader discovers that Tam Lin, in his younger days, accidentally killed twenty schoolchildren while attempting to assassinate the Prime Minster (176). The consequences of his action, his crippling guilt, and his status as a criminal, are a result of his choices.

Tam Lin makes it his mission to secretly share the lesson he learned the hardest way possible. Later on, Matt is accused of killing María's dog, and the evidence points to him. Tam Lin tells him, "Any rat in the sewer can lie. It's how rats are. It's what makes them rats. But a human doesn't run and hide in dark places, because he's something more" (134). Tam Lin's accusation of dishonesty hurts Matt, since he did not kill the dog, but he realizes that the man considers him human in the way he "treated Matt as an equal" (138). When Tam Lin helps Matt escape the farm, he articulates the truth of the situation: "'Here's the dirty little secret.' Tam Lin bent down and whispered, as though he had to hide the information from the swallows, the duck, and the dragonflies. 'No one can tell the difference between a clone and a human. That's because there *isn't* any difference. The idea of clones being inferior is a filthy lie'" (245). Because Tam Lin treats Matt like a fellow human, Matt learns that he has a choice to be either kind or evil. His choices, rather than his genetics, direct his future. The relationship between Matt and his friend enables him to be something more than the younger copy of a wicked man. Tam Lin's friendship, as well as Celia's love and María's compassion, are essential to Matt's development, a process worthy of exploration in a college setting.

As a result of Tam Lin's instructions Matt learns that he must think about his actions, but an exploration of some of his most significant choices is important in further understanding how *The House of the Scorpion* is relevant in an academic environment. Matt's admirable decisions stem from a vehement desire to end others' suffering. The first time Matt ventures out with Tam Lin, they see a dead "eejit" worker who did not hear the command to stop working. Matt cannot fathom why the worker has been neglected: "Why hadn't the man gone home when he got sick? Why hadn't the other workers helped him? *Why was he being left out there like a piece of trash?*" (78). At the time, Matt does not know that the farm workers were people who had been stripped of the ability to think for themselves.

Images of the forgotten worker haunt Matt's dreams and fill him with guilt. He realizes "what a terrible thing it would be to be an eejit" after seeing his old jailer Rosa as a robot-like servant: "He hadn't known any of the others before their operation. They were simply there to do boring jobs. But Rosa had been a real, though cruel and violent, person. Now she was merely a shadow with the life sucked out of her" (147). Although the eejits do not actually know that their lives are miserable, Matt recognizes the need to help them. After escaping the Alacrán farm, Matt agrees to return to stop the drug trade and liberate the "eejits" by removing the implants in their brains that prevent them from being functional humans (365). The protagonist's experiences in seeing humans treated cruelly resonate with him, and he wants to end their suffering.

On a less extravagant scale, Matt displays his noble nature, after escaping the Alacrán farm, when he is captured by "Keepers" and put to work at a water purification plant. Each night the Keepers force the boys to confess their sins, and Matt refuses to participate in the spirit-breaking activity, even when that means getting a beating. The Keeper Jorge, realizing that he cannot break Matt by using violence against him, begins to thrash Matt's malnourished friend Fidelito. Matt and his friend Chacho attack Jorge, using the Keeper's cane against him. Chacho blindly rages, but Matt regains his head: "He grabbed Chacho and pulled him back. 'We mustn't kill him!'" (319). Matt is adamant about protecting those weaker than himself, yet he retains the ability to control his anger. While attacking Jorge is not a plan in the way Matt's eventual return to the Alacrán farm is, defending Fidelito is a choice. Both instances display Matt's desire to prevent inhumane treatment, a desire that may not be innate for him, considering the cruelty of the old scorpion El Patrón. Farmer's protagonist learns to be compassionate from the example of a handful of others, and he consciously chooses to stand up for those unable to defend themselves.

Matt's development into an admirable individual may seem overtly romantic, but Farmer's novel illustrates the potential of humanity to be both base and benign. Her protagonist is not perfect, nor is he blissful. He regrets his immoral choices, such as when he intentionally humiliates María by demanding that she give him—a clone—a kiss in front of the entire Alacrán family (109). Yet, he remembers his mistakes and learns to make choices that help, rather than hurt, others. Although Matt is only fourteen by the end of the novel, his experiences in learning the importance of love and compassion apply beyond the intended audience. *The House of the Scorpion* is not so much a tale of morality as it is a tale of how morality helps define humanity. It is obvious which characters are heroes and which are villains; this evident division between good and bad individuals translates to an exploration of how choice is at the core of ethical living. The idea is not unique to the novel, but Farmer's simplification of morality's sources in the form of a children's novel helps illustrate what it means to be human. From Plato to Shakespeare to James Joyce, the exploration of our ability to conceive of ourselves as a species and as individuals has informed philosophy, literature, and art for thousands of years. This ability to ask questions such as "Who am I?" and "What is right?" is what makes us human, an idea that Matteo Alacrán embodies as he comes to realize that his choices dictate his future.

Works Cited

Farmer, Nancy. *The House of the Scorpion*. New York: Simon & Schuster, 2002. Print.

My Lady Hero
H. J. BATES

Young adult (YA) fiction is a distinct genre, one that functions in a number of ways. As the genre's title suggests, it is marketed to a young audience including preteens and teenagers, often because the subject matter appeals to those who are beginning to question who they are and how they should deal with the challenges that budding adults face. YA literature necessarily explores identity, self, and the human experience, all of which are obviously important to those of middle school and high school age. This literature can encourage readers to make thoughtful, reflective choices while forging their identities. But preteens and teenagers aren't the only ones who are browsing the bookshelves in the Young Adult section at Barnes & Noble. YA literature often tackles some of the most challenging questions of what it means to live in a certain culture, struggle in daily life, and question the significance of every event, whether big or small. This genre can be relevant to a reader regardless of age because of the ways it encourages reflection on humanity and what it means to be human.

YA literature can raise a number of interesting issues for readers, and one interesting issue is the treatment of gender within a culture. It is easy to think of roles this type of literature would play in a college classroom, as easy as it is to see the literature's importance in the life of younger readers. Authors like Tamora Pierce and Patricia Wrede introduce readers to ideas about gender roles within a culture and question the value of such roles being firmly established for each gender. Both Song of the Lioness (Pierce) and The Enchanted Forest Chronicles (Wrede) are series that show strong young women with diverse interests, sometimes interests that defy cultural expectations for their gender. These ideas and questions, and the stories that convey them, can help a middle school student learn to accept others despite differences, or the stories can be used in any number of courses at universities to challenge students to think more pointedly about the effects of culture on an individual. The study of YA texts like Pierce's series can be effective in a class studying developmental psychology, in addressing issues of social norms and those who deviate from the status quo. It could be useful in business courses, in studying targeted consumers and actual consumers of the product (the literature). Communications courses can use YA texts like Wrede's series to elicit discussion on how to strategize a communications plan based on who the audience is and what that audience values (is the audience a group of dragons, an angry mob of villagers, or the Society of Wizards?). YA literature is quite suitable for English courses, where it can serve as a gateway form of literature for composition students learning literary analysis, or it can find its way into upper-level courses that deal with gender issues or critical reflection of self. Like all forms of literature, YA literature recognizes and addresses issues of what the human experience can be like. It raises questions. It brings forth discussion. It inspires reflection.

All that said, it is no shock that Pierce and Wrede write literature that voice questions over controversial issues. Both authors challenge ideas that are deeply entrenched within the cultures that many readers belong to or have backgrounds in. Some cultures and older generations still—sometimes strongly—believe in normative gender roles, and Pierce and Wrede encourage readers to think differently and to be outspoken in their ideas and opinions. They accomplish this largely through their protagonists, both of which are girls who grow into women during each series. In Pierce's novel, Alanna is a young girl who dreams of becoming a knight, despite the cultural belief in the novel that girls are incapable of the strength and willpower it takes to become a knight. Alanna proves herself and challenges skeptics when she uses her sheer determination to train and develop skills to earn her shield. Similarly, Wrede's young Cimorene is a girl who feels stifled by all of the expectations her world has for her as a princess. Pursuing her interests, she puts an end to her family's plans for her future and takes it into her own hands, saving kingdoms and going on adventures with dragons, the King of the Enchanted Forest, and a zany witch. Through these protagonists, Pierce and Wrede communicate a number of poignant themes and ideas. As for the idea of gender roles within both works, there are three major thoughts that readers are faced with while reading.

Girls Can Like to Do "Boy Things"

A child's interests can be influenced from birth. A nursery decked out in pink princess décor versus a mobile of dinosaurs above a crib in a room of blue: such decorations are completely acceptable and often even expected in today's culture. For years, little girls have been given Barbie dolls and toy jewelry on their birthdays. Boys get action figures and toy trucks. When these kids hit kindergarten and have "When I grow up, I want to be _____" days when they get to dress up, many little girls come as a princess or teacher, while little boys frequently dress as doctors, firemen, and astronauts. But what about the girl who likes to play with her brother's action figures and toy trucks? What about the little girl who imagines growing up to become a fireman? Cultural expectations often discourage such interests. Not everywhere, of course, but in many places, young girls experience obstacles if they have nontraditional interests or passions. Heroes like Cimorene and Alanna can encourage young readers to follow their dreams despite discouragement and can challenge older readers to think critically about gender expectations.

In *Song of the Lioness*, Alanna is characterized as a girl who originally has no interest in the normal life of a noblewoman. She is an excellent archer from a young age, a good outdoorsperson and fighter, and loves adventure. When she comes of age and must go to the Mithran priestesses to learn how to be a noblewoman, which involves the study of skills she finds to be dull and uninteresting, she makes a plan. Her twin brother is about to be sent off to train as a knight, although he has no interest in the fighting arts or adventure and would rather be a sorcerer. In the first book of the series, Alanna easily convinces him to go to the priestesses (where young boys start their training as sorcerers before going to the Mithran priests to train) (*Alanna: The First Adventure*, 3), and she dresses as a boy and takes his place, training first as a page, then becoming a squire and finally a knight. She gains friends along the way who support her even when they learn of her secret, though she does have many who oppose her choice of lifestyle once her secret is made public. But by following her interests and passions, Alanna defeats a traitor who would have stolen the kingdom and killed the royal family; she saves the life of the prince multiple times; she defeats powerful evil creatures who steal children from their families; she makes peace with the desert people who had been in constant disagreement with her kingdom; she seeks and finds a fabled artifact that helps rulers and nearly dies to bring it to her king; and she kills the traitor a second time when he rises from the dead to fulfill his earlier plan. By the end of the series, it is clear that women can like to do "boy things" and that women can be successful in jobs or fields that are typically dominated by men.

In The Enchanted Forest Chronicles, Cimorene is a girl who likes to do anything that interests her. While she enjoys cooking, cleaning, and working in the library, she also enjoys the novel's more "masculine" pursuits of fencing,

Latin, and philosophy, until her father finds out and puts a stop to her lessons in such pursuits. Her parents continually forbid her to do each successive thing because it "isn't proper" for a princess (*Dealing with Dragons* 3). Cimorene finally gets tired of being told that she cannot pursue her interests (or get rid of an unwanted princely suitor) because "it's simply not done" (3) so, following the advice of a frog, she runs off to a hovel, discovers a magical cave full of dragons, and becomes a dragon's princess. Starting off, she doesn't know what to expect. Cimorene only wants to *do* something to take control of her own life and pursue her own interests, so she purposefully leaves those who try to force her to be someone she does not want to be. Because of her interest in Latin and cooking, she is a great success at her new position, where she alphabetizes the library (*Dealing with Dragons*, 62) and cooks for her dragon and the occasional company (*Dealing with Dragons*, 48). She discovers and foils a plot by evil wizards to fix the succession of the next dragon king. She becomes the King's Cook and Librarian to the next dragon king, Kazul, whom she later rescues from being trapped by the same evil wizards. When Cimorene wants to learn something or try something new, she does it. What is "appropriate" for her to do as a girl, or as a princess, rarely factors into the equation, and her boldness serves her and her friends well. Cimorene's choices are examples of how to both recognize and dismiss the misguided expectations of family or peers, especially when those expectations are merely cultural and arbitrary.

Success Depends Upon the Individual

Another major lesson of these two series is that of individuality. Women can be as good as, if not better than, men at typically masculine roles. The misconception that men are inherently stronger and faster is one that can block the potential of a society's female denizens. Limiting a person based on gender can teach a girl to seek marriage as her highest goal, or pressure a boy into athletics instead of nursing. That girl could be the next great mind in engineering, and that boy could be one of the century's greatest nurses. This potential is one of the greatest losses caused by gender expectations. These young men and women might not know that they can be just as successful in a career field as those of its predominant gender are, whether male or female. Literature can offer narratives to encourage readers in overcoming this daunting fear and following their dreams despite criticism.

Alanna is an excellent example of how achievement rests upon the shoulders of the individual, regardless of gender. While many who experience the fear of failure because of some limitation often get hung up on that limitation (gender, physical strength, wealth, etc.), Alanna refuses to let herself be distracted by ideas about how her gender "should" perform at any given task. The few moments when she does question if a girl would be able to succeed at a task, such as the inevitable fight with a bully twice her size with years more of experience, she lets it galvanize her into action: she trains more frequently, seeks more experienced fighters to teach her, and learns different styles of combat. She develops her mind and body to face the challenge, instead of falling into her culture's insistence that she is doomed to fail because a girl cannot hope to beat a bigger, stronger boy in a fight. She becomes the greatest swordsman in all of Tortall because she deliberately trains to overcome her size limitation. She practices with a heavy sword that her massive man-at-arms carries, so that, when she wields a sword balanced for her, she can move it easily without wearing out quickly (*Alanna: The First Adventure*, 131). She trains to learn how to use her body as a weapon so that she can always protect herself and others as a knight, even without a sword. Eventually, she even learns to use her magic, despite her dislike of it, and becomes a skilled shaman of the desert people. Her success inspires numerous other young girls to seek adventure, become shamans, and practice the fighting arts. While the world she lives in stays largely the same, the potential of female warriors and wielders of magic is unlocked through her example; the kingdom does not fall into turmoil as critics claimed it would; and the culture she lives in shifts to adapt to letting people establish themselves based on talent and skill instead of gender. She is the first to realize that success or failure depends upon her resolve, not on her gender. Inspired by her understanding that individual potential is separate from gender expectations, others are able to understand their own potential and make something of it.

Cimorene seems to innately understand that if another person can do something, so can she. When it comes to doing magic or wielding a sword, she sees no reason that she cannot do it just as well as her opponent or those who've gone before her. This self-assurance helps her accomplish a fire-proofing spell that saves her life, helps her defeat wizards over and over again, and aids her in doing things that no other princess, or even human, has ever done before in her world. She shares cookware with giants (*Dealing with Dragons*, 119–21), haggles with genies (47), and categorizes sword sheaths based on their magical properties (90). She also handles her *own* knights, those who are often misguided in their attempts to "rescue" her from the dragons that she enjoys working for. Cimorene demonstrates that individuals succeed because of their own choices, not because of their gender. Her accomplishments defy gender expectations and are impressive for any person, male or female, to have accomplished. Her potential is her own, not her gender's. This is a principle that the dragons within the series seem to understand well; when it comes to choosing their king, all dragons, regardless of gender, are given the chance to take the magical test and become king. Only one dragon can succeed at carrying Colin's Stone to the Ford of Whispering Snakes, and that dragon becomes king and rules over the dragons. The queen of dragons is a secretarial position, also gender neutral. Kazul explains the idea to Cimorene, who is surprised and tries to wrap her head around the idea, saying, "You mean the dragons don't care whether their king is male or female; the title is the same no matter who the ruler is" (*Dealing with Dragons* 85). The roles depend on ability—nothing else. In this, the dragons clearly embody the idea that the human culture in the novel so clearly lacks: success depends upon the individual's potential, drive, and discipline, not his or her gender.

Girls Can Like "Girl Things," Too

There is a danger in creating female protagonists who excel in male-dominated fields; if a woman hero only likes swordplay or adventure, then activities like cooking, reading, sewing, or even dressing in clothes one enjoys can be seen as weaker or less valuable traits. Both Song of the Lioness and The Enchanted Forest Chronicles are careful to show their strong female protagonists demonstrating a variety of interests, and this variety is what truly shows a breakdown of gender divisions. It does not degrade specific interests but is merely an attempt to show that they do not need to be limited to one gender or another. If a person is interested in learning a skill, that person should be free to learn it and practice it without regard to gender.

In Tortall, Alanna eventually discovers that she finds dresses pretty and envies the girls at court who get to wear them—just a little. She also discovers that she does not necessarily want to be a warrior *maiden*, roaming the lands without ever being tied down to a man, and she has three lovers throughout the series. At first, she is afraid to love; Alanna sees it as giving part of herself to another person, and thinks such an action—or feeling—would be "girly" and weak. She eventually overcomes this fear and, by the end of the series, accepts a proposal of marriage (*Lioness Rampant*, 383–84). This marriage is important for various reasons. Alanna has always thought marriage would take her away from knighthood and freedom, forcing her to become a wife and fulfill the expected wifely duties of staying at an estate as a lady and bearing children. In marrying the ex–King of Thieves, George Cooper, Alanna finds a person who understands her desires to fight for Tortall and to find adventure. George shares the same desires, and Alanna realizes that settling down with a family is something that she wants to eventually do, no matter if it is characterized as feminine or not. She comes to realize that "girly" is not such a bad thing, and that she has merely been repulsed by the future as a lady that had originally been arranged for her. Since she had earned her shield and changed her fate, Alanna is free to choose what she enjoys, whether culture designates it masculine or feminine. She develops this mindset further when she spends time among the desert people, where there is a clear social hierarchy in which women are below men. When Alanna becomes part of a tribe and eventually becomes a shaman, she has to combat the misogyny of one of the younger boys whom she is tasked with instructing in magic. She is the instructor of two young girls and one boy, and the boy constantly speaks down to the girls and even to Alanna at times. When the girls talk about weaving, the boy dismisses it as "women's work" that is "all right if you have nothing better to do" (*The Woman Who Rides Like a Man* 111). His arrogance is quickly upended when Alanna shows the girls thread magic, where one twists a string to alter the world around oneself. She chastises him and explains that he "can't treat Kara and Kourrem as the men of the tribe treat the women" and continues to say "these women are your equals" to him (112). Because she is interested, Alanna does not let the disdain with which many men view weaving keep her from learning the skill of weaving cloth from the women in the tribe. She decides what she enjoys and what she will learn, instead of being influenced by cultural evaluations of certain skills.

Cimorene also demonstrates androgyny of interests, as is seen from the very beginning of the series. She likes cooking and sorting books. These skills couple well with her fighting skills and magic when she is in the Enchanted Forest or living with the dragons. And, similar to Alanna, Cimorene shows a disinterest in marriage early on in her series, only to eventually find someone who is compatible with her. Cimorene has not entirely sworn off men before she meets Mendanbar, but she has not found one that she likes. She has always been more interested in exploring and adventuring than seeking out a man who is intelligent to talk to and has some common sense, so she never actually has had an opportunity for romance. When she meets Mendanbar, they come to know each other and like each other. Cimorene finally does the "appropriate" things when they become engaged and plans the wedding ceremony to include all of the guests that ought to be invited (*Searching for Dragons*, 236–37). This shows that Cimorene does not just rebel against cultural norms for the sake of rebellion, but simply does what she enjoys doing. Cimorene wants to have a beautiful ceremony with the adventurer she loves. And she likes to cook and organize the library, which are more "feminine" tasks when cultures assign the role to a specific gender. Cimorene really never seems to care if her culture calls an activity appropriate, feminine, or masculine. She just does what interests her and makes choices for herself.

Conclusions

The consequences of society perpetuating gender roles is a serious matter. Traditional culturally-inculcated gender roles can discourage boys from becoming great dancers, elementary school teachers, caregivers, nurses, or any number of things that are often categorized as "feminine." Gender expectations can discourage girls from becoming outstanding politicians, lawyers, doctors, craftsmen, soldiers, professors, scientists, mathematicians, or any number of things that are often coded as "masculine" or "manly." By encouraging interest in roles regardless of gender, society unleashes the potential of one who might become a medical researcher who discovers the cure to cancer or a politician who finds a way to diminish poverty. Overcoming the illusion that one gender is inherently always better at a job than another, and recognizing that an individual can become successful at any given role, is vital. One's interests should not be limited by his or her gender. Society, and those who make up society, should recognize that encouraging young women and men to pursue "appropriate" interests based on gender limits the potential for greater success in each field of work. Little is to be gained by such gender divisions, but much to be lost.

In this matter, literature serves a pivotal role. YA literature can intercede when a child or young adult is coerced to follow a socially-acceptable path based on gender. Ideas about limited gender roles can come from peers, family, teachers, coworkers, employers, or even passing remarks from strangers. YA literature, like that by Patricia Wrede and Tamora Pierce, functions to show an alternative way of thinking to these young people, who might not find an alternative opinion anywhere else. In this way the literature is subversive. For those older readers of YA literature, such literature can challenge previous notions of gender roles, opening discussions in places like a university classroom. Both The Enchanted Forest Chronicles and Song of the Lioness show strong and reserved female and male characters, some who adhere to gender expectations and some who defy these expectations. The courage of these characters in defying a firm status quo within their worlds can give courage to young readers. The success and failures of each character can reassure young readers that sometimes they, too, can succeed in standing out, and that they can survive failures, too, even when laughed at by peers or others. These series do not teach young readers that it is only good and admirable to rebel against societal expectations: this would only serve to make girls "masculine" or boys "feminine" in their actions, thus continuing to encourage gendering certain actions as masculine or feminine. No, the novels have characters who excel at or enjoy a variety of jobs and skills, mixing or critiquing traditionally masculine and feminine roles. The works espouse equality of opportunity, discourage typing roles based on gender, and show the importance of the individual and his or her interests.

Works Cited

Pierce, Tamora. *Alanna, the First Adventure.* New York: Atheneum, 1983. Print.
_____. *In the Hand of the Goddess.* New York: Atheneum, 1984. Print.
_____. *Lioness Rampant.* New York: Atheneum, 1988. Print.
_____. *The Woman Who Rides Like a Man.* New York: Atheneum, 1986. Print.
Wrede, Patricia C. *Calling on Dragons.* New York: Jane Yolen Books, 1993. Print.
_____. *Dealing with Dragons.* New York: Harcourt Brace, Jovanovich, 1990. Print.
_____. *Searching for Dragons.* New York: Harcourt Brace, 1991. Print.
_____. *Talking to Dragons.* New York: HMH, 2003. Print.

Tulsa's Coming-of-Age Stories

Jessica Limke

For a purely factual, intellectual study of societies and the people who comprise them, history and sociology textbooks are excellent resources. Moreover, the best of these sources convey their information chronologically, creating a story that guides the reader through each progression of the society or social group in question. However, ironically, one of the most important elements of a story is often notably absent from such academic accounts: the human component. What passions and fears, what heartaches and joys influenced the citizens of a given group or multiple groups in a given society? What emotional atmosphere prevailed in the various stages of a society's existence? Although history and sociology may not provide suitable answers, young adult literature can illuminate these aspects of humanity that are regrettably buried in more objective, fact-oriented material. For in young adult literature, whether fiction or non-fiction, the broad spectrum of human emotion is at its pinnacle as the young characters fight to define themselves and their place in the society in which they live. Thus, through their own experiences, these characters provide a unique glimpse into the emotional and cultural dynamics of their setting. A striking example of this elucidative power of young adult fiction is also a local one for Oklahoma readers, with the works telling much more—despite their author's admission—than simple stories.

The Storyteller

When Oklahoma author Susan Eloise Hinton became a member of the Oklahoma Writers Hall of Fame in 1998, she did not boast of exquisite writing prowess or of the literary merit of her regional works. Rather, she humbly stated, "'I'm just a storyteller. If you put me in the hall of fame for my story-telling, then you might as well put me in for breathing because I can't help it'" (qtd. in Kjelle 81).

What stories did she tell? According to her biographer Marylou Morano Kjelle, Hinton began chronicling through fiction the challenges of life as a teenager, including "peer pressure, gangs, violence, drugs, and abusive parents," when she was fifteen in the 1960s (7–8). Moreover, Hinton experts agree that *The Outsiders*, Hinton's breakout novel first illustrating these challenges in vivid detail, was the impetus for the creation of "'The New Realism,'" a literary subgenre within young adult fiction that depicts unabashedly "life as it is" for youth (Howard 8, 24; Daly 15). Although *The Outsiders* is Hinton's only novel written while she, herself, was a teenager witnessing the struggles similar to those of the novel's characters, she continued to produce works depicting the "sobering realism" of the teenage existence into the late 1980s (Howard 8). In each of her first four young adult novels, Hinton portrays the growing pains of a male Oklahoma teenager through the voice of that young man, thereby centering the novel's story on the coming-of-age experiences of the narrator. Furthermore, since various characters from the previous novels reappear in the subsequent ones, all four novels form a continuous story arc. However, this unified story's emphasis rests not on the characters' relationships with one another but rather on the narrators' connection to the principal backdrop of all four novels: Tulsa.

In a sense, as will be discussed in the following section, each of Tulsa's identities from its birth in the late 1800s up until World War II had been arbitrarily assigned to it, forced upon it as various social factions fought to claim the city as their own. As a result, the true nature or essence of Tulsa did not have a chance to blossom organically until after the Second World War ended. However, Tulsa would discover that the problems left unattended in its infancy and childhood would resurface in the years ahead and hinder the city from finding itself. Through the words and experiences of fictional but realistic Oklahoma teenage boys, Hinton is also telling Tulsa's own coming-of-age story.

In each of Hinton's novels, changing social conditions link the fictional narrator to historical Tulsa and emphasize the struggles of both the narrators and the city to discover their identity and place in the world. The narrators' experiences with various social changes during the 1960s through 1980 reflect the city's efforts during its adolescence to create a cultural identity that captured the essence of Tulsa.

Oklahoma and Tulsa: The Early Years

Decades before Hinton began her series of novels depicting the trials of growing up for Oklahoma teenagers, both the state and the city in which her novels are set fought to achieve a unified identity. According to professors David Baird and Danney Goble in their book *Oklahoma: A History*, Oklahoma was geographically and politically divided during the years preceding its official designation as a state of the Union (163). Called the "Twin Territories," Oklahoma was split into Indian Territory in the east and Oklahoma Territory in the west, with members of the five civilized Native American tribes fighting to maintain their political autonomy in the eastern half (Baird and Goble 163; 167). However, as Baird and Goble note, the Native Americans could not win against the incoming droves of white settlers demanding that the tribal governments, which denied political participation and crucial public services to non-tribal members, be eliminated (154–55). Therefore, with the enactment of the Curtis Act of 1898, Oklahoma's first attempt to unite its two territories commenced as the dissection of Indian Territory into individual parcels of land effectively stripped the tribes of their political power (Baird and Goble 156–57). Moreover, through the exploitation of various legal loopholes, unscrupulous white settlers conned numerous Native Americans out of their allotted property, thereby contributing, albeit immorally, to the eventual combination of Oklahoma's two sections (Baird and Goble 158–61; 176). Nevertheless, despite Oklahoma joining the Union as one state in 1907, the ramifications of the cruel unification methods would define one Oklahoma town's search for wholeness in the years to come.

For Tulsa, the eradication of the Native American governments was only the beginning of the city's decades-long identity crisis. As Danney Goble describes in *Tulsa! Biography of the American City*, the Curtis Act, which was implemented just months after Tulsa became an official city in January 1898, facilitated the city's expansion much like the law expedited the abolition of Indian Territory (46). Creek Nation people, who were responsible for Tulsa's formation in the early 1800s, were allocated plots of Tulsa property which were then promptly sold at a discount to white bidders if the Creeks could not purchase their plots or if the land was vacant (Goble 13; 46). Therefore, in the two decades following, not only did control over Tulsa shift from the Native Americans to whites but also from the lower class to what Goble calls "the elite" (56). Throughout the oil boom in the 1910s and 1920s, businessmen and oil tycoons used their wealth and influence to construct and control downtown Tulsa's first banks and office buildings, helping the city "[earn] its title of Oil Capital of the World" (Goble 85–99; 108). However, despite this impressive status, Tulsa remained a city divided by wealth and racism.

As the oil moguls built their empire on the east side of the Arkansas River, their laborers lived in squalor on the west side due to poor wages and dilapidated housing (Goble 118–19). Perhaps more telling of the city's dichotomous identity was Tulsa's behavior towards its small African American population, a group consisting of freedmen who were formerly slaves to Creeks and whites in Oklahoma and the rest of the nation (Goble 123). Not only did the government of Tulsa restrict African Americans to the Greenwood district in the northern part of the city, but also the city's citizens set the district ablaze after reports that a black man "assaulted" a white woman in a store elevator (Goble 123–24). In the Tulsa Race Riot of 1921, as the event came to be known, unknown numbers of individuals were slaughtered as an entire community was nearly destroyed (Goble 127).

Unfortunately, as the years passed, Tulsa seemed to forget about the incident in Greenwood and its overall social divide. Instead, as Goble mentions, Tulsa focused on surviving economic crises, including plummeting oil prices and the Great Depression, as well as restoring its former magnificence by switching from the oil to aircraft industry during World War II (Goble 137–40; 169–73; 174–81). However, the end of World War II signaled the end of Tulsa's tumultuous childhood and the beginning of an even more turbulent adolescence, one in which the teenaged city would be forced once again to confront its class and racial divisions. As the first of Hinton's novels demonstrates, these internal conflicts posed significant challenges for the city determined to establish an enduring identity.

Ponyboy Curtis in The Outsiders: Class Division and Social Warfare

In Hinton's debut 1967 novel, the narrator's account of local socioeconomic division and resulting civil warfare in the mid–1960s sheds light on Tulsa's fractured identity during the same timeframe. Told by fourteen-year-old Tulsa hoodlum Ponyboy Curtis, The Outsiders depicts with raw realism the intense conflict between the poor "East Side" Greasers and the "West-side rich kids" called the Socs and the efforts of these two teenage groups to reach mutual understanding (The Outsiders 2). As Ponyboy notes, the Socs are known for attacking the Greasers without reason, causing the social outcasts to band together in gangs and fight off their oppressors in staged "rumbles," even though the Greasers "can't win" against the group possessing so much social influence (*The Outsiders* 2–3, 11). However, when Ponyboy finds himself in the company of popular Soc Cherry Valance at the local drive-in theater, his perceptions of the upper-class teenagers begin to transform (*The Outsiders* 26). As the story progresses, Ponyboy gradually realizes that Greasers and Socs are separated only by label, with members of both groups searching for identity and meaning in a city where "'[t]hings are rough all over'" (*The Outsiders* 35). Unfortunately, his new understanding and attempts to reach out to receptive Socs like Cherry are met with staunch resistance from Cherry's boyfriend, Bob Sheldon. One of the hardened, violent Socs bent on keeping the class division alive, Bob seeks revenge on Ponyboy and Johnny for associating with his girlfriend by attacking the boys in their own territory (*The Outsiders* 53–56).

Once Johnny murders Bob in self-defense, the boys are forced to flee, and, as Dallas Winston reports later, the sporadic fighting between the groups escalates into "'all-out warfare all over the city'" (*The Outsiders* 83). Ponyboy and Cherry work to maintain their groundbreaking alliance, but Johnny's role in Bob's death reignites the loyalty each feels towards his and her own class (*The Outsiders* 128–29). Although the two soon reconcile and Ponyboy reaffirms his insight that "Socs [are] ... human too," he discovers that other Greasers and Socs are not ready to accept this truth and that possibly others, like Dally, will die in hatred and hopelessness (*The Outsiders* 108, 179). Ponyboy's revelation about the obstacles to reconciliation between the Socs and Greasers reflects the problems Tulsa encountered as it strived to unite its people and its identity.

Throughout the novel, Ponyboy's mostly unfruitful attempts to make peace with the Socs are obliquely similar to the struggles Tulsa faced in bridging the gap between its African-American and white citizens during the 1960s. As *Tulsa World* reporter Nora Froeschle notes, since the state's inception in 1907, Oklahoma mandated racial segregation via a constitutional provision dictating "that black and white students in all public schools be separated by race" ("Discrimination Rooted"). For Tulsa especially, this divide pervaded not only the education system but also all spheres of city life. Goble indicates that harsh "[r]estrictive covenants" enabled geographical segregation of Tulsa by forcing African Americans to live mostly in the north Tulsa community of Greenwood (211). Furthermore, according to some of Tulsa's first African-American students to attend previously all-white schools, African Americans who did venture past Greenwood for necessity or recreation were met with unequal treatment in the form of denials-of-service at restaurants and segregated movie theater seating (Woosley A-9). Thus, Tulsa was divided into black northern and white southern portions with members of each race rarely interacting with the other.

Amazingly, despite the prevalence of the racial division, forced integration of the nation's public schools in the late 1950s was met with little resistance and violence in Tulsa, as Leigh Woosley notes in her article "For Tulsa, Desegregation Was Tense but Peaceful" (A-1). However, as the years passed, Tulsa demonstrated that it, like Bob Sheldon, still found reconciliation between its two halves unpalatable. Instead of conducting violent physical warfare like the Greasers and Socs, Tulsa leaders employed cunning legal ordinances that maintained school segregation while appearing to remedy the division. As Goble describes, Tulsa "redrew attendance zones" in order to facilitate integration but simultaneously created a "majority-to-minority" provision in which students comprising the minority population in schools could move to other schools where they would be the predominant race (210–11).

In effect, these counteracting measures extended, rather than eliminated, the north-south racial boundary as fearful white parents removed their children from the northernmost schools as quickly as African Americans moved in, resulting in de facto segregation of Tulsa once more (Goble 214–15). Therefore, Ponyboy's observation throughout his narrative of the resistance of many Greasers and Socs to live harmoniously is, in a small way, similar to Tulsa's opposition to racial integration, and, thus, to a unified identity. Moreover, his and Cherry's gradual awareness of the other's humanity, as symbolized by their seeing "the same sunset" despite living on opposite sides of town, and their ensuing friendship echo the efforts of black and white families to implement actual integration of Tulsa's schools in the late '60s and early '70s once the United States Supreme Court ruled Tulsa's prior desegregation "practices indefensible" (*The Outsiders* 4; Goble 282, 284–85). However, as the heartbreaking account of Hinton's second narrator reveals, Tulsa struggled with other, newer internal conflicts when a new social group and form of recreation emerged during the havoc of integration.

Bryon Douglas in That Was Then, This Is Now: *The Counterculture and Drug Abuse*

Published in 1971 and set one or two years after *The Outsiders*, Hinton's second novel illustrates Tulsa's worsening social chaos and crumbling image through the eyes of a young man disillusioned by the coming-of-age process.

In *That Was Then, This Is Now*, Tulsa teenager Bryon Douglas recounts both his and his brother's treachery amidst the backdrop of the counterculture and illicit drug use of the late 1960s. As Bryon recalls throughout the novel, he and Mark Jennings were inseparable even before Mark became his adopted brother (*That Was Then* 12–13). However, the boys' encounters with members of the countercultural movement and their fascination with hallucinogenic drugs irreparably fracture Bryon and Mark's relationship. Initially, Bryon and Mark's exposure to counterculture is limited to their friendship with the intelligent yet innocent M&M Carlson and their brief encounter with a college student who intrigues Mark with his experiences of living in a hippie commune in another part of town (*That Was Then* 26–27). Once M&M's older sister Cathy Carlson returns home and captures Bryon's heart, the brothers find themselves drifting apart.

As Bryon spends more time with Cathy and M&M, he observes both the prejudicial insults M&M receives from his father and grapples with the heartbreak Cathy and her family experience after M&M runs away from home (*That Was Then* 50–52, 104–105). Meanwhile, Mark separates himself from Bryon out of his growing animosity towards Cathy and seems to sever ties with the new crowd altogether as he devotes his time to acquiring substantial income from an unknown source (*That Was Then* 97–100, 107). Therefore, when Mark takes Bryon to the commune where M&M is living, Bryon is surprised to discover that Mark not only is well-acquainted with the inhabitants but also defends their questionable form of living (*That Was Then* 121–24). Only after Bryon and Cathy find M&M suffering from a "'bad trip'" on LSD does Bryon unearth the devastating truth: Mark is selling the kinds of drugs that permanently altered M&M's mental faculties and shattered the boy's family (*That Was Then* 138, 142–46). In a burst of disloyalty, Bryon reports Mark to the police and watches in silence as his traitorous brother is taken away (*That Was Then* 148–49). Despite his disgust at Mark's appalling behavior, Bryon feels guilty for betraying his brother, and, as a result, he "'[gets] even with Cathy for Mark'" by breaking up with her (*That Was Then* 152–53, 156). Thus, Bryon concludes his narrative in apathy and confusion, unsure of both himself and the soundness of his actions (*That Was Then* 159). Bryon's tale runs parallel to Tulsa's identity conflict in the midst of the countercultural movements' emergence.

The rampant infidelity Bryon witnesses and participates in throughout *That Was Then, This Is Now* may be read as an echo of Tulsa's betrayal of its counterculturally-aligned citizens and the drug underworld during the late 1960s and early 1970s. Although Tulsa was beginning to rectify its long-standing discrimination against African Americans as integration took effect, Tulsa turned against itself in a new way by rejecting another group of citizens. Just as Bryon watched strangers and M&M's own family ridiculing the boy's appearance and personality, so did an inquisitive Tulsan witness see the city's antiestablishment youth being scorned by the masses. In her series of *Tulsa Daily World* articles describing the weeks she observed and joined in the countercultural lifestyle, reporter Terry Black notes Tulsa "held little love" for its young people who often congregated in Woodward Park on 21st Street and Peoria to relax and survive "living in a city hostile" to them ("Life with the Hippies"; "'Hip' Youth Set" 19). According to Black, the park served as the last refuge from the "glares" of mainstream Tulsa citizens and the inhospitable treatment by local restaurants and retail stores wary of serving such unusual clientele ("Life with the Hippies"). However, even in Woodward they could not escape persecution by the police who frequently either forced the peaceful teenagers out of the park on false charges of disturbing the peace or arrested them for "'loitering'" during normal park hours ("Life with the Hippies"). Therefore, adolescents faced with compromising their values, decided instead to join like-minded outcasts pursuing "something different, something better and more meaningful" in a city with a history of intolerance to diversity ("Defiance Symbol").

However, similar to Bryon's double-betrayal, Tulsa also fought against those responsible for supporting substance abuse. As Edward J. Reilly notes in *The 1960s*, drugs such as marijuana and lysergic acid diethylamide (LSD) proliferated among youth during the latter half of the decade as a form of "relaxation" and a method of "dropping out from mainstream society" (31–32). Tulsa was by no means insulated from such controversial recreation and declared war against dealers. Initially, Tulsa relied mainly on its police force to expose and reduce the drug trafficking throughout the city through subversive techniques. For example, a six-person raid in 1967 of individuals selling marijuana to minors resulted from police detective Charlie Jones's posing as a legitimate purchaser of the illegal substance and then using the marijuana as incriminating evidence against the sellers (Ridenour and Storms 1). Once the sale of LSD became grounds for a felony conviction in 1968, the workload of Jones and other policemen increased as LSD distributors were included among the other narcotics sellers arrested for drug trafficking (Ridenour 1; 4A). Therefore, in order to perpetuate the war against the drug dealers, Tulsa rallied the masses to the police's aid.

Launched by the *Tulsa Tribune* in September 1971, the "Nail-the-Pusher" program offered individuals monetary rewards for providing tips on drug-selling activity in the city (Butler 169; The Associated Press 1). The effectiveness of this public call-to-action was impressive. The program resulted in the arrests of fifteen pushers in one month alone in 1972, and local police remarked that three of the twenty-one pushers arrested later that year for selling marijuana, LSD, and other drugs were identified solely through "Nail-the-Pusher" informants (Butler 169; Storms 1).

Thus, like Bryon, Tulsa faced internal tension. As a result, coupled with the concurrent failure of integration, the city's conflict further splintered Tulsa's adolescent identity. In the years ahead, Tulsa would attempt to leave its conflicts behind and forge a new image of stability and unity. However, similar to the narrator in Hinton's next novel, Tulsa would discover that forgetting is neither an easy nor a quick process.

Rusty-James in Rumble Fish: *The Inability to Forget Past Failures*

Comprised by a young adult's recollection of his ruined hopes for the future, Hinton's third novel, published in 1975, also reflects the dis-integration of Tulsa's identity. Narrated by an older, despondent Rusty-James, *Rumble Fish* depicts the teenager's failure to establish himself as a true gang leader. When an unexpected encounter with his former best friend, Steve, triggers painful memories of home, Rusty-James recalls the last days he spent with his brother, The Motorcycle Boy. Confident and brash, the young Rusty-James thrives on his authority over his peers, the security of his relationship with Patty, and the certainty that he will follow in The Motorcycle Boy's footsteps as a local gang kingpin of old. However, when The Motorcycle Boy returns from an extended absence in California, the foundation of Rusty-James's dreams begins to crumble. As Rusty-James shadows his idol throughout the city, he grasps that he shares neither the "different" perspective through which The Motorcycle Boy views society nor the respect and awe his older brother effortlessly draws from those around him (*Rumble Fish* 31–36). Although initially Rusty-James remains assured that these qualities will pass to him as he matures, his continued interaction with his brother and the assertions by both friends and strangers that he will never be "'royalty in exile'" slowly undermine his confidence (*Rumble Fish* 66, 71–71, 92).

The Motorcycle Boy's insight into Rusty-James's fear of abandonment and his musing on the insignificance of gang fighting scare and confuse Rusty-James because they contradict his own naïve perceptions of himself and the glory of gang warfare (*Rumble Fish* 83–85, 101–103). Furthermore, rival Smokey Bennett's cunning overthrow of Rusty-James's control and acquisition of Patty's affection reveal to Rusty-James that the nuances of leadership are exceedingly more complex than "one and one [making] two" (*Rumble Fish* 118–19). As a result, in his bewilderment and fear over his decaying life, Rusty-James clings to The Motorcycle Boy, his last link to a past that will never be revived (*Rumble Fish* 130–31). After his brother is shot by the police, Rusty-James falls apart as he gains a brief glimpse into the colorless, hopeless world of The Motorcycle Boy (*Rumble Fish* 131–32).

Returning to the present, Rusty-James says goodbye to Steve, focusing on forgetting the collapse of the world he once was certain he would rule. Nevertheless, as Rusty-James comments at the end of his account, disregarding such a momentous failure and moving on to discover self is nearly impossible (*Rumble Fish* 133–35). Rusty-James's epiphany mirrors Tulsa's own finding that its past mistakes, despite its efforts to rectify and forget them, still haunted the city as it fought to assemble an intact identity from the shards of its society.

Rusty-James's desire to bury the past is a reverberation of Tulsa's attempted restoration of its structural and social vitality from the late 1960s through the mid–1970s after its failure to keep its population centralized and its identity unified. According to Goble in *Tulsa! Biography of the American City*, increased traffic congestion in downtown Tulsa, coupled with the increasingly southeastern shift of retail and residential establishments following World War II, prompted Tulsa officials to construct an intricate expressway system (252–54). As Michael D. Bates notes in his editorial "A Tulsa Turning Point: 1957 Comes Back to Haunt and Remind Us," the Tulsa Metropolitan Area Planning Commission (TMAPC) hoped the building of such routes as the Inner Dispersal Loop (IDL), the Skelly Bypass, and other expressways would resolve the city's "lack of radial routes" that hindered individuals' commute to and excursions in downtown ("A Tulsa Turning Point"). However, only during and after construction of the interstate highways from approximately 1960 through 1975 did Tulsa realize that the reunification plan created further division and decay (Bates). For example, Goble explains that the destruction and isolation of homes and businesses by the Red Fork Expressway's construction contributed to west Tulsa's financial demise during that period (256).

Furthermore, the community that had survived both the physical and emotional flames of hatred in the early 1920s faced ruin as the new expressway system encroached. In his 1967 article "An Old Tulsa Street Is Slowly Dying: Greenwood Fades Away Before Advance of Expressway," *Tulsa Tribune* reporter Joe Looney describes how the Crosstown Expressway overpass cut through the heart of Greenwood's business district ("An Old Tulsa Street"). As Looney indicates, the overpass resulted in several building demolitions and forced other owners to close their businesses and relocate ("An Old Tulsa Street"). Moreover, this overpass would forever overshadow and isolate the street from Tulsa's population. The expressway system escalated downtown's deterioration as its efficient routes from downtown to the outlying suburbs enticed Tulsa's citizens to live farther away, effectively gutting the city's heart (Bates).

As the ramifications of the expressway system became apparent, Tulsa, like Rusty-James, strived in vain to keep its hopes alive for a future in which status would be assured. Tulsa planned extensive reconstruction of the areas adversely affected by the expressways. Called "urban renewal" and implemented by the Tulsa Urban Renewal Authority (TURA) throughout the late 1960s and well into the 1970s, the efforts to reestablish downtown and the surrounding areas as Tulsa's social center included extensive property acquisition, demolition of older structures, and construction of new buildings (Bachelder 4; Goble 260). Land in the northwest corner of downtown, as well as the area west of the Arkansas River, became updated as existing homes were renovated, new ones were built, and corporate and manufacturing buildings were constructed (Bachelder 5). In addition, the TURA projects attempted to breathe new life into Greenwood by razing older neighborhoods in favor of upscale housing, retirement establishments, and the Greenwood Cultural Center (Goble 262). Moreover, downtown Tulsa received a "facelift" as structures of "bygone eras" like the Lynch Building, Grand Opera House, and Hunt Building were demolished in order to erect buildings such as the Performing Arts Center, Williams Center complex, the Doubletree Hotel, and the Center Plaza (Lester 175, 189; Goble 260).

Like the everlasting influence of The Motorcycle Boy, the social divide already present and enhanced by the expressways would plague Tulsa for years to come, sealing the separation of downtown from its citizens and permanently obstructing Tulsa's goal of making a name for itself as a city with one identity. In the aftermath of these projects, the northern part of the city would face abandonment at the expense of the expansion of the southern half, alterations observed by Hinton's fourth narrator who is keenly aware of the nature of change.

Tex McCormick in Tex: *Abandonment and Growth*

Entering the market in 1979, the fourth installment of Hinton's coming-of-age saga exposes the disheartening consequences of Tulsa's separation as the narrator grapples with his impending isolation. In *Tex*, rural Oklahoma teenager Tex McCormick describes his ongoing battle with fear of abandonment while becoming aware of the vastness of Tulsa. Living with his older brother Mason in the small town of Garyville, Tex is intimately connected to the people around him. Since his father is rarely home, Tex is dependent upon Mason not only for food and shelter but also for companionship. However, as Mason's preoccupation with leaving for college threatens Tex's closeness to his brother, the narrator's anxiety grows. Since solitude is a form of living foreign to Tex, he balks at the thought of remaining alone in Garyville without Mason, seeing the years ahead as "a foggy pit" into which he must inevitably plunge (*Tex* 26, 54). As a result of his heightened understanding of the loneliness involved with Mason's departure, Tex is more cognizant of Tulsa's immense size and growth when he and his brother visit.

As the brothers drive to the hospital for Mason's appointment, Tex recognizes his separation from the other drivers and is perplexed by the fleeting nature of human interaction in the city's large population (*Tex* 90–91). Later, while waiting for Mason, Tex wanders the stores in Westmall on the other side of town, mentioning his strange sensation of feeling "lonesome in a place full of people" (*Tex* 92). Furthermore, the vast number of stores and the indication that "enough people" live and shop in the area to warrant such growth enhance Tex's sense of isolation and fear of abandonment by his brother (*Tex* 94–95). In the days following the boys' trip to Tulsa, a series of emotionally trying events nearly cause Tex to sever ties with Mason and embrace life in the city out of spite for the brother who will soon leave him (*Tex* 113–86). However, once he realizes his love for Mason will ease the pain of parting, Tex eventually accepts his brother's departure, recognizing that some individuals must change their physical locations in order to change themselves (*Tex* 187–211). Although Tex realizes he will still successfully mature in Mason's absence, Tulsa could not find its true character via physical division.

Tulsa's effort to unify its identity in the late 1960s only compounded its social division as white citizens fled the legally mandated integration of the public schools. Moreover, the newly built expressways—once Tulsa's hope for a united city—contributed to the exodus from downtown Tulsa throughout the 1960s, as businesses and their customers "moved out by the [Interstate 44] bypass" and away from the city's center, according to Froeschle ("Highways Road" 8). According to Dan Osborne in his *Tulsa Tribune* article "Tulsa in 70s; Time of Change," the city's "growth" in the mid–1970s actually constituted a "population shift" as white Tulsans relocated south and east, dividing the city once again into two distinct northern and southern halves (10D).

Moreover, Goble notes that as "money that might have been spent to maintain the city's decaying infrastructure ... went instead to playing catch-up with the developers" in the southeast, north Tulsa deteriorated (268). The exiting affluent and middle-class whites did not look back as they invaded southeast Tulsa, creating an expansive metropolis that intimidated Tex and enlarging the suburbs in the surrounding areas. As the white population shifted, so did Tulsa's commercial center, with the construction of Woodland Hills Mall on 71st Street resulting in the growth and development of that area (Goble 267–68; Tippee G-1).

In addition, the expressways stretching from Tulsa to nearby smaller communities such as Broken Arrow resulted in substantial suburban growth, albeit to the detriment of the metropolitan area's population (Stanley 5). For example, student enrollment in Broken Arrow schools increased by nearly 70 percent and by over 100 percent in Jenks from "1968 to 1974" (Goble 268). However, the corresponding decrease in Tulsa's student population forced the city to close many of its schools since, as Goble explains, the city "disproportionately lost the kind of families who had originally contributed to making its public schools work: the young, middle- and upper-middle-class families who were most involved in their children's schooling" (269). The shifts in Tex's world arguably parallel Tulsa's population shifts along racial and economic class lines. However, Tulsa's shifts facilitated an apparently permanent, unhealthy split in its identity. Thus, while Tex eventually finds "'contentment,'" as one Hinton reviewer terms it, with himself and with his future in Garyville (qtd. in Daly 89), Tulsa had failed to create a unified identity, instead.

Tulsa's Story

In and of themselves, the stories of Ponyboy, Bryon, Rusty-James, and Tex portray some of the numerous hardships both Oklahoma teenagers and youth worldwide confront as they approach adulthood. However, when each tale is considered in tandem with the others, the overall story also becomes one of the maturation of the city in which the novels are based. Thus, the struggles of each narrator to discover self amid social chaos throughout the 1960s and 1970s symbolize Tulsa's own trouble uniting its people, and, therefore, fashioning an identity representative of all its citizens. Therefore, when she stated at her inauguration into the Oklahoma Writers Hall of Fame that she just "can't help" being a storyteller, Susan Hinton showed amazing self-awareness, for her first four young adult novels tell more than just the coming-of-age stories of four Oklahoma teenage boys. They tell Tulsa's story: one that is, true to Hinton form, a grimly realistic depiction of the adversities the city faced as it entered adulthood and one that, in contrast to mere historical or sociological accounts, captures the human emotions and motivations fueling Tulsa's changes during its adolescence. Thus, S. E. Hinton's novels, along with similar works of young adult literature, remind the reader that without insight into the people, the studies of history and sociology are ultimately incomplete. For only through the eyes of its individuals, especially its youth—those who not only existed but lived, loved, and lost—can one truly comprehend the nature of a society, historical or contemporary.

Works Cited

The Associated Press. "Newspapers Erect Schemes to Help Oklahoma Police." *Ada Evening News* 11 Mar. 1973: 1–2. NewspaperArchive.com. NewspaperArchive.com, 2014. Web. 7 Apr. 2014.

Bachelder, Don. "Tulsa's Changing Face." *Tulsa Sunday World* 2 Mar. 1975: 4–5. Print. Local History Collection, Research Center Annex, Tulsa City-County Library, Tulsa, OK.

Baird, David W., and Danney Goble. *Oklahoma: A History.* Norman: University of Oklahoma Press, 2008. Print.

Bates, Michael D. "A Tulsa Turning Point: 1957 Comes Back to Haunt and Remind Us." *Urban Tulsa Weekly* 11–17 Oct. 2007: n.p. Print. Archives, Tulsa Historical Society, Tulsa, OK.

Black, Terry. "Defiance Symbol Often Defied: Hairy Hippy Problems Can't Be Brushed Off." *Tulsa Daily World* 29 Sept. 1968: n.p. Print. Local History Collection, Research Center Annex, Tulsa City-County Library, Tulsa, OK.

_____. "Hip Youth Set in Tulsa Fits No Stereotype." *Tulsa Daily World* 15 Sept. 1968: 19–20. Print. Local History Collection, Research Center Annex, Tulsa City-County Library, Tulsa, OK.

_____. "Life with the Hippies: Unusual Appearance Jolts Many People." *Tulsa Daily World* n.d.: n.p. Print. Local History Collection, Research Center Annex, Tulsa City-County Library, Tulsa, OK.

Butler, William. *Tulsa 75: A History of Tulsa, Oklahoma.* Tulsa: The Metropolitan Chamber of Commerce, 1974. Print.

Daly, Jay. *Presenting S. E. Hinton: Updated Edition,* 2d ed. Boston: Twayne, 1989. Print. Twayne's United States Authors Series: Young Adult Authors.

Froeschle, Nora. "Discrimination Rooted in Oklahoma History." *Tulsa World* n.d.: n.p. Print. Archives, Tulsa Historical Society, Tulsa, OK.

_____. "Highways Road to City's Success." *Tulsa World* 29 Dec.1999: 8. Print. Archives, Tulsa Historical Society, Tulsa, OK.

Goble, Danney. *Tulsa! Biography of the American City.* Tulsa: Council Oak Books, 1997. Print.

Hinton, S. E. *The Outsiders*. 1967. New York: Speak, 2012. Print.

_____. *Rumble Fish*. 1975. New York: Delacorte Press, 2013. Print.

_____. *Tex*. 1979. New York: Delacorte Press, 2013. Print.

_____. *That Was Then, This Is Now*. 1971. New York: Speak, 2008. Print.

Howard, Todd. *Understanding* The Outsiders. San Diego: Lucent Books, 2001. Print. Understanding Great Literature Series.

Kjelle, Marylou Morano. *S. E. Hinton: Author of* The Outsiders. Berkeley Heights: Enslow Publishers, 2008. Print. Authors Teens Love Series.

Lester, Terrell, ed. *Tulsa Times: A Pictorial History: Coming of Age*. Vol. 3. 1988. Tulsa: World Publishing, 1997. Print. 3 vols.

Looney, Joe. "An Old Tulsa Street Is Slowly Dying: Greenwood Fades Away Before Advance of Expressway." *Tulsa Tribune* 4 May 1967: n.p. *Tulsa City-County Library*. Web. 19 Mar. 2014.

Osborne, Dan. "Tulsa in 70s; Time of Change." *Tulsa Tribune* 15 Oct. 1975: 1D+. Print. Local History Collection, Research Center Annex, Tulsa City-County Library, Tulsa, OK.

Reilly, Edward J., ed. *The 1960s*. Westport, CT: Greenwood Press, 2003. Print. American Popular Culture Through History.

Ridenour, Windsor. "Raiders Arrest 6 in LSD and Pot Sweep." *Tulsa Tribune* 18 June 1969: 1+. Print. Local History Collection, Research Center Annex, Tulsa City-County Library, Tulsa, OK.

_____, and John Storms. "6 Charged in Marijuana Sale After Parent Tip." *Tulsa Tribune* 15 Sept. 1967: 1+. Print. Local History Collection, Research Center Annex, Tulsa City-County Library, Tulsa, OK.

Stanley, Tim. "Where There's a Will, There's an Expressway: School Growth." *Tulsa World* 14 Nov. 2007: 4–5. Print. Archives, Tulsa Historical Society, Tulsa, OK.

Storms, John. "Drug Raids Net 21 Arrests." *Tulsa Tribune* 28 Apr. 1972: 1+. Print. Local History Collection, Research Center Annex, Tulsa City-County Library, Tulsa, OK.

Tippee, Bob. "Business Drawn to Area Around 1-Year-Old Mall." *Tulsa World*: 4 Sept. 1977: G-1–G-2. Print. Archives, Tulsa Historical Society, Tulsa, OK.

Woosley, Leigh. "For Tulsa, Desegregation Was Tense but Peaceful." *Tulsa World* 11 Feb. 2007: A-1+. Print. Archives, Tulsa Historical Society, Tulsa, OK.

Into the Swamp
Davey Rumsey

When I hear the term "young adult literature," I think of the kind of novels that my sister reads and cries over. I think of the YA Lit section at Barnes and Noble that only seems to display the next saga about a vampire boy who falls in love with a mortal girl. I'm not knocking those novels; however, I feel that a lot more can be said for the genre when it's not restricted to romantic vampires and that merit can be found in the most unsuspecting of places.

Young adult literature is taught in college classes with the guiding rule that whatever work is being discussed should be relatable to genre lovers, to the population at large, and to discerning, discriminating, and educated readers. A typical reader, outside a classroom, of YA lit would be an adolescent between the ages of twelve and eighteen. The question then presents itself, "What would be important to a youth aged twelve to eighteen?" Themes, such as a dream deferred, unrequited love, and isolation, come to mind. Understanding the proper context, types of characters, and presentation also go into determining if a work is considered young adult or not. Many titles are no-brainers, such as *The Hunger Games, Twilight*, and *Divergent*. How about *The Saga of the Swamp Thing*? I admit that this title is unconventional, but I believe that the work holds merit and should be celebrated as a work of young adult fiction. It even has vampires in it, too.

The Saga of the Swamp Thing is unconventional in the fact that Swamp Thing was originally published as monthly comic issues beginning in 1983. A young writer by the name of Alan Moore took over this failing DC property and breathed life into what many people considered a tired and simple monster story. In Moore's hands, Alec Holland became more than a man who had been transformed into a swamp creature. He became a symbol for loss and hopelessness. Moore took the simple monster story and crafted a deeper meditation on what it means to be human: the reputation of Swamp Thing began to rise. Throughout Moore's run on the title, he consistently produced a work that looked inside the human condition. It is because of this glimpse into humanity that I believe Swamp Thing is a great example of how educators can relate to their students.

The Anatomy Lesson (Vol. 1) was the second issue that Alan Moore wrote for Swamp Thing, and it was a game-changing issue for the mythology. The previous issues of the book introduced the protagonist, Alec Holland. Holland was a scientist working on a bio-restorative formula—a formula that could produce vegetation in the most dry and arid of environments. In the original mythology, Holland is killed after an unfortunate accident results in an explosion. The fire-ridden body of Holland flees from his laboratory and into the swamps of Louisiana. Shortly after, he rises again as the Swamp Thing—a plant-like creature that has the semblance and mind of Alec Holland.

Before *The Anatomy Lesson*, Alec Holland believed himself to be a man trapped in the body of a swamp monster. He felt that beneath the green foliage of his body lay the essence of his humanity. Underneath it all, he was still Alec Holland. In *The Anatomy Lesson*, everything changed. After seemingly being killed in an attack by the Sunderland Corporation, a shady agency with criminal dealings and government ties, Swamp Thing's body is taken into the care of the sadistic Mr. Sunderland himself. Sunderland procures the release of Jason Woodrue, a DC villain called The Floronic Man, to perform the autopsy on the body. The Floronic Man is a true plant/human hybrid and is fascinated at the discovery of this swamp monster.

After completing the autopsy, Jason Woodrue finds that there is nothing human about this creature at all. Everything about the creature gives the impression of a human; however, it is all an imitation made of plants. Woodrue determines that Alec Holland, the man, died in the fire. Once his body lay at the bottom of the swamp, somehow the plants absorbed Holland's consciousness. What rose from the swamp was not human, but a sentient plant-like creature.

Sunderland is not happy with these findings. He dismisses Woodrue as a lunatic and tells him to leave. An angry Woodrue then turns the temperature up in the freezer that the Swamp Thing is being held in. In the comic "universe," plants can be frozen but they cannot die. This causes the Swamp Thing to rise. Being that the creature has the consciousness of Alec Holland, he finds Woodrue's report on his autopsy and is crushed at what he finds: his hopes and dreams of becoming human again die as he reads the report. He goes on a rampage throughout the Sunderland compound, and the issue culminates in the murder of Mr. Sunderland at the hands of the Swamp Thing.

This plot turn solves a looming problem in the Swamp Thing mythology. What would happen when Swamp Thing finally cured himself and became human Alec Holland again? Moore completely eliminates this as a possibility, which allows him to take the book in a number of directions not possible before. With no hope of ever becoming human again, what does the Swamp Thing do with his life now? What is his goal or his endgame? This plot turn creates an existential crisis at the heart of the character, a crisis that is now far more fascinating than a monster trying to become human again. The narrative becomes about a monster dealing with feelings that he can never act on, hopes that can never come true, and a life that he never asked for. This issue illuminates the essence of a dream deferred, hopes crushed in an instant.

This theme resonates with people of all ages and positions. When I was a freshman in high school, my hopes and dreams were crushed, demolished, and burned to the ground. I had taken the leap of faith that is the single most defining moment of a fifteen-year-old boy's life and laid it on the line for the girl of my dreams. Well, I laid it on the line to a friend of her friend who then relayed the message to her. Her devastating response came back down the line of text messages, and I went on a rampage that was not unlike Swamp Thing's. Maybe I didn't commit murder, but I did begrudgingly make my way through school all day and then holed myself up in my room with a gallon of ice cream once I got home. I remember a friend of mine coming over that night with the sole purpose of cheering me up and convincing me to get over her. It was as if I had read the Floronic man's report myself. What would I do with all of these feelings? They were useless now. My endgame, my goal was suddenly destroyed, and the existential crisis left me staggering. Forget being graduated from high school and going to college and finding a career; the sole purpose of my life was burning before my eyes.

Admittedly, I am exaggerating. But what about the student who comes home to find that his parents are divorcing after many years of marriage? Or the sibling who finds out a brother or sister has tragically died? Or the healthy student who is suddenly and inexplicably stricken with cancer? All of these events have happened to many of my friends and family. The aftermath of these tragedies always involves anger, isolation, and desperation. This is what makes Swamp Thing so compelling as a piece of young adult literature to me. It's a book that can speak to all of these issues. Taught in a college class, it can be a doorway into how college students currently cope or teacher candidates later deal with students who face these struggles. Literature like this helps us understand the feelings we think no one else has. It puts a foothold where there was nothing before.

If you turn on the news, it is almost a guarantee that the image of a youth in crisis will be on the screen. As the details of that youth's crime are spouted off by the news anchor, most people easily label that student as "delinquent," "wayward," or, in extreme instances, "monster." These labels are thrown around because people fear what they do not understand.

In the chapter "Monster Culture: Seven Theses," Jeffrey Cohen states, "We have seen that the monster arises at the gap where difference is perceived as dividing a recording voice from its captured subject; the criterion of this division is arbitrary, and can range from anatomy of skin color to religious belief, custom, and political ideology" (14). Cohen believes that we create monsters when we do not understand something. Throughout history, this has proved to be true. From the Medieval Crusades to Nazi Germany, cultures have created monsters out of the things—and people—they do not understand. Images of medieval maps with the warning "Here Be Monsters" at the outer edges come to mind. The unknown and the mysterious, "the gap" that Cohen talks about, are all breeding grounds of people we perceive as monsters.

And so a young adult internalizes the struggles he or she faces and attempts to carry him or her self through life day by day. Eventually, something snaps. To the casual viewer, this snap is "the gap." It is the end result of a string of events that we have not seen. Our lack of understanding of the big picture makes it easy for us to say the words "delinquent," "wayward," or "monster." To Mr. Sunderland, the creature that chased him throughout his compound and brought about his death was a monster. We, the readers, understand the deep, complex nature of this sentient plant, however ridiculous that may sound. Put into teacher candidate or college student hands, Swamp Thing's plight can be the lens in which they view themselves or younger students.

Misunderstanding what it means to be human, what it means to be a person and not "the Other," continues throughout Alan Moore's Swamp Thing mythology. In Issue 51, *Home Free*, Swampy returns home from doing battle in the underworld. (That's right, you read that correctly.) Upon arrival, he finds that the love of his life, Abigail Arcane, has been arrested for committing "crimes against nature" (Vol. 5, 15). The relationship between Abigail and Swampy is a demented take on the star-crossed lovers mythos. Abigail, being a human, and Swampy, being a sentient plant, must keep their relationship secret. When pictures of the two of them being intimate (it's not quite like you're thinking) surface, Abigail is quickly taken into police custody while Swampy is out saving the day. Swampy is not happy when he finds that his beloved has been taken away.

In a brilliant move of plot, Alan Moore sends Abigail fleeing from her small Louisiana hometown to the big city of Gotham. That's right, Batman's home turf. All of this leads to some of my favorite issues in comic book history. In Issues 52 and 53 (Vol. 5), Swampy wages an ecological war on the city of Gotham to win back his beloved Abigail. The words that Moore pens for his titular character in the Gotham issues are the words of a misunderstood and desperate creature, a monster that has risen from "the gap" of human understanding.

In the middle of Issue 52, *Natural Consequences*, Swampy bursts into the courtroom in which Abigail is being tried. One police officer shrieks, "I don't know what you are, but that woman is in the custody of this city" (Vol. 5, 49). The police officer holding the gun only sees a monster, a fierce plant-like creature bursting through the floorboards of the courtroom. Faced with this being that defies his understanding, the police officer reacts out of fear. Upon being warned, Swamp Thing declares, "Do you warn the hurricane? Do you warn the earthquake? You have taken that which I love away from me. I have come to reclaim it!" (Vol. 5, 49).

I believe the character of Swamp Thing is the mouthpiece for the misunderstood and maligned of this world. Never able to interact with humanity, he exists on the boundaries of this world, in a space that humans do not understand. Many times, youth can exist in that same liminal place, too. For one thing, each youth often feels that he or she is the "only one" who has ever felt the way he or she does. Edgar Allan Poe said this in 1875: "From childhood's hour I have not been / As others were—I have not seen / As others saw—I could not bring / My passions from a common spring" (1–4). Poe's speaker states that he is the "only one" who has ever felt as he feels. And today, the time in which many young adults are growing up is quite different in many ways from generations past. Young adults are dealing with issues—or feel they are dealing with issues—never thought of by their parents. I have an example before I bring my case for Swamp Thing to a close.

I recently completed my student teaching in a Senior English class in an urban area. The school had a very diverse demographic of students from all walks of social life that made my day-to-day very interesting. All of my students were great, and I had a fruitful, inspiring time learning the profession of teaching with them. One student, in particular, affected me more than I thought possible, however.

For the sake of confidentiality, I shall refer to her as Student A for the rest of the story. Student A came from a Latino household of low socio-economic status. Her parents were deadbeats and only valued their daughter if she brought home money to support their habits of buying and selling drugs. This, of course, meant that they forced their daughter into buying and selling drugs. Over time, Student A developed a reputation of being a dealer and got involved with local drug lords. (I wish I were making this entire story up.)

One day, Student A approached my mentor teacher and me. She confessed to all the rumors about her and began to weep openly. She told us that she had recently confronted her parents and said that she was no longer going to sell drugs, that she wanted to change her life. Her parents kicked her out of the house. Student A was then forced to move in with a friend who was a single mother living on food stamps. I'll never forget how she wept and cried out, "I need help!"

To the outside world, Student A would be another gang-banger who sold drugs. To the outside world, the only place for Student A to exist would be a jail cell. To me, Student A was a student who had been dealt a bad hand in life and desperately wanted to change. To me, Student A was someone for whom I deeply cared. She was not a monster, but a human being worthy of empathy.

Stories like Student A's are the reason why I believe Swamp Thing should be taught as valid young adult literature—and as literature in college classes. Alan Moore created a character that spoke for the outsiders, the marginalized, the "Others." Whether it is a superficial issue, such as the one I experienced in high school, or the difficult struggles of a high school girl in the drug trade, every child, at some point, feels isolated and alone. Every child, teen, young adult, feels misunderstood. It is important for educators to understand that literature can be a stepping-stone into understanding and out of that situation for those students. We must not force readings on them that they have no chance of relating to and expect them to make excellent scores on a test. Education isn't just about helping students get good grades; it's about showing them how to navigate the storms of this life. I can't think of a time when the storms of life seem more overwhelming than young adulthood. Stories like the Swamp Thing have a unique ability to speak to students, both college and high school, right where they are, no matter how ridiculous and fantastical the story may be.

Swamp Thing can be a tool that will greatly impact students because it creates discussions that many students, high school and/or college, can relate to. By understanding the dynamic of young adult life in this day and age, future educators and college professors can take better steps to teaching those students. I propose college educators use Swamp Thing as a springboard to discuss these issues that I have talked about in their classes. It doesn't hurt that the material being discussed involves swamp monsters, vampires, werewolves, magic, and time travel.

Works Cited

Cohen, Jeffrey Jerome. "Monster Culture: Seven Theses." *Monster Theory: Reading Culture.* Ed. Jeffrey Jerome Cohen. Minneapolis: University of Minnesota Press, 1996. 3–25. Print.

Moore, Alan. *Saga of the Swamp Thing: Book 1.* Illus. Stephen Bissette and John Totleben. New York: Vertigo, 2012. Print.

_____. *Saga of the Swamp Thing: Book 2.* Illus. Stephen Bissette and John Totleben. New York: Vertigo, 2012. Print.

_____. *Saga of the Swamp Thing: Book 3.* Illus. Stephen Bissette and John Totleben. New York: Vertigo, 2012. Print.

_____. *Saga of the Swamp Thing: Book 4.* Illus. Stephen Bissette and Stan Woch. New York: Vertigo, 2012. Print.

_____. *Saga of the Swamp Thing: Book 5.* Illus. Rick Veitch and John Totleben. New York: Vertigo, 2012. Print.

_____. *Saga of the Swamp Thing: Book 6.* Illus. Rick Veitch and Alfredo Alcala. New York: Vertigo, 2012. Print.

Poe, Edgar Allan. "Alone." PoeStories.com. 2014. Web. 10 Aug. 2014.

Epilogue

Sara N. Beam

I had read Margaret Wise Brown's *Goodnight Moon* before, but I didn't "get it" until I had an infant daughter and started reading it to her every evening to establish a nighttime routine at eight weeks in. I didn't know that it was hard to put a child to bed when she was that tiny, to worry that she wouldn't wake up, to start awake several times a night to listen for her breathing in her Rock 'n Play™ sleeper by my feet. I didn't know that later I'd fret internally (needlessly, ridiculously) about her being kidnapped from her bedroom, just next door to my own, when we moved her into her own room at three months old.

I didn't know that the book was *for me*, the nervous young parent, too.

A few months later, when I introduced the *Goodnight Moon* to my Freshman Seminar Writing class, I tried to recite the lines from memory like I did for my daughter every night—and I still do it—she's three years old now. I faltered and felt embarrassed and had to look up the words online on the computer in my classroom. (Why didn't I just bring the damn book to class? Ugh.) After hearing the words aloud, we then looked at the accompanying pictures. Next, we talked about allusions, repetition, ways that visual and verbal style can complement each other ... and then we talked about the publication year. 1947. Think about it, I told them. Think about 1947 and think, not only about the infant or child as audience, but also about the person *reading* this book.

What had that person been through? Think about history, sociology, and psychology.

What will it be like to put a child to bed every night in those early years? Think about parenting.

What does a child know about going to sleep? How do they understand dreams? Think about transitions and rites of passage.

The essays you've already read have discussed children's and YA literature as a hook (Katz Amburn), a stepping stone (Rumsey), a leveling device (Taylor). They've explained that the books blossom under intellectual examination and when they are approached with an open, critical mind, one that is curious and wonder-seeking. These essays have also told you that kiddie lit, as co-editor Emily affectionately calls it (because we've decided to co-opt a term others call demeaning but we think rhetorically and pedagogically useful), meets learners where they are in a welcoming manner; in doing so, the texts in this collection have helped us think about literacy, privilege, and access. Like Tino's grandfather (Kerlin), at first glance—or second or third—we don't always see what younger or less experienced learners have to offer.

Kiddie lit can be a finely-crafted, sophisticated (McKeon) bridge to assist transfer of knowledge (Blakely and Williams). It can be a bridge, too, to a different land, a different way of thinking, a transformation (Newcomb, Carter, Evusa, Emmons, Foley).

Most importantly, throughout the essay collection there's a reminder to notice the overlooked, the taken-for-granted, and the disrespected. There's a message that balancing intellectual readings and less critical readings is important; keeping pleasure readings sacred, letting the literature do its job of soothing, empowering, providing medicine—fostering rooted wonder—all are necessary for the learning process. The takeaway is that, if we were kinder to each other, to our students, or to ourselves, and if we recognized that "beginner's mind" (Suzuki) is a benefit, not a hindrance, we could all get a bit more enrichment into and out of the college classroom experience.

Also, we'd have more fun. "These things are fun, and fun is good," winks *One Fish Two Fish Red Fish Blue Fish* (Seuss 51).

So, though it's hard to walk away, I'll put this thing to bed so you can have a turn to respond.

Works Cited

Brown, Margaret Wise. *Goodnight Moon*. Illus. Clement Hurd. 1947. New York: Harper-Collins, 2006. Print.

Seuss, Dr. *One Fish Two Fish Red Fish Blue Fish*. 1960. New York: Beginner Books, 1988. Print.

Suzuki, Shunryu. *Zen Mind, Beginner's Mind*. Ed. Trudy Dixon. New York: Walker/Weatherhill, 1970. Print.

About the Contributors

Jacqueline **Bach** is the Elena and Albert LeBlanc associate professor of English education and curriculum theory at Louisiana State University. Her work has appeared in *Changing English, The English Journal,* and the *Journal of Curriculum Theory.* In addition to her work with *Buffy the Vampire Slayer,* she studies the representations of classrooms in school films and television shows.

H. J. **Bates** is a recent graduate of Rogers State University, where she received a bachelor of liberal arts in English. She loves literature and writing but spends most of her time working in search and rescue within the U.S. with her canine partner.

Sara N. **Beam** is the writing center coordinator and an English instructor at Rogers State University. Her areas of academic specialty include composition, literature for children and young adults, and 19th-century British literature.

David **Blakely** is the theatre program director and an associate professor at Rogers State University. A director, actor, designer, and musician, his area of expertise is playwriting. His award-winning plays have been produced all over the United States.

Erika **Carter** is a teacher of English at Legacy Christian School. She earned a bachelor of liberal arts degree at Rogers State University, where she also worked as a tutor in the writing center.

Holly **Clay-Buck** is an instructor at Rogers State University in English and developmental studies. She wrote her master's thesis on Flannery O'Connor but also studied pedagogy and popular culture. Additionally, her time working for nonprofits led her to an interest in interpersonal and business communication.

Emily **Dial-Driver** is a professor of English at Rogers State University. She serves as fiction editor of RSU's *Cooweescoowee: A Journal of Arts and Letters.* She has served as co-editor of books on *Buffy the Vampire Slayer* and the use of fantasy media in a classroom setting.

Sally **Emmons** is a professor in the English and humanities program at Rogers State University. She teaches Native American literature, creative writing, technical writing, apocalyptic/dystopian literature, and graphic novels. She serves as the managing editor of RSU's academic and literary journal, the *Cooweescoowee*.

Juliet **Evusa** is an associate professor at Rogers State University with nine years of experience teaching communication studies. She considers herself a follower of Stuart Hall's cultural studies tradition and research related to the empowerment of women in Sub-Saharan Africa through her publications and conference presentations.

Hugh **Foley** is a professor of fine arts at Rogers State University. He teaches cinema and coordinates the university's Native American studies courses. His award-winning video documentaries on American Indian life and music in Oklahoma have been shown nationwide on public television and at national conferences.

Jim **Ford** is the director of academic enrichment and professor of humanities, philosophy, and religious studies at Rogers State University, where he has also served as director of the honors program since 2004. He has been a co-editor and contributor to collections on *Buffy the Vampire Slayer* and the use of fantasy media in the classroom setting.

Francis A. **Grabowski** III is an associate professor of philosophy at Rogers State University.

Laura **Gray** is a professor of English and the writing faculty coordinator at Rogers State University. She teaches courses in women's studies and the humanities as well as English and rhetoric. She has previously contributed other essays on the practice of teaching.

Paul B. **Hatley** is an associate professor of history at Rogers State University. He served as an intelligence officer with the United States Army in the Federal Republic of Germany. He teaches American, world, and military history, as well as German language courses.

Melanie **Hundley** is an assistant professor in the Department of Teaching and Learning at Vanderbilt University. Her work has appeared in *Journal of Adolescent and Adult Literacy* and *The ALAN Review*. In addition to her work with young adult literature, she studies the digital and multimodal composition practices of pre-service English teachers.

D. Sue **Katz Amburn** is a professor of biology at Rogers State University. She has been active with the Education Division of the American Society for Microbiology and has attended meetings of the American Society for Microbiology Conference for Undergraduate Educators (ASMCUE) and Gordon Research Conferences on Microbiology Education and Visualization in Science and Teaching.

Gioia **Kerlin** is an assistant professor of Spanish at Rogers State University. Her areas of academic specialty include 16th- and 17th-century Spanish theater, the works of Spain's Morisco writers, and anything that helps her bridge the gap between students and teacher.

Jessica **Limke** is a senior at Rogers State University and is working on a B.S. in business administration with an emphasis in accounting. With the exception of an uncredited inclusion of a Composition I assignment in the 4th and 5th editions of *The Everyday Writer* customized for RSU, this is her first publication.

Peter **Macpherson** is the John W. Norman Chair in business information technology at Rogers State University. He teaches computer programming, computer architecture, networking, game development, and 3D modeling.

Macy **McDonald** is a graduate teaching assistant at Oklahoma State University pursuing a master's in English literature with a certificate option in TESL. Her areas of academic specialty include young adult metafiction, gender, fat, and beast studies.

Michael **McKeon** is an assistant professor of fine arts at Rogers State University, where he teaches courses in art history and theory. He donates time to serve on the Higher Education Cultural Roundtable and academic interests lie at the intersection of Renaissance texts and images.

Gary **Moeller**, a Rogers State University art professor, has served as a mentor for fine artists, designers, and teachers of art in the United States and abroad. Primarily a painter, his work has been exhibited in galleries in museums and private collections in Oklahoma, New Mexico, Arkansas, Missouri, Louisiana, and Umbria, Italy.

Frances E. **Morris** is an assistant professor at Rogers State University. She has been a medical technologist, English bulldog breeder, and cattle rancher. She returned to school to study literature and subsequently to her profession of teaching composition.

Robin M. **Murphy** is an associate professor of English at East Central University in Ada, Oklahoma. Her main research interests are civic literacy, trauma rhetoric, pop culture studies, and feminist theory. She serves on the review board of *Computers and Composition Online* and print journals and teaches different writing classes.

David **Newcomb** has taught at the college and university level for more than twenty-five years, primarily in the American southwest (specifically Texas, New Mexico, and Oklahoma). Major interests include how symbolic interactions result in meaning and purpose for individuals.

Kimberly **Qualls** is a recent graduate of Rogers State University, where she earned a bachelor of liberal arts degree.

Scott **Reed** worked for the University of Central Oklahoma and Chickasaw Nation Industries as a grant writer before becoming a teacher of English composition, literature, and humanities.

Nataliya **Romenesko** is an ELL teacher and language arts consultant at Craig High School in Janesville, Wisconsin. She earned a master's degree in English studies from Western Illinois University where she specialized in composition theory and practice. She taught composition at Western Illinois University and Rogers State University.

Davey **Rumsey** is a former student of Rogers State University. He completed a bachelor in secondary English education degree at Northeastern State University in May of 2014. He is a worship pastor at LifeChurch.tv.

Jesse **Stallings** is a teacher of English at the Tulsa School of Arts and Sciences. He earned a bachelor of liberal arts degree at Rogers State University.

Gregory **Stevenson** is a professor of New Testament at Rochester College in Rochester Hills, Michigan. His teaching and research interests are varied with a focus on biblical interpretation, apocalyptic literature, and Greco-Roman culture on the one hand, and the intersection of religion and popular culture on the other.

Emily **Tarver** is an instructor at the Louisiana State University Laboratory School. She teaches tenth grade English literature. Her work has appeared in *Australasian Journal of Gifted Education* and *Journal of Research in International Education*.

Carolyn **Taylor** is a professor of political science at Rogers State University. Her areas of academic specialty include American federal, state, and local government. She served in the Oklahoma House of Representatives from 1984 to 1992.

Mike **Turvey** retired in 2011 after a 40-year career in education. He taught all high school levels of English literature, creative writing, dramatic literature, psychology, government, and a college preparatory course in term paper writing for seniors.

Weldon Lee **Williams** is an assistant professor of communications at Rogers State University. He spent thirty years in television news, mostly in management as an award-winning news director and executive producer, and also as an investigative, political, and science reporter and photographer.

Index